A History of Philosophy

VOLUME V

Modern Philosophy:
The British Philosophers

PART II

Berkeley to Hume

by Frederick Copleston, S.J.

IMAGE BOOKS
A Division of Doubleday & Company, Inc.
Garden City, New York

Image Books Edition 1964
by special arrangement with The Newman Press and
Burns & Oates, Ltd.
Image Books edition published February, 1964

DE LICENTIA SUPERIORUM ORDINIS:
J. D. Boyle, S.J.
Praep. Prov. Angliae

NIHIL OBSTAT:
J. L. Russell, S.J.
Censor Deputatus

IMPRIMATUR:
✠ Franciscus Archiepiscopus Birmingamiensis
Birmingamiae die 25 Julii 1957

CONTENTS

A HISTORY OF PHILOSOPHY

Volume V Part II

Chapter Eleven

BERKELEY (1)

Life — Works — Spirit of Berkeley's thought — Theory of Vision.

1. George Berkeley was born at Kilcrene near Kilkenny in Ireland on March 12th, 1685, his family being of English descent. In his eleventh year he was sent to Kilkenny College, and in March 1700 he entered Trinity College, Dublin, being then fifteen years old. After studying mathematics, languages, logic and philosophy he took his B.A. degree in 1704. In 1707 he published his *Arithmetica* and *Miscellanea mathematica*, and in June of that year he became a Fellow of the College. He had already begun to doubt the existence of matter, his interest in this subject having been stimulated by the study of Locke and Malebranche. In fulfilment of statutory requirements he was ordained deacon in 1709 and priest in 1710 in the Protestant Church and held various academic offices first as Junior Fellow and later, from 1717, as Senior Fellow. But in 1724 he obtained the post of dean of Derry and was thus compelled to resign his Fellowship. His residence at the college had not been without a break, of course. He had visited London, where he had made the acquaintance of Addison, Steele, Pope and other notables; and he had twice visited the Continent.

Soon after his installation as dean of Derry, Berkeley left for London in order to interest the Crown and government circles in his project of founding a college in the island of Bermuda for the education of the sons of English planters and of native Indians. He apparently envisaged English youths and Indians coming a very considerable distance from the mainland of America for general, and especially religious, education, after which they would return to the mainland.

Berkeley succeeded in obtaining a charter and parliamentary approval of a proposed grant, and in 1728 he set sail with some companions for America and made his way to Newport in Rhode Island. Having become doubtful of the wisdom of his earlier plan, he made up his mind to apply for leave, once the grant was given, to build the projected college in Rhode Island rather than in Bermuda. But the money was not forthcoming, and Berkeley returned to England, reaching London at the end of October 1731.

After his return to England Berkeley waited in London, hoping for preferment, and in 1734 he was in fact appointed bishop of Cloyne. It is to this period of his life that there belongs his famous propaganda on behalf of the virtues of tarwater which he regarded as a panacea for human diseases. Whatever one may think of this specific remedy Berkeley's zeal for the relief of suffering is undoubted.

In 1745 Berkeley refused the offer of the more lucrative bishopric of Clogher, and in 1752 he settled at Oxford with his wife and family, where he took a house in Holywell Street. He died peacefully on January 14th, 1753, and was buried in Christ Church chapel, the cathedral of the diocese of Oxford.

2. Berkeley's most important philosophical works were written at an early period in his career, during his first years as a Fellow of Trinity College. *An Essay towards a New Theory of Vision* appeared in 1709. In this work Berkeley dealt with problems of vision, analysing, for example, the foundations of our judgments of distance, size and position. But though he was already convinced of the truth of immaterialism he did not express in the *Essay* the doctrine for which he is famous. This doctrine was put forward in A *Treatise concerning the Principles of Human Knowledge*, Part I, which was published in 1710, and in *Three Dialogues between Hylas and Philonous*, published in 1713. Preliminary work for the *Essay* and for the *Principles* was contained in Berkeley's notebooks which were written in 1707 and 1708. These were published by A. C. Fraser in 1871 under the title *Commonplace Book of occasional Metaphysical Thoughts* and by Professor A. A. Luce in 1944 under the title *Philosophical Commentaries*. In 1712 Berkeley published a pamphlet on *Passive Obedience*, in which he maintained the doctrine of passive obedience though he qualified it by admitting the right of revolt in extreme cases of tyranny.

Berkeley's Latin treatise *De motu* appeared in 1721, and in the same year he published *An Essay towards preventing the*

Ruin of Great Britain which contained a call to religion, industry, frugality and public spirit in view of the calamities caused by the South Sea Bubble. While he was in America he wrote *Alciphron or the Minute Philosopher*, which he published in London in 1732. Comprising seven dialogues, it is the longest of his books and is essentially a work of Christian apologetic, directed against free-thinkers. In 1733 appeared *The Theory of Vision or Visual Language showing the immediate Presence and Providence of a Deity Vindicated and Explained* in answer to a newspaper criticism of the *Essay*; and in 1734 Berkeley published *The Analyst or a Discourse addressed to an Infidel Mathematician* in which he attacked Newton's theory of fluxions and argued that if there are mysteries in mathematics it is only reasonable to expect them in religion. A Dr. Jurin published a reply, and Berkeley retorted with *A Defence of Free-thinking in Mathematics*, published in 1735.

In 1745 Berkeley published two letters, one addressed to his own flock, the other to the Catholics in the diocese of Cloyne. In the latter he urged non-participation in the Jacobite rising. His ideas about the question of an Irish bank appeared anonymously at Dublin in three parts in 1735, 1736 and 1737 under the title of *The Querist*. Berkeley took a considerable interest in Irish affairs, and in 1749 he addressed *A Word to the Wise* to the Catholic clergy of the country, urging them to join in a movement for the promotion of better social and economic conditions. In connection with his propaganda on behalf of the virtues of tar-water, he published in 1744 *Siris*, a work which also contained a certain amount of philosophy. His last known writing was *Farther Thoughts on Tar-water*, included as the opening piece in his *Miscellany*, published in 1752.

3. Berkeley's philosophy is exciting in the sense that a brief statement of it (for instance, there exist only God, finite spirits and the ideas of spirits) makes it appear so remote from the ordinary man's view of the world that it arrests the attention. How, we may wonder, could an eminent philosopher think himself justified in denying the existence of matter? Indeed, when Berkeley published the *Principles of Human Knowledge* he not unnaturally became the target of criticism and even of ridicule. To many minds it appeared that he had denied what was most obvious, so obvious that no ordinary man would call it in question, and asserted what was by no means so obvious. Such a philosophy was nothing but a fan-

tastic extravagance. Its author might be mentally unbalanced, as some thought, or a hunter after paradoxical novelties or a humorous Irishman perpetrating an elaborate joke. But nobody who believed or who affected to believe that houses and tables and trees and mountains were the ideas of spirits or minds could reasonably expect other men to share his opinions. Some conceded that Berkeley's arguments were ingenious and subtle and difficult to refute. At the same time there must be something wrong with arguments which led to such paradoxical conclusions. Others thought that it was easy to refute Berkeley's position. Their reaction to his philosophy is well symbolized by Dr. Samuel Johnson's famous refutation. The learned doctor kicked a great stone, exclaiming, 'I refute him thus.'

Berkeley himself, however, was very far from regarding his philosophy as a piece of extravagant fantasy, contrary to common sense, or even as being at variance with the spontaneous convictions of the ordinary man. On the contrary, he was convinced that he was on the side of common sense, and he explicitly classed himself with 'the vulgar' as distinct from the professors and, in his opinion, misguided metaphysicians who propounded strange and bizarre doctrines. In his notebooks we read the significant entry: 'Mem: To be eternally banishing metaphysics, etc., and recalling men to common sense.'[1] One may not, indeed, be inclined to regard Berkeley's philosophy as a whole as being an example of banishing metaphysics; but his denial of Locke's theory of occult material substance was certainly for him an example of this activity. And he did not regard his doctrine that bodies or sensible objects are dependent on perceiving minds as incompatible with the views of the ordinary man. True, the latter would say that the table exists and is present in the room even when there is nobody there to perceive it. But Berkeley would reply that he has no wish to deny that the table can be said to exist in some sense when there is nobody in the room to perceive it. The question is not whether the statement is true or false, but in what sense it is true. What does it mean to say that the table is in the room when nobody is present and perceiving it? What can it mean except that if someone were to enter the room, he would have the experience which we call seeing a table? Would not the ordinary man argue that this is what he means when he says that the table is in the room even when nobody is perceiving it? I do not suggest that the matter is as simple as these questions may seem to imply. Nor do I wish to commit myself to Berkeley's view. But I wish to indicate very briefly in advance how the latter could maintain that opinions which his contemporaries were inclined to look on as fantastic were in point of fact quite consonant with common sense.

Mention has just been made of the question, what does it mean to say of a body or sensible thing that it exists when it is not actually perceived? Berkeley was not only one of those philosophers who are capable of writing their own language well: he was also greatly concerned with the meanings and uses of words. This is, of course, one of the principal reasons for the interest which is taken in his writings today by British philosophers. For they see in him a precursor of the movement of linguistic analysis. Berkeley insisted, for example, on the need for an accurate analysis of the term 'existence'. Thus in his notebooks he remarks that many ancient philosophers ran into absurdities because they did not know what existence was. But ''tis on the discovering of the nature and meaning and import of Existence that I chiefly insist'.[2] In Berkeley's view the conclusion, *Esse est percipi*, was the result of an accurate analysis of the term 'exist' when we say that sensible things exist. Again, Berkeley gave particular attention to the meaning and use of abstract terms, such as those occurring in the Newtonian scientific theories. And his analysis of their use enabled him to anticipate views about the status of scientific theories which have later become common coin. Scientific theories are hypotheses, and it is a mistake to think that because a scientific hypothesis 'works', it must necessarily be the expression of the human mind's natural power of penetrating the ultimate structure of reality and attaining final truth. Further, terms such as 'gravity', 'attraction', and so on, certainly have their uses; but it is one thing to say that they possess instrumentalist value and quite another thing to say that they connote occult entities or qualities. The use of abstract words, though it cannot be avoided, tends to contaminate physics with metaphysics and to give us a wrong idea of the status and function of physical theories.

But though Berkeley spoke about banishing metaphysics and recalling men to common sense, he was himself a metaphysician. He thought, for example, that, given his account of the existence and nature of material things, it follows with certainty that God exists. There is no material substance (Locke's occult and unknown substratum) to support the qualities which Berkeley called 'ideas'. Material things can therefore be reduced to clusters of ideas. But ideas cannot exist on their own apart from some mind. At the same time it is obvious that there is a difference between the ideas which we frame for ourselves, creatures of the imagination (for instance, the idea of a mermaid or of a unicorn), and the phenomena or 'ideas' which a man perceives in normal circumstances and conditions during his waking life. I can create an imaginative world of my own; but it does not depend on me what I see when I raise my eyes from my book and look out of the window. These 'ideas' must, therefore, be presented to me by a mind or spirit; that is to say, by God. This is not exactly how Berkeley expresses the matter; but it will suffice as a brief indication of the fact that in his view phenomenalism entails theism. Whether it does or not is, of course, another question. But Berkeley thought that it does; and this is one reason why he considered that belief in God is a matter of plain common sense. If we take a common-sense view of the existence and nature of material things, we shall be led to affirm the existence of God. Conversely, belief in material substance promotes atheism.

This is a matter of some importance if we are considering the spirit of Berkeley's philosophizing. For he made it quite plain that he regarded his criticism of material substance as serving to pave the way for an acceptance of theism in general and of Christianity in particular. As has been said, his philosophy was looked on by many contemporaries as a fantastic extravagance. And his willingness to sacrifice a career in the Protestant Church in Ireland[3] in order to carry out his Bermuda project was considered by some as a symptom of madness. But his immaterialistic philosophy and his Bermuda project reveal the same character and bent of mind which are revealed in another way in his concern for the sufferings of the Irish poor and in his enthusiastic propaganda for the virtues of tar-water. Whatever value may be attached to his philosophy and whichever elements in it may be stressed by later generations of philosophers, his own estimate of it is admirably summarized in the closing words of the *Principles*. 'For after all, what deserves the first place in our studies, is the consideration of God, and our duty; which to promote, as it was the main drift and design of my labours, so shall I esteem them altogether useless and ineffectual, if by what I have said I cannot inspire my readers with a pious sense of the presence of God: and having shown the falseness or vanity of those barren speculations, which make the chief employment of learned men, the better dispose them to reverence and embrace the salutary truths of the Gospel, which to know and to practise is the highest perfection of human nature.'[4]

Berkeley was thus quite explicit about the practical function of his philosophy. The full title of the *Principles* is *A Treatise concerning the Principles of Human Knowledge, wherein the chief causes of error and difficulty in the Sciences, with the grounds of Scepticism, Atheism and Irreligion, are inquired into.* Similarly, the aim of the *Three Dialogues* is said to be 'plainly to demonstrate the reality and perfection of human knowledge, the incorporeal nature of the soul and the immediate providence of a Deity, in opposition to sceptics and atheists'.[5] But the conclusion should not be drawn from these and similar declarations that Berkeley's philosophy is so coloured by preconceptions and preoccupations of a religious and apologetic character that it has nothing of value to offer for philosophical reflection. He was a serious philosopher; and whether one agrees or not with the arguments which he employed and the conclusions at which he arrived, his lines of thought are well worth consideration, and the problems which he raised are of interest and importance. In general, he is remarkable as an empiricist who was also a metaphysician and a phenomenalist who did not think that phenomenalism has the last word in philosophy. His philosophy may, of course, appear to be a hybrid. It inevitably appears in this light if we regard it simply as a stepping-stone on the way from Locke to Hume. But it is, I think, of interest for its own sake.

4. It has already been mentioned that Berkeley did not give his immaterialist philosophy to the world without having made some effort to prepare men's minds for its reception. For though he was convinced of the truth of his views and of their compatibility with common sense, he was aware that his statements would appear strange and bizarre to many readers. He sought, therefore, to prepare the way for the *Principles of Human Knowledge* by publishing first his *Essay towards a New Theory of Vision.*

It would be a mistake, however, to imagine that this *Essay* was merely a device for predisposing men's minds to accord a sympathetic hearing to what Berkeley intended to say in later publications. It is a serious study of a number of problems connected with perception, and it is of interest for its own sake, quite apart from its prefatory function. The construction of optical instruments had stimulated the development of theories of optics. A number of works had already appeared, such as Barrow's *Optical Lectures* (1669); and in the *Essay* Berkeley made his own contribution to the subject. His aim, as expressed in his own words, was 'to show the manner wherein we perceive by sight the distance, magnitude, and situation of objects. Also to consider the difference there is betwixt the ideas of sight and touch, and whether there be any idea common to both senses.'[6]

Berkeley assumes as agreed that we do not immediately perceive distance of itself. 'It remains therefore that it be brought into view by means of some other idea that is itself immediately perceived in the act of vision.'[7] But Berkeley rejects the current geometrical explanation by means of lines and angles. For one thing, experience does not support the notion that we compute or judge distance by geometrical calculation. For another thing, the lines and angles referred to are hypotheses framed by mathematicians with a view to treating optics geometrically. Instead of the geometrical explanation Berkeley offers suggestions on these lines. When I am looking at a near object with both eyes, the interval between my pupils is lessened or widened according as the object approaches or recedes. And this alteration in the eyes is accompanied by sensations. The result is that an association is set up between the different sensations and different distances. Thus the sensations act as intermediate 'ideas' in the perception of distance. Again, if an object is placed at a certain distance from the eye and is then made to approach, it is seen more confusedly. And thus 'there ariseth in the mind an habitual connection between the several degrees of confusion and distance; the greater confusion still implying the lesser distance, and the lesser confusion the greater distance of the object'.[8] But when an object, placed at a certain distance from the eye, is brought nearer, we can, for some time at least, prevent its appearance becoming confused by straining the eye. And the sensation accompanying the effort of strain helps us to judge the distance of the object. The greater the effort of straining the eye, the nearer is the object.

As for our perception of the magnitude or size of sensible objects, we must first distinguish between two sorts of objects apprehended by sight. Some are properly and immediately visible; others do not fall immediately under the sense of sight but are rather tangible objects, and these are seen only mediately, by means of what is directly visible. Each sort of object has its own distinct magnitude or extension. For example, when I look at the moon, I see directly a coloured disc. The moon, as a visible object, is greater when it is situated on the horizon than when it is situated on the meridian. But we do not think of the magnitude of the moon, when it is considered as a tangible object, as changing in this way. 'The magnitude of the object, which exists without the mind, and is at a distance, continues always invariably the same. But the visible object still changing as you approach to, or recede from, the tangible object, it hath no fixed and determinate greatness. Whenever, therefore, we speak of the magnitude of anything, for instance a tree or a house, we must mean the tangible magnitude, otherwise there can be nothing steady and free from ambiguity spoken of it.'[9] 'Whenever we say an object is great or small, of this or that determinate measure, I say it must be meant of the tangible, and not the visible extension which, though immediately perceived, is nevertheless taken little notice of.'[10] The magnitude of tangible objects, however, is not directly perceived; it is judged by the visible magnitude, according to the confusion or distinctness, faintness or vigour, of the visible appearances. There is, indeed, no necessary connection between visible magnitude and tangible magnitude. For instance, a tower and a man, when situated at appropriate distances, might have more or less the same visible magnitude. But we do not on that account judge that they have the same tangible magnitude. Our judgment is affected by a variety of experimental factors. This does not, however, alter the fact that before we touch an object its tangible magnitude is suggested by its visible magnitude, though the latter has no necessary connection with the former. 'As we see distance, so we see magnitude. And we see both in the same way that we see shame or anger in the looks of a man. Those passions are themselves invisible, they are nevertheless let in by the eye along with colours and alterations of countenance, which are the immediate object of vision: and which signify them for no other reason than barely because they have been observed to accompany them. Without experience we should no more have taken blushing for a sign of shame than of gladness.'[11]

Berkeley's ideas about visual perception were by no means all original. But he utilized the ideas which he borrowed in the construction of a carefully worked out theory which, apart from particular points of value, possess the great merit of being the result of reflection, with the aid of particular examples, on the ways in which we do as a matter of fact perceive distance, magnitude and situation. He had, of course, no wish to question the utility of a mathematical theory of optics; but it was clear to him that in ordinary visual perception we do not judge distance and size by mathematical calculations. We can, indeed, employ mathematics to determine distances; but this process obviously presupposes the ordinary visual perception of which Berkeley is speaking.

It is unnecessary to enter here into further details of Berkeley's account of perception. The point to notice is the distinction which he makes between sight and touch and between their respective objects. We have already seen that he distinguishes between objects which are, properly speaking, the objects of sight or vision and objects which are only mediately objects of visual perception. Visible magnitude or extension is distinct from tangible extension. But we can go further and say, in general, that 'there is no idea common to both senses'.[12] That this is so can be easily shown. The immediate objects of sight are light and colours, and there is no other immediate object.[13] But light and colours are not perceived by touch. Hence there are no immediate objects common to both senses. It may seem perhaps that Berkeley is contradicting himself when he says that the only immediate objects of sight are light and colours, though at the same time he speaks of visible extension. But what we see are colour-patches, as it were extended colours. And visible extension, visible as patches of colour, is, Berkeley insists, entirely distinct from tangible extension.

It may be said that to assert the heterogeneity of the objects of sight and touch is to assert a truism. Everyone knows, for example, that we perceive colours by sight and not by touch. We say, for instance, that a thing looks green, and not that it feels green. All of us are just as much aware that light and colours are the proper objects of sight as we are that sounds are heard and not smelt. But insisting on the heterogeneity of the objects of sight and touch Berkeley has an ulterior aim. For he wishes to maintain that visual objects, the 'ideas of sight', are symbols or signs which suggest to us tangible ideas. There is no necessary connection between the two; but 'these signs are constant and universal, (and) their connection with tangible ideas has been learnt at our first entrance into the world'.[14] 'Upon the whole, I think we may fairly conclude that the proper objects of vision constitute an universal language of the Author of nature, whereby we are instructed how to regulate our actions in order to attain those things that are necessary to the preservation and well-being of our bodies, as also to avoid whatever may be hurtful and destructive of them. . . . And the manner wherein they signify and mark unto us the objects which are at a distance is the same with that of languages and signs of human appointment, which do not suggest the things signified by any likeness or identity of nature, but only by an habitual connection that experience has made us to observe between them.'[15]

The words 'signify and mark unto us the objects which are at a distance' should be noted. The implication is that the objects of sight or vision are not at a distance. That is to say, they are in some sense within the mind, not 'out there'. Berkeley has already implied this by remarking that 'the magnitude of the object which exists without the mind and is at a distance, continues always the same',[16] and by contrasting this external and tangible object with the visible object. The objects of sight are in some sense within the mind, and they act as signs or symbols of objects outside the mind, tangible objects.

This distinction between visible and tangible objects is not compatible with the view afterwards maintained in the *Principles*, that all sensible objects are 'ideas', existing in some sense within the mind. But this does not mean that Berkeley changed his view in the interval between writing the *Essay* and writing the *Principles*. It means rather that in the *Essay* he wishes to give only a partial version of his general theory. He speaks, therefore, as though visible objects were in the mind and tangible objects outside the mind. In the *Principles*, however, all sensible objects are brought within the mind, and it is no longer objects of sight alone which constitute a language determined by God. In other words, in the *Essay*, where he is primarily discussing a number of particular problems connected with perception, he introduces the reader to a part only of his general theory, and then only incidentally, whereas in the *Principles* he expounds the general theory. It should be added that even on Berkeley's general theory problems connected with our perception of distance, magnitude and situation can still be raised; but distance and situation can be, of course, only relative, and not absolute, if there are no mind-independent material things.

Chapter Twelve

BERKELEY (2)

*Words and their meanings — Abstract general ideas —
The* esse *of sensible things is* percipi — *Sensible things
are ideas — Material substance is a meaningless term —
The reality of sensible things — Berkeley and the representative theory of perception.*

1. In the last chapter attention was drawn to Berkeley's concern with language and with the meanings of words. In the
Philosophical Commentaries, that is, in his notebooks, he remarks that mathematics has this advantage over metaphysics
and ethics, that mathematical definitions are definitions of
words not yet known to the learner, so that their meaning is
not disputed, whereas the terms defined in metaphysics and
ethics are for the most part already known, with the result
that any attempt to define them may meet with preconceived
ideas and prejudices about their meanings.[1] Further, in many
cases we may understand what is meant by a term used in
philosophy and yet be unable to give a clear account of its
meaning or define it. 'I may clearly and fully understand my
own soul, extension, etc., and not be able to define them.'[2]
And he attributes difficulty in defining and talking clearly
about things to 'the fault and scantiness of language' as much
as to confusion of thought.[3]

Linguistic analysis is, therefore, of importance in philosophy. 'We are frequently puzzled and at a loss in obtaining
clear and determined meanings of words commonly in use.'[4]
It is not words such as 'thing' or 'substance' which have caused
mistakes so much as 'the not reflecting on their meaning. I
will be still for retaining the words. I only desire that men
would think before they speak and settle the meaning of their
words.'[5] 'The chief thing I do or pretend to do is only to re-

move the mist or veil of words. This has occasioned ignorance and confusion. This has ruined the Schoolmen and mathematicians, lawyers and divines.'[6] Some words do not express any meaning, that is to say, their supposed meaning vanishes under analysis; they are seen not to refer to anything. 'We have learned from Mr. Locke that there may be and that there are several glib, coherent, methodical discourses which nevertheless amount to just nothing.'[7] An example of Berkeley's meaning is given by a jotting expressing an idea which evidently occurred to him, though he did not develop it and indeed rejected the point of view to which he alludes. 'Say you the mind is not the perceptions but that thing which perceives. I answer you are abused by the words "that" and "thing"; these are vague, empty words without a meaning.'[8] We need analysis, therefore, to determine meanings when these are not clear and to reveal the meaninglessness of nonsignificant terms.

Berkeley applied this line of thought to Locke's doctrine of material substance. One can say that his attack on Locke's theory took the form of an analysis of material-object sentences. He argued that analysis of the meaning of sentences containing the names of sensible objects or bodies does not support the view that there is any material substance in Locke's sense, that is to say, a hidden and unknowable substrate. Things are simply what we perceive them to be, and we perceive no Lockean substance or substrate. Statements about sensible things can be analysed in terms of phenomena or translated into statements about phenomena. We can talk about substances if we simply mean things as we perceive them, but the term 'material substance' does not signify anything distinct from and underlying phenomena.

The whole matter is complicated, of course, by Berkeley's doctrine that sensible things are 'ideas'. But this doctrine can be left aside for the moment. And if we look at his procedure from one point of view only, we can say that for Berkeley those who believe in material substance have been misled by words. Because we predicate qualities of a rose, for example, philosophers such as Locke have been inclined to think that there must be some invisible substance which supports the perceived qualities. But Berkeley argues, as will be seen later, that no clear meaning can be attached to the word 'supports' in this context. He does not wish to deny that there are substances in any sense of the word, but only in the philosophical sense. 'I take not away substances. I ought not to be accused of discarding substance out of the reasonable world. I only reject the philosophic sense (which in effect is no sense) of the word "substance". . . .'[9]

Again, as we saw in the last chapter, Berkeley insisted on the need for a clear analysis of the word 'existence'. When he says of sensible things that their existence is to be perceived (*esse est percipi*), he does not intend to say that it is untrue that they exist; he is concerned to give the meaning of the statement that sensible things exist. 'Let it not be said that I take away Existence. I only declare the meaning of the word so far as I can comprehend it.'[10]

These remarks about language in the *Philosophical Commentaries* find their echo, of course, in the *Principles of Human Knowledge*; for the former contained preparatory material for the latter, as well as for the *Essay towards a New Theory of Vision*. In his introduction to the *Principles* Berkeley remarks that in order to prepare the mind of the reader for understanding his doctrine about the first principles of knowledge it is proper to say something first 'concerning the nature and abuse of language'.[11] And he has some interesting observations to make about the function of language. It is commonly supposed, he says, that the chief and indeed only function of language is the communication of ideas marked by words. But this is certainly not the case. 'There are other ends, as the raising of some passion, the exciting to, or deterring from an action, the putting the mind in some particular disposition; to which the former (that is, the communication of ideas) is in many cases barely subservient, and sometimes entirely omitted, when these can be obtained without it, as I think both not infrequently happen in the familiar use of language.'[12] Here Berkeley draws attention to the emotive use or uses of language. It is necessary, he thinks, to distinguish the various functions or purposes of language and of particular kinds of words and to discriminate between controversies which are purely verbal and those which are not, if one is to avoid 'being imposed on by words'.[13] This is obviously excellent advice.

2. It is in the setting of these general remarks about language that Berkeley discusses abstract general ideas. His contention is that there are no such things, though he is prepared to admit general ideas in some sense. 'It is to be noted that I do not deny absolutely there are general ideas, but only that there are any *abstract general ideas*.'[14] But this contention stands in need of some explanation.

In the first place there are no abstract general ideas, the emphasis being on the word 'abstract'. Berkeley is primarily concerned with refuting Locke's theory of abstract ideas. He mentions the Schoolmen too; but it is Locke whom he quotes. Further, he takes Locke to mean that we can form abstract general images, and he has, of course, no difficulty in refuting Locke's position when it is so understood. 'The idea of man that I frame to myself must be either of a white, or a black, or a tawny, a straight, or a crooked, a tall, or a low, or a middle-sized man. I cannot by any effort of thought conceive the abstract idea above described.'[15] I cannot, that is to say, frame an image of man which both omits and includes all the particular characteristics of real individual men. Similarly, 'what more easy than for anyone to look a little into his own thoughts, and there try whether he has, or can attain to have, an idea that shall correspond with the description that is here given of the general idea of a triangle, which is *neither oblique, nor rectangle, equilateral, equicrural, nor scalenon, but all and none of these at once?*'[16] I cannot have an idea (that is, an image) of a triangle which includes all the characteristics of different types of triangles and which at the same time is itself not classifiable as the image of a particular type of triangle.

This last illustration is taken directly from Locke, who speaks about forming the general idea of a triangle which 'must be neither oblique, nor rectangle, neither equilateral, equicrural, nor scalenon; but all and none of these at once'.[17] But Locke's accounts of abstraction and its products are not always consistent. Elsewhere he says that 'ideas become general by separating from them the circumstances of time, and place, and any other ideas, that may determine them to this or that particular existence. By this way of abstraction they are made capable of representing more individuals than one. . . .'[18] And he tells us that in the general idea of man the characteristics of individual men as individuals are omitted, only those characteristics being retained which all men have in common. Moreover, though Locke sometimes implies that abstract general ideas are images, he does not by any means always do so. Berkeley, however, who is himself speaking throughout of ideas of objects presented in sense-perception, persists in interpreting Locke as though the latter were speaking of abstract general images. And it is easy for him to show that there are no such things. True, he seems to suppose that composite images must be clearer than they are; but this does not alter the fact that there cannot be, for instance, an abstract general image of a triangle which fulfils all the conditions mentioned above. Nor, to take another example given by Berkeley, can we have an idea (image) of motion without a moving body and without any determinate direction or velocity.[19] But if we consider that part of Berkeley's theory which consists in an exegesis of Locke, we must say, I think, that he was definitely unfair to the latter, however much some admirers of the good bishop may have tried to dispose of this charge.

As we have seen, Berkeley appeals to introspection. And a natural comment to make is that on looking into his mind for abstract general ideas he sees only images and proceeds to identify the image with the idea. And as even the composite image is still a particular image, though it can be made to stand for a number of particular things, he denies the existence of abstract general ideas. This may, indeed, be true to a great extent; but Berkeley did not admit that we have universal ideas, if by this it is meant that we can have ideas, with a positive universal content, of sensory qualities which cannot be given alone in perception (such as motion without a moving body) or of purely general sensory qualities such as colour. If he had been accused of confusing images with ideas, he might have replied by challenging his critic to show that there are any abstract general ideas. It must be remembered that in Berkeley's philosophy 'essences' go by the board.

How, then, can Berkeley say that though he denies abstract general ideas he does not intend to deny general ideas absolutely? His view is that 'an idea, which considered in itself is particular, becomes general by being made to represent or stand for all other particular ideas of the same sort'.[20] Thus universality does not consist 'in the absolute, positive nature or conception of anything, but in the relation it bears to the particulars signified or represented by it'.[21] I can attend to this or that aspect of a thing; and if this is what is meant by abstraction, abstraction is obviously possible. 'It must be acknowledged that a man may consider a figure merely as triangular, without attending to the particular qualities of the angles, or relations of the sides. . . . In like manner we may consider Peter so far forth as man, or so far forth as animal. . . .'[22] If I consider Peter only in relation to the characteristics which he possesses in common with animals, abstracting or prescinding from the characteristics which he possesses in common with other men but not with

animals, my idea of Peter can be made to represent or stand
for all animals. In this sense it becomes a general idea; but
universality belongs to it only in its function of representing
or standing for. Considered in itself, with regard to its positive content, the idea is a particular idea.

If there are no abstract general ideas, it follows that reasoning must be about particulars. It obviously cannot be about
abstract general ideas if there are none. The geometer makes
a particular triangle stand for or represent all triangles, by attending to its triangularity rather than to its particular characteristics. And in this case properties demonstrated of this
particular triangle are held to be demonstrated of all triangles.
But the geometer is not demonstrating properties of the abstract general idea of triangularity; for there is no such thing.
His reasoning is about particulars, and its universal scope is
made possible by the power we have of rendering a particular
idea universal, not by its positive content, but in virtue of a
representative function.

Berkeley does not, of course, deny that there are general
words. But he rejects Locke's theory that general words denote, as he says, general ideas, if we mean by this ideas which
possess a positive universal content. A proper name, such as
William, signifies a particular thing, while a general word
signifies indifferently a plurality of things of a certain kind.
Its universality is a matter of use or function. If we once
understand this, we shall be saved from hunting for mysterious entities corresponding to general words. We can utter the
term 'material substance', but it does not denote any abstract general idea; and if we suppose that because we can
frame the term it must signify an entity apart from the
objects of perception, we are misled by words. Berkeley's
nominalism is thus of importance in his attack on Locke's
theory of material substance. 'Matter' is not a name in the
way in which William is a name, though some philosophers
seem to have thought mistakenly that it is.

3. Already at the beginning of the *Principles* Berkeley
speaks about sensory objects of knowledge as 'ideas'. But it
will perhaps be better to leave aside this complicated subject
for the moment, and to start with an approach to the theory
that sensory objects have no absolute existence of their own
apart from their being perceived, which does not necessarily
involve talking about these objects as 'ideas'.

According to Berkeley, anyone can have knowledge of the
fact that sensible things do not and cannot exist independ-

ently of being perceived if he attends to the meaning of the
term 'exist' when applied to these things. 'The table I write
on, I say, exists, that is, I see and feel it; and if I were out
of my study I should say it existed, meaning thereby that if
I was in my study I might perceive it, or that some other
spirit actually does perceive it.'[23] Berkeley thus challenges
the reader to find any other meaning for the proposition, 'the
table exists', than 'the table is perceived or perceivable'. It is
perfectly true to say, as any ordinary man would say, that
the table exists when nobody is in the room. But what can
this mean, asks Berkeley, save that if I were to enter the
room I should perceive the table or that if another person
were to enter the room he or she would, or could, perceive
the table? Even if I try to imagine the table existing out of
all relation to perception, I necessarily imagine myself or
someone else perceiving it; that is to say, I covertly introduce
a percipient subject, though I may not advert to the fact that
I am doing so. Berkeley can say, therefore, that 'the absolute
existence of unthinking things without any relation to their
being perceived, that seems perfectly unintelligible. Their
esse is *percipi*, nor is it possible they should have any existence
out of the minds or thinking things which perceive them.'[24]

Berkeley's contention, therefore, is that to say of a sensible
thing or body that it exists is to say that it is perceived or
perceivable: in his opinion, there is nothing else that it can
mean. This analysis, he maintains, does not affect the reality
of things. 'Existence is *percipi* or *percipere*. The horse is in
the stable, the books are in the study as before.'[25] In other
words, he does not assert that it is untrue to say that the
horse is in the stable when there is nobody about: he is concerned with the meaning of the statement. The following
note has already been quoted, but it is worth re-quoting. 'Let
it not be said that I take away Existence. I only declare the
meaning of the word so far as I can comprehend it.'[26] Further, Berkeley considers that his analysis of existential statements about sensible things is in accordance with the outlook
of the plain man whose mind has not been misled by metaphysical abstractions.

It might well be objected, of course, that though the ordinary man would certainly agree that to say that the horse
is in the stable when nobody is about means that if someone
enters the stable he would or could have the experience which
we call seeing a horse, he would boggle at the statement that
the horse's existence is to be perceived. For when he admits

that to say that the horse is in the stable 'means' that if someone entered the stable he would or could perceive a horse,
he really only intends to say that the second statement is a
consequence of the first. If the horse is in the stable, then
anyone with normal eyesight who enters the stable can perceive the horse, given the other requisite conditions for perception. But it does not follow that the horse's existence
consists in being perceived. Berkeley's position, however,
seems to approach very closely to that of some of the modern
neopositivists when they maintained that the meaning of an
empirical statement is identical with the mode of its verification. To enter the stable and perceive the horse is a way of
verifying the statement that there is a horse in the stable.
And when Berkeley says that the latter statement can only
mean that if a percipient subject enters the stable, he will
have or could have certain sensory experiences, this seems to
be another way of saying that the meaning of the statement
that there is a horse in the stable is identical with the mode
of its verification. This is not, of course, an adequate account
of his view. For it omits all mention not only of his theory
that sensible objects are ideas but also of his subsequent
introduction of God as a universal and omnipresent perceiver. But as far as the linguistic analysis aspect of his doctrine goes, there does seem to be some similarity between
his position and that of a number of modern neopositivists.
And Berkeley's position is subject to the same sort of criticism
which can be brought against the view of the neopositivists in
question.[27]

Before we go any further it may be as well to draw attention to the two following points. First, when Berkeley says
esse est percipi, he is talking only about sensible things or
objects. Secondly, the full formula is, *esse est aut percipi aut
percipere*, existence is either to be perceived or to perceive.
Besides sensible 'unthinking' things, the existence of which
consists in being perceived, there are minds or percipient
subjects, which are active and whose existence is to perceive
rather than to be perceived.

4. Already in the *Philosophical Commentaries* we can find
a statement of Berkeley's theory that sensible things are
ideas or collections of ideas and of the conclusion which he
draws, namely, that they cannot exist independently of
minds. 'All significant words stand for ideas. All knowledge
(is) about our ideas. All ideas come from without or from
within.'[28] In the first case the ideas are called sensations, in

the second, thoughts. To perceive is to have an idea. When, therefore, we perceive colours, for example, we are perceiving ideas. And as these ideas come from without, they are sensations. But 'no sensation can be in a senseless thing'.[29] Therefore ideas such as colours cannot inhere in material substance, an inert substrate. Hence it is quite unnecessary to postulate such a substance. 'Nothing like an idea can be in an unperceiving thing.'[30] To be perceived implies dependence on a perceiver. And to exist means either to perceive or to be perceived. 'Nothing properly but persons, i.e. conscious things, do exist; all other things are not so much existence as manners of the existence of persons.'[31] To show, therefore, that sensible objects are ideas is one of Berkeley's chief ways, if not the chief way, of showing the truth of the statement that the existence of these objects is to be perceived and of ruling out Locke's theory of material substance.

In the *Principles* Berkeley speaks of sensible things as collections or combinations of 'sensations or ideas' and draws the conclusion that they 'cannot exist otherwise than in a mind perceiving them'.[32] But though he asserts that it is evident that the objects of our knowledge are ideas,[33] he feels that this doctrine is not altogether in accordance with what most people believe. For he remarks that 'it is indeed an opinion strangely prevailing amongst men, that houses, mountains, rivers, and in a word all sensible objects have an existence natural or real, distinct from their being perceived by the understanding'.[34] But this strangely prevalent opinion is, none the less, a manifest contradiction. 'For what are the aforementioned objects but the things we perceive by sense, and what do we perceive besides our own ideas or sensations; and is it not plainly repugnant that any one of these or any combination of them should exist unperceived?'[35] The notion that these things can exist on their own, without relation to perception, 'will, perhaps, be found at bottom to depend on the doctrine of *abstract ideas*. For can there be a nicer strain of abstraction than to distinguish the existence of sensible objects from their being perceived, so as to conceive them existing unperceived?'[36]

Of course, if sensible things are ideas in the ordinary sense of the word, it is evident that they cannot exist apart from some mind. But what is the justification for calling them ideas? One line of argument pursued by Berkeley runs as follows. Some people make a distinction between secondary qualities, such as colour, sound and taste, and primary qualities, such as extension and figure. They admit that the former, as perceived, are not resemblances of anything existing outside the mind. They admit, in other words, their subjective character, that they are ideas. 'But they will have our ideas of the primary qualities to be patterns or images of things which exist without the mind, in an unthinking substance which they call *matter*. By matter therefore we are to understand an inert, senseless substance, in which extension, figure, and motion, do actually subsist.'[37] But this distinction will not do. It is impossible to conceive primary entirely apart from secondary qualities. 'Extension, figure, and motion, abstracted from all other qualities, are inconceivable.'[38] Further, if, as Locke thought, the relativity of secondary qualities provides a valid argument for their subjectivity, the same sort of argument can be employed with regard to the primary qualities. Figure or shape, for example, depends on the position of the perceiver, while motion is either swift or slow, and these are relative terms. Extension in general and motion in general are meaningless terms, depending 'on that strange doctrine of *abstract ideas*'.[39] In fine, primary qualities are no more independent of perception than are secondary qualities. The first no less than the second are ideas. And if they are ideas, they cannot exist or inhere in an unthinking substance or substrate. We can, therefore, get rid of Locke's material substance; and sensible things become clusters or collections of ideas.

Locke, as we saw earlier, did not actually say that secondary qualities are subjective. For in his technical terminology secondary qualities are the powers in things which produce in us certain ideas; and these powers are objective; that is, not dependent for their existence on our minds. However, if we mean by secondary qualities the qualities as perceived, colours, for example, we can say that for Locke they are subjective, being ideas in the mind. And it is from this point that Berkeley starts in the argument mentioned above. But the validity of the argument is certainly questionable. Berkeley seems to think that the 'relativity' of qualities shows that they are in the mind. There are no qualities in general, over and above the particular qualities perceived. And each particular quality perceived is perceived by and is relative to a particular subject. But it is not immediately evident that because the grass looks to me now green, now yellow or golden, the greenness and yellowness are ideas in the sense of being in my mind. Nor is it immediately evident that be-

cause a particular thing looks to me large in these circumstances and small in those circumstances or of one shape at
one time and of another shape at another time, extension
and figure are ideas. If, of course, we assume that, given the
objectivity of qualities, things must necessarily appear the
same to all people or to one person at all times and in all circumstances, it follows that if they do not so appear, they are
not objective. But there does not seem to be any cogent reason for making this assumption.

5. However, if we assume that sensible things are ideas, it
is evident that Locke's theory of a material substrate is an
unnecessary hypothesis. But we can go further than this, according to Berkeley, and say that the hypothesis is not merely
unnecessary but unintelligible. If we try to analyse the meaning of the term, we find that it consists of 'the idea of being
in general, together with the relative notion of its supporting
accidents. The general idea of being appeareth to me the
most abstract and incomprehensible of all other; and as for
its supporting accidents, this, as we have just now observed,
cannot be understood in the common sense of those words;
it must therefore be taken in some other sense, but what
that is they do not explain.'[40] The phrase 'supporting accidents'[41] cannot be taken in its ordinary sense, 'as when we
say that pillars support a building'. For material substance
is supposed to be logically prior to extension, an accident,
and to support it. 'In what sense therefore must it be
taken?'[42] In Berkeley's opinion, no definite meaning can be
given to the phrase.

The same line of thought is expressed more at length in
the *First Dialogue*. Hylas is brought to acknowledge that the
distinction between sensation and object, between an action
of the mind and its object, is untenable when we are talking
about perception. Sensible things are reducible to sensations;
and it is inconceivable that sensations should exist in an unperceiving substance. 'But then on the other hand, when I
look on sensible things in a different view, considering them
as so many modes and qualities, I find it necessary to suppose a material *substratum*, without which they cannot be
conceived to exist.'[43] Philonous then challenges Hylas to
explain what he means by material substrate. If he means
that it is spread under sensible qualities or accidents, it must
be spread under extension. In this case it must itself be extended. And then we are involved in an infinite regress.
Moreover, the same conclusion follows if we substitute the

idea of standing under or supporting for the idea of being a substratum or of being spread under.

Hylas protests that he is being taken too literally. But Philonous retorts: 'I am not for imposing any sense on your words: you are at liberty to explain them as you please. Only I beseech you, make me understand something by them. . . . Pray let me know any sense, literal or not literal, that you understand in it.'[44] In the end Hylas finds himself compelled to admit that he cannot assign any definite meaning to phrases such as 'supporting accidents' and 'material substrate'.[45] The upshot of the discussion, therefore, is that the statement that material things exist absolutely, without dependence on the mind, is meaningless. 'The absolute existence of unthinking things are words without a meaning, or which include a contradiction. This is what I repeat and inculcate, and earnestly recommend to the attentive thought of the reader.'[46]

6. Berkeley is at pains to show that the statement that sensible things are ideas is not equivalent to the statement that sensible things possess no reality. 'Say you, at this rate all's nothing but idea, mere phantasm. I answer that every thing is as real as ever. I hope that to call a thing "idea" makes it not the less real. Truly I should perhaps have stuck to the word "thing", and not mentioned the word "idea", were it not for a reason, and I think a good one too, which I shall give in the second Book.'[47] Again, 'On my principles there is a reality, there are things, there is a *rerum natura*'.[48] In the *Principles* Berkeley raises the objection that on his theory 'all that is real and substantial in Nature is banished out of the world: and instead thereof a chimerical scheme of ideas takes place. . . . What therefore becomes of the sun, moon, and stars? What must we think of houses, rivers, mountains, trees, stones; nay, even of our own bodies? Are all these but so many chimeras and illusions of the fancy?'[49] To this he answers that 'by the principles premised, we are not deprived of any one thing in Nature. Whatever we see, feel, hear, or any wise conceive or understand, remains as secure as ever, and is as real as ever. There is a *rerum natura*, and the distinction between realities and chimeras retains its full force.'[50]

If, however, sensible things are ideas, it follows that we eat and drink and are clothed with ideas. And this way of speaking sounds 'very harsh'. Of course it does, replies Berkeley; but the reason why it sounds harsh and strange is simply that in ordinary discourse the word 'idea' is not normally used for the things which we see and touch. The principal requirement is that we should understand in what sense the word is being used in the present context. 'I am not for disputing about the propriety, but the truth of the expression. If therefore you agree with me that we eat and drink and are clad with the immediate objects of sense which cannot exist unperceived or without the mind: I shall readily grant it more proper or conformable to custom, that they should be called things rather than ideas.'[51]

What, then, is the justification for using the term 'idea' in a sense which is admittedly not in accordance with common usage? 'I answer, I do it for two reasons: first, because the term *thing*, in contradistinction to *idea*, is generally supposed to denote somewhat existing without the mind: secondly, because *thing* hath a more comprehensive signification than *idea*, including spirits or thinking things as well as ideas. Since therefore the objects of sense exist only in the mind, and are withal thoughtless and inactive, I chose to mark them by the word *idea*, which implies those properties.'[52]

Because, therefore, Berkeley uses the word 'ideas' to refer to the immediate objects of sense, and because he does not deny the existence of the objects of sense-perception, he can maintain that his theory of ideas makes no difference to the reality of the sensible world. All that he gets rid of is Locke's material substance, which is not an object of sense and which will therefore not be missed by any ordinary man. 'I do not argue against the existence of any one thing that we can apprehend, either by sense or reflexion. That the things I see with mine eyes and touch with my hands do exist, really exist, I make not the least question. The only thing whose existence we deny, is that which philosophers call matter or corporeal substance. And in doing of this, there is no damage done to the rest of mankind, who, I dare say, will never miss it. The atheist indeed will want the colour of an empty name to support his impiety; and the philosophers may possibly find they have lost a great handle for trifling and disputation.'[53]

It is arguable that there is some confusion or inconsistency in Berkeley's use of the term 'idea'. In the first place he protests that he simply uses the term to signify what we perceive, sensible objects. And though this use of the term may be uncommon its use does not affect the reality of the objects of sense-perception. This suggests to the reader that the term is for Berkeley a purely technical one. To call sensible things ideas in this purely technical sense does not reduce them to ideas in the ordinary sense. At the same time Berkeley speaks, as we have seen, of 'sensations or ideas', as though the terms were synonymous. And, quite apart from the general impropriety of equating ideas and sensations, this inevitably suggests that sensible things are mere subjective modifications of our minds. For the word 'sensation' refers to something subjective and, indeed, to something private. It suggests that there is no real public sensible world, but rather as many private sensible worlds as there are percipient subjects. The sensible world then becomes something very like a dream world.

At this point, however, it is relevant to introduce Berkeley's distinction between ideas and images of things, even though it means touching on aspects of his philosophy which will be considered in the next chapter. Ideas, that is, sensible things, are said to be 'imprinted on the senses by the Author of Nature': they are called 'real things'.[54] When, for example, I open my eyes and see a piece of white paper, it does not depend on my choice that I see a piece of white paper, except in the sense that I can choose to look in one direction rather than in another. I cannot look in the direction of the paper and see a piece of green cheese instead. In Berkeley's language the ideas or qualities which compose the piece of white paper are imprinted on my senses. I can, however, have images of things which I have seen, and I can combine images at will, to form, for example, the image of a unicorn. In ordinary language the piece of white paper which I see on my table is not called an idea, whereas we do talk about having the idea of a unicorn. But though in Berkeley's terminology the piece of white paper is spoken of as a collection or cluster of ideas, these ideas are not dependent on the finite mind in the same way that the image of a unicorn is dependent on it. And thus there is room in Berkeley's theory for a distinction between the sphere of sensible reality and the sphere of images. This distinction is of importance; for Berkeley insisted, as will be mentioned in the next chapter, that there is an 'order of Nature', a coherent pattern of ideas which does not depend on human choice. At the same time, though real things, sensible things that is to say, do not depend simply on the human perceiver, they are none the less ideas, and they cannot exist in absolute independence of a mind. For Berkeley, therefore, these two statements are both true and important, namely, that ideas (in his sense of the term) are not entirely dependent on the *human* mind and that they are none the less ideas and so dependent on some mind.

I do not suggest that this distinction clears up all difficulties and answers all possible objections. For one thing, it still seems to follow from Berkeley's theory that there are as many private worlds as there are percipient subjects, and that there is no public world. Berkeley was not, of course, a solipsist. But to say that he was not a solipsist is not the same thing as saying that solipsism cannot be derived from his premisses. He believed, indeed, in a plurality of finite minds or spirits. But it is very difficult to see how on his premisses he can assure himself of the validity of this belief. However, the distinction described in the last paragraph does at least help us to understand how Berkeley could feel justified in maintaining that on his theory there is still a *rerum natura* and that sensible things are not reduced to the level of chimeras, even if there is some discrepancy between the common-sense aspect of this theory (sensible things are simply what we perceive or can perceive them to be) and its idealist aspects (sensible things are ideas, equivalent to sensations). The discrepancy can be expressed in this way. Berkeley sets out to describe the world of the ordinary man, excluding the unnecessary and indeed meaningless additions of metaphysicians; but the result of his analysis is a proposition which, as Berkeley himself was aware, the ordinary man would not be disposed to accept.

7. As a conclusion to this chapter we can raise the question whether Berkeley's use of the term 'idea' implies the representative theory of perception. Locke frequently, though not always, speaks about perceiving ideas rather than things. And inasmuch as ideas for him often represent things, this way of speaking implies the representative theory of perception. This is one reason, of course, why Locke depreciates sensitive knowledge and physics in comparison with mathematics. The question is, therefore, whether Berkeley is involved in the same theory and in the same difficulties.

The proper answer to this question seems to be clear enough, provided that we attend to Berkeley's own philosophy rather than to the fact that Locke furnished him with a point of departure. If we consider merely the last-mentioned fact, we may easily be inclined to father on Berkeley the

representative theory of perception. But if we attend carefully to his own philosophy, we shall recognize that he was
not involved in this theory.

What Berkeley calls ideas are not ideas of things: they *are*
things. They do not represent entities beyond themselves:
they are themselves entities. In perceiving ideas we perceive,
not images of sensible things, but sensible things themselves.
In the *Philosophical Commentaries* Berkeley says explicitly:
'the supposition that things are distinct from ideas takes
away all real truth and consequently brings in a universal
scepticism, since all our knowledge and contemplation is
confined barely to our own ideas'.[55] Again, 'the referring
ideas to things which are not ideas, the using the term "idea
of", is one great cause of mistake. . . .'[56] This is certainly
not the representative theory of perception, which is indeed
incompatible with Berkeley's philosophy. For on his premisses there is nothing for 'ideas' to represent. And, as can be
seen from the first of the two quotations just given, he objects against the theory that it leads to scepticism. For if the
immediate objects of sensible knowledge are ideas which are
supposed to represent things other than themselves, we can
never know that they do in fact represent things. Berkeley
doubtless borrowed from Locke the use of the term 'idea'
for the immediate object of perception; but this does not
mean that ideas fulfil the same function or have the same
status in Berkeley's philosophy that they do in Locke's. With
the latter, according at least to his prevalent way of speaking,
ideas act as intermediaries between the mind and things, in
the sense that though they are the immediate objects of
knowledge, they represent external things which are not dependent on our minds. With the former ideas are not intermediaries; they are sensible things themselves.

Chapter Thirteen

BERKELEY (3)

Finite spirits; their existence, nature and immortal char-
acter — The order of Nature — Berkeley's empiricist in-
terpretation of physics, especially as seen in the De motu
— The existence and nature of God — The relation of
sensible things to ourselves and to God — Causality —
Berkeley and other philosophers — Some remarks on
Berkeley's ethical ideas — A note on Berkeley's influence.

1. If sensible things are ideas, they can exist only in minds
or spirits. And spirits are thus the only substances. Ideas are
passive and inert: spirits, which perceive ideas, are active.
'*Thing* or *being* is the most general name of all, it comprehends under it two kinds entirely distinct and heterogeneous,
and which have nothing common but the name, to wit, *spirits*
and *ideas*. The former are *active, indivisible substances*: the
latter are *inert*, fleeting, dependent beings, which subsist
not by themselves, but are supported by[1] or exist in minds
or spiritual substances.'[2]

Spirits, therefore, cannot be ideas or like ideas. 'It is therefore necessary, in order to prevent equivocation and confounding natures perfectly disagreeing and unlike, that we
distinguish between *spirit* and *idea*.'[3] 'That this *substance*
which supports or perceives ideas should itself be an *idea* or
like an *idea*, is evidently absurd.'[4] Further, we cannot have,
properly speaking, any idea of spirit. Indeed, 'it is manifestly
impossible there should be any such *idea*'.[5] 'A spirit is one
simple, undivided, active being: as it perceives ideas, it is
called the *understanding*; and as it produces or operates about
them, it is called the *will*. Hence there can be no idea formed
of a soul or spirit: for all ideas whatever, being passive and

inert, they cannot represent unto us, by way of image or likeness, that which acts.'[6]

When he says that we can have no idea of spirit, Berkeley is using the term 'idea' in his technical sense. He does not mean that we have no knowledge of what is signified by the word 'spirit'. It must be admitted that 'we have some notion of soul, spirit, and the operations of the mind, such as willing, loving, hating, inasmuch as we know or understand the meaning of those words'.[7] A distinction is thus made by Berkeley between 'notion', namely, the mental or spiritual as object, and 'idea', namely, the sensible or corporeal as object. We can have a notion of spirit but not an idea in the technical sense. 'In a large sense indeed, we may be said to have an idea, or rather a notion of *spirit*; that is, we understand the meaning of the word; otherwise we could not affirm or deny anything of it.'[8] A spirit can be described as 'that which thinks, wills, and perceives; this, and this alone, constitutes the signification of that term'.[9] It will be remembered that an entry in Berkeley's notebooks[10] suggests that the possibility had occurred to him of applying to the mind the same sort of phenomenalistic analysis which he applied to bodies. But he rejected this idea. It seemed evident to him that if sensible things are reduced to ideas, there must be spirits or spiritual substances which have or perceive these ideas.

The question arises, how do we know of the existence of spirits, that is, of a plurality of finite spirits or selves? 'We comprehend our own existence by inward feeling or reflexion, and that of other spirits by reason.'[11] That I exist is, after all, evident; for I perceive ideas, and I am aware that I am distinct from the ideas which I perceive. But I know the existence of other finite spirits or selves only by reason, that is, by inference. 'It is plain that we cannot know the existence of other spirits, otherwise than by their operations, or the ideas excited by them in us. I perceive several motions, changes, and combinations of ideas, that inform me there are certain particular agents like myself, which accompany them, and concur in their production. Hence the knowledge I have of other spirits is not immediate, as is the knowledge of my ideas; but depending on the intervention of ideas, by me referred to agents or spirits distinct from myself, as effects or concomitant signs.'[12] Berkeley returns to this matter in *Alciphron*. 'In a strict sense I do not see Alciphron, i.e. that individual thinking thing, but only such visible signs and

tokens as suggest and infer the being of that invisible thinking principle or soul.'[13] And he draws an analogy between
our mediate knowledge of other finite spirits and our mediate
knowledge of God. In both cases it is through sensible signs
that we come to know the existence of an active agent.

Apart from any other possible criticism, this account of
our knowledge of the existence of other finite spirits or selves
seems to labour under the following difficulty. According to
Berkeley, 'when we see the colour, size, figure, and motions
of a man, we perceive only certain sensations or ideas excited
in our own minds: and these being exhibited to our view in
sundry distinct collections serve to mark out unto us the
existence of finite and created spirits like ourselves'.[14] 'We
do not see a man, if by *man* is meant that which lives,
moves, perceives, and thinks as we do: but only such a certain collection of ideas as directs us to think there is a distinct
principle of thought and motion like to ourselves, accompanying and represented by it.'[15] But even if I do think in
this way, can I be certain that the ideas produced in me
which I attribute to other finite spirits are not really the
effects of God? If God produces in me, without there being
any material substance, the ideas which on the substance-
accident theory would be regarded as accidents of material
or corporeal substance, how can I be certain that he does not
produce in me, without there being any other finite selves,
the ideas which I take to be signs of the presence of such
selves, that is, of spiritual substances other than myself?

At first sight Berkeley may appear to have felt this difficulty. For he asserts that the existence of God is more evident
than the existence of human beings. But his reason for saying
this is that the number of signs of God's existence is greater
than the number of signs of any given man's existence. Thus
Alciphron asks: 'What! Do you pretend you can have the
same assurance of the being of a God that you can have of
mine, whom you actually see stand before you and talk to
you?'[16] And Euphranor answers: 'The very same, if not
greater.' He goes on to state that whereas he is convinced of
the existence of another finite self by only a few signs, 'I do
at all times and in all places perceive sensible signs which
evince the being of God.' Similarly, in the *Principles* Berkeley says that 'we may even assert, that the existence of God
is far more evidently perceived than the existence of men;
because the effects of Nature are infinitely more numerous
and considerable than those ascribed to human agents'.[17]

But he does not tell us how we can be certain that the ideas which we take to be signs of the presence of finite spiritual substances really are what we think they are. Perhaps, however, he would reply that we do in point of fact discriminate between the particular effects which we ascribe to finite agents and the general order of Nature which is presupposed by these effects; and that his theory does not demand any further grounds for discrimination than those which we in fact possess and utilize. From ideas or observable effects which are analogous to those which we are conscious of producing, we infer the existence of other selves; and this is sufficient evidence. But if anyone is dissatisfied with such an answer and wishes to know what justification there is, on Berkeley's premisses, for making this inference, he will not receive much help from Berkeley's writings.

Some of Berkeley's descriptions of the nature of a spirit have already been mentioned. But it can hardly be successfully claimed, I think, that his descriptions are always consistent. In the *Philosophical Commentaries* the suggestion is made that the mind is 'a congeries of perceptions. Take away perceptions and you take away the mind: put the perceptions and you put the mind.'[18] As has been noted, Berkeley did not pursue this phenomenalistic analysis of mind. But even later he says that the existence (*esse*) of spirits is to perceive (*percipere*), which implies that a spirit is essentially the act of perceiving. However, he also tells that the word 'spirit' means 'that which thinks, wills and perceives; this, and this alone, constitutes the signification of that term'.[19] Hence we can say in general that Berkeley rejected the idea of applying to mind the type of phenomenalistic analysis which he applied to bodies, and that he accepted Locke's theory of immaterial or spiritual substance.[20] And it is on this basis, of course, that he maintains the immortality of the human soul or spirit.

If, as some held, the soul of man were a thin vital flame or a system of animal spirits, it would be corruptible like the body. It could not survive 'the ruin of the tabernacle, wherein it is enclosed'.[21] But 'we have shown that the soul is indivisible, incorporeal, unextended, and it is consequently incorruptible'.[22] This does not mean that the human soul is incapable of annihilation even by the infinite power of God; 'but only that it is not liable to be broken or dissolved by the ordinary Laws of Nature or motion'.[23] This is what is meant by saying that the soul of man is naturally immortal;

namely, that it cannot be affected by the motions, changes and decay 'which we hourly see befall natural bodies'.[24] The notion that the soul of man is corporeal and corruptible 'hath been greedily embraced and cherished by the worst part of mankind as the most effectual antidote against all impressions of virtue and religion'.[25] But the soul, as spiritual substance, is naturally immortal; and this truth is of great importance for religion and morality.

2. Returning from spirits to bodies, we have seen that according to Berkeley his analysis of the latter leaves intact the *rerum natura*. 'There is a *rerum natura*, and the distinction between realities and chimeras retains its full force.'[26] It is quite proper, therefore, to speak of laws of Nature. 'There are certain general laws that run through the whole chain of natural effects: these are learned by the observation and study of Nature. . . .'[27] Berkeley is thus quite ready to speak of 'the whole system, immense, beautiful, glorious beyond expression and beyond thought'.[28] We have to remember that for him sensible things or bodies are precisely what we perceive or can perceive them to be, and that he calls these phenomena 'ideas'. These ideas form a coherent pattern: we can discern more or less regular sequences. Regular sequences or series can be expressed in the form of 'laws', statements about the regular behaviour of sensible things. But connections in Nature are not necessary connections: they may be more or less regular, but they are always contingent. Ideas are imprinted on our minds in more or less regular series by the Author of Nature, God. And to say that Y regularly follows X is to say that that God imprints in us ideas in this order. And since all particular regular series, and the whole order of Nature in general, depend on the unceasing divine activity and will, what we call Nature is shot through and through, as it were, with contingency.

Physics, therefore, or natural philosophy is not denied by Berkeley. But physical laws which state, for example, that certain types of bodies attract one another state connections which are purely factual and not necessary. That certain bodies behave in a certain way depends on God; and though we may expect that God will act uniformly for the most part we cannot know that He will always behave in the same way. If, generally speaking, Y always follows X, and if on a given occasion it does not do so, we may have to speak of a miracle. But if God acts miraculously, that is to say, in a

manner quite different from the way in which He normally
acts, He does not, so to speak, break a hard and fast law of
Nature. For a law of Nature states the way in which things
generally behave as a matter of fact, as far as our experience
goes, not the way in which they must behave. 'By a diligent
observation of the phenomena within our view, we may discover the general laws of Nature, and from them deduce
the other phenomena. I do not say demonstrate; for all deductions of that kind depend on a supposition that the Author of Nature always operates uniformly, and in a constant
observance of those rules we take for principles: which we
cannot evidently know.'[29] In the language of ideas God is
accustomed to imprint ideas on us in a certain order or in
certain regular sequences. And this enables us to state 'laws
of Nature'. But God is in no way bound to imprint ideas on
us always in the same order. Miracles, therefore, are possible.
They do not involve any interference with necessary connections between distinct ideas. For there are no such necessary connections. There is, indeed, a *rerum natura*, and
there is an order of Nature, but it is not a necessary order.

3. In the foregoing section I assumed the existence of
God and Berkeley's view of the way in which God acts. For
I wished to bring out the fact that for him the order of Nature is not a necessary order. In the present section I wish to
illustrate Berkeley's markedly empiricist, even positivistic,
interpretation of physics, especially as seen in the *De motu*.

Berkeley's attack on abstract general ideas naturally has
its repercussions in his interpretation of physics. He does not
say that the use of abstract terms is illegitimate and serves
no useful purpose; but he does suggest that the use of such
terms may lead people to imagine that they possess more
knowledge than they actually have, because they can employ
a word to cover their ignorance. 'The great mechanical principle now in vogue is *attraction*. That a stone falls to the
earth, or the sea swells towards the moon, may to some appear sufficiently explained thereby. But how are we en-
lightened by being told this is done by attraction?'[30] The
physicist (Berkeley frequently speaks of 'mathematicians') or
natural philosopher may come to think that a term like 'attraction' signifies an essential quality inherent in bodies,
which acts as a real cause. But it is no such thing. As a matter
of pure empirical fact the observed relations between some
bodies are of such a kind that we describe them as cases of
mutual attraction; but the word 'attraction' does not signify

an entity, and it is idle to suppose that the behaviour of bodies is explained by the use of such a term. The physicist is concerned with description and with the grouping of analogies under general 'laws' with a view to prediction and practical utility: but he is not concerned with causal explanation, if we mean by 'cause' an active efficient cause. And it is a great mistake to suppose that phenomena *a*, *b* and *c* are explained by saying that they are due to P, where P is an abstract term. For to suppose this is to misunderstand the use of the term. It does not signify any entity which could be an active efficient cause.

In the *De motu* Berkeley develops this point of view. He begins the treatise with the remark that 'in the pursuit of truth we must beware of being misled by terms which we do not rightly understand. Almost all philosophers utter the caution; few observe it.'[31] Take terms such as 'effort' and 'conation'. Such terms are properly applicable only to animate things: when applied to inanimate things they are used metaphorically and in a vague sense. Again, natural philosophers are accustomed to use abstract general terms, and there is a temptation to think they signify actual occult entities. Some writers speak, for example, of absolute space as though it were something, a distinct entity. But we shall find on analysis that 'nothing else is signified by these words than pure privation or negation, that is, mere nothing'.[32]

According to Berkeley, we ought to 'distinguish mathematical hypotheses from the natures of things'.[33] Terms such as 'force', 'gravity' and 'attraction' do not denote physical or metaphysical entities; they are 'mathematical hypotheses'. 'As for attraction, it is certainly employed by Newton, not as a true, physical quality, but only as a mathematical hypothesis. Indeed Leibniz, when distinguishing elementary effort or solicitation from impetus, admits that these entities are not really found in nature, but have to be formed by abstraction.'[34] Mechanics cannot progress without the use of mathematical abstractions and hypotheses, and their use is justified by their success, that is, by their practical utility. But the practical usefulness of a mathematical abstraction does not prove that it denotes any physical or metaphysical entity. 'The mechanician employs certain abstract and general terms, imagining in bodies force, action, attraction . . . which are of great utility for theories and formulations, as also for computations about motion, even if in the truth of things, and in bodies actually existing, they would be sought in vain, just like the things which are fictions made by the geometers through mathematical abstraction.'[35]

One main reason why people are inclined to be misled by abstract terms as used in physics is that they think that the physicist is concerned with finding the true efficient causes of phenomena. They are inclined, therefore, to think that a word such as 'gravity' signifies an existent entity or quality which is the true efficient cause of certain motions and which explains the latter. But 'it does not belong to physics or mechanics to give efficient causes. . . .'[36] One reason why Berkeley says this is, of course, that in his view the only true causes are incorporeal agents. This is apparent in the following quotation. 'In physical philosophy we must seek the causes and solutions of phenomena from mechanical principles. Physically, therefore, a thing is explained not by assigning its truly active and incorporeal cause but by demonstrating its connection with mechanical principles, such as *action and reaction are always contrary and equal*. . . .'[37] What is meant by mechanical principles? The primary laws of motion, 'proved by experiments, developed by reasoning and rendered universal . . . are fittingly called principles, since from them are derived both general mechanical theorems and particular explanations of phenomena'.[38] To give a physical explanation of an event, therefore, is to show how it can be deduced from a high-level hypothesis. And explanations of this kind are concerned with behaviour rather than with existence. The existence of phenomena is explained in metaphysical philosophy by deriving it from its true efficient cause, which is incorporeal. The physicist is concerned to this extent with 'causes', that when he finds B constantly following A and never occurring when A has not preceded, where A and B are phenomena, he speaks of A as cause and B as effect. But phenomena are ideas, and ideas cannot be active efficient causes; and if this is what is understood by causes, the physicist is not concerned with them.

Berkeley's contention, therefore, is that science is left unimpaired by his theory of ideas and by his metaphysics, provided that the nature of science is understood. Metaphysics must be eliminated from physics, and the two should not be confused. This elimination will purify physics of obscurities and vague verbiage and will save us from being misled by words which, however useful they may be, do not denote entities or actual qualities of entities. At the same time Berkeley did not eliminate metaphysics from physics in order to dissolve the former. His desire was rather to point the way to metaphysics. For if we once understand that physical science is not concerned with the truly active efficient causes of phenomena, we shall not only be saved from interpreting wrongly the function and meaning of words such as gravity and attraction but also be prompted to look elsewhere for the cause of the existence of phenomena. Berkeley spoke in a positivistic way about physics; but at the back of his mind was the desire to disabuse people of the notion that an adequate causal explanation of phenomena can be given in terms of gravity, attraction, and so on, which do not signify entities, or existent qualities, but are used for convenience in hypotheses which are validated by their success in grouping phenomena and deducing them from certain principles describing the behaviour of bodies. And he wished to disabuse people of a mistaken interpretation of the function of physical science because he wished to show them that the true causal explanations of phenomena can be found only in metaphysics, which establishes the relation of phenomena to God, the ultimate incorporeal and true efficient cause. 'Only by meditation and reasoning can truly active causes be brought out of the darkness with which they are surrounded and be so to some extent known. To deal with them pertains to first philosophy or metaphysics.'[39]

In this section reference has been made to physics or physical science, understood as including mechanics. But in the *De motu* Berkeley makes a curious distinction between physics and mechanics. 'In physics sense and experience, which reach only to apparent effects, hold sway; in mechanics the abstract notions of mathematicians are admitted.'[40] In other words, physics is concerned with the description of phenomena and their behaviour, while mechanics involves theorizing and explanatory hypotheses which employ mathematics. The reason why Berkeley makes this distinction is that he wishes to distinguish between the observed facts and the theories constructed to understand or explain these facts. For unless we make this last distinction, we shall be inclined to postulate occult entities corresponding to the abstract terms 'of the mathematicians'. Words such as 'gravity' or 'force' do not denote observable entities. Therefore, we may be inclined to think, there must be occult entities or qualities corresponding to these terms. 'But what an occult quality is, or how any quality can act or do anything, we can scarcely conceive—indeed we cannot conceive. . . . What is itself

occult explains nothing.'[41] But if we distinguish carefully
between observed effects and the hypotheses constructed to
explain them, we shall be in a better position to understand
the function of the abstract terms employed in these hypotheses. 'In part the terms have been invented by common
habit to abbreviate speech, and in part they have been
thought out for the purpose of teaching.'[42] In reasoning
about sensible things we reason about particular bodies. But
we require abstract terms for our universal propositions about
particular bodies.

4. There is, therefore, for Berkeley an order of Nature, a
system of phenomena or ideas which renders possible the
construction of the natural sciences. But, as we have just
seen, it is idle to look to the scientist for knowledge of the
cause or causes of the existence of phenomena. And this
suggests at once that Berkeley's proof of the existence of
God will be an *a posteriori* proof, a variant of the causal
argument. When he says in the *Philosophical Commentaries*, 'Absurd to argue the existence of God from his idea. We
have no idea of God. 'Tis impossible,'[43] he is doubtless
thinking primarily of his technical use of the word 'idea'.
For it is obvious that there can be no idea of God, if 'God'
means a spiritual being and 'idea' is used for the object of
sense-perception. And when Alciphron is made to say that
he is not to be persuaded by metaphysical arguments, 'such,
for instance, as are drawn from the idea of an all-perfect
being',[44] we have to remember that Alciphron is the 'minute philosopher' and the defender of atheism. Nevertheless,
it is safe to say that Berkeley did not accept the so-called
ontological argument, as used in different ways by St. Anselm
and Descartes. His proof is a causal argument, based on the
existence of sensible things. And the characteristic feature
of Berkeley's argument for God's existence is the use which
he makes of his theory of 'ideas'. If sensible things are ideas,
and if these ideas are not dependent simply on our minds,
they must be referred to a mind other than our own. 'It is
evident to everyone, that those things which are called the
works of Nature, that is, the far greater part of the ideas or
sensations perceived by us, are not produced by, or dependent on the wills of men. There is, therefore, some other
spirit that causes them, since it is repugnant that they should
subsist by themselves.'[45]

In the *Dialogues* the proof of God's existence is put in
this succinct form. '*Sensible things do really exist: and if they*

exist, they are necessarily perceived by an infinite mind: therefore there is an infinite mind, or God. This furnishes you with a direct and immediate demonstration, from a most evident principle, of the *being of a God.*'[46] Berkeley does not enter at any length into the question of the unicity of God; he seems to proceed more or less straight from the statement that sensible things or ideas do not depend on our minds to the conclusion that they depend on one infinite mind. He practically takes it for granted that the system and harmony and beauty of Nature show that Nature is the product of one infinitely wise and perfect spirit, God, who upholds all things by His power. We do not, of course, see God. But we do not, for the matter of that, see finite spirits. We infer the existence of a finite spirit from 'some one finite and narrow assemblage of ideas', whereas 'we do at all times and in all places perceive manifest tokens of the divinity'.[47]

The blemishes and defects of Nature do not constitute any valid argument against this inference. The apparent waste of seeds and embryos, and the accidental destruction of immature plants and animals, may seem to point to faulty and careless management and organization, if we judge by human standards. But 'the splendid profusion of natural things should not be interpreted (as) weakness or prodigality in the agent who produces them, but rather be looked on as an argument of the riches of his power'.[48] And many things which appear to us to be evil, because they affect us painfully, can be seen to be good if they are regarded as part of the whole system of things. In *Alciphron* the speaker with this name is depicted as saying that while it may plausibly be alleged that a little evil in creation sets the good in a stronger light, this principle cannot account for 'blots so large and so black. . . . That there should be so much vice and so little virtue upon earth, and that the laws of God's kingdom should be so ill observed by His subjects, is what can never be reconciled with that surpassing wisdom and goodness of the supreme Monarch.'[49] To this Berkeley answers that moral faults are a result of human choice, and also that we ought not to exaggerate the position of human beings in the universe. 'It seems we are led not only by revelation, but by common sense, observing and inferring from the analogy of visible things, to conclude there are innumerable orders of intelligent beings more happy and more perfect than man.'[50]

It would be wrong to conclude from Berkeley's somewhat summary exposition of the proof of God's existence that the philosopher who was so ready to apply a critical analysis to terms such as 'material substance' was blind to the difficulties which can be encountered in analysing the meaning of the terms predicated of God. Thus he makes Lysicles speak as follows: 'You must know then that at bottom the being of God is a point in itself of small consequence, and a man may make this concession without yielding much. The great point is what sense the word God is to be taken in.'[51] There have been people, says Lysicles, who have maintained that terms such as wisdom and goodness, when predicated of God, 'must be understood in a quite different sense from what they signify in the vulgar acceptation, or from anything that we can form a notion of or conceive'.[52] Thus they were able to meet objections brought against the predication of such attributes of God by denying that they were predicated in any known sense. But this denial was equivalent to denying that the attributes belonged to God at all. 'And thus denying the attributes of God, they in effect denied His being, though perhaps they were not aware of it.'[53] In other words, to assert that the terms predicated of God are to be understood in a purely equivocal sense is to assert agnosticism. Such people so whittled away the meaning of the word 'God' by qualifications that 'nothing (was) left but the name without any meaning annexed to it'.[54]

Lysicles takes it that this agnostic position was maintained by a number of Fathers and Schoolmen. But Crito, with an apology for introducing such unpolished and unfashionable writers as the Schoolmen into good company, gives a summary historical account of the doctrine of analogical predication, in which he shows that the position of Schoolmen such as St. Thomas Aquinas and Suárez was not the same as that of the Pseudo-Dionysius. These Schoolmen did not deny, for example, that knowledge can be attributed to God in a proper sense, but only that we can properly attribute to God the imperfections of knowledge as it is found in creatures. When, for instance, Suárez says that 'knowledge is said not to be properly in God it must be understood in a sense including imperfection, such as discursive knowledge. . . . (But) of knowledge taken in general for the clear evident understanding of all truth, he expressly affirms that it is in God, and that this was never denied by any philosopher who believed a God.'[55] Similarly, when the Schoolmen said that

God must not be supposed to exist in the same sense as
created beings, they meant that He exists 'in a more eminent
and perfect manner'.[56]

This represents Berkeley's own position. On the one hand,
the terms which are first predicated of creatures and afterwards of God must be predicated of Him 'in the proper
sense, . . . in the true and formal acceptation of the
words. Otherwise, it is evident that every syllogism brought
to prove those attributes or (which is the same thing) to
prove the being of a God, will be found to consist of four
terms, and consequently can conclude nothing.'[57] On the
other hand, the terms predicated of God cannot be predicated
in the same imperfect manner or degree in which they are
predicated of creatures. My notion of God, Berkeley argues,
is obtained by reflecting on my own soul, 'heightening its
powers, and removing its imperfections'.[58] I conceive God
according to the notion of spirit which I obtain by self-reflec-
tion. The notion remains essentially the same, though in
conceiving God I remove the limitations and imperfections
attaching to the notion of finite spirit as such.

It cannot be said that Berkeley carried the analysis of the
meaning of the terms predicated of God any further than
the Scholastics had done. Nor did he give much, if any,
consideration to the possible objection that in the process of
removing imperfections we also remove the positive describ-
able content of the term in question. He did, however, understand that there is a problem connected with the meaning of
the terms predicated of God. And among the eminent modern philosophers who stood outside the Scholastic tradition
he was one of the very few who paid any serious attention to
the problem. Analogy in this context was scarcely considered
by the non-Scholastic philosophers. And this is one reason
why discussion of the problem by analytic philosophers today
not infrequently appears to believers as being purely destructive in character. On occasion, of course, it has been
destructive. But one ought also to understand that this discussion represents the resuscitation of a problem with which
the Schoolmen, and Berkeley, concerned themselves, but
which was scarcely touched by the majority of the better-
known modern philosophers.

5. Now, Berkeley frequently speaks of sensible things as
though they existed in our minds. Thus we read that God
'excites those ideas in our minds',[59] and that ideas are 'imprinted on the senses'.[60] This suggests that the world is be-

ing constantly renewed or rather re-created. 'There is a mind which affects me every moment with all the sensible impressions I perceive.'[61] Again, though the metaphysical hypothesis of seeing all things in God is to be rejected, 'this optic language is equivalent to a constant creation, betokening an immediate act of power and providence'.[62] And Berkeley speaks of 'the instantaneous production and reproduction of so many signs, combined, dissolved, transposed, diversified, and adapted to such an endless variety of purposes. . . .'[63] It is also suggested, as has been already remarked, that there are as many private worlds as there are percipient subjects. And, indeed, Berkeley admits that while in the vulgar acceptation of the word 'same' we can be said to perceive the same objects, we do not do so, strictly speaking, any more than a given individual sees the same object which he touches or perceives the same object with the microscope that he perceives with the naked eye.[64]

But Berkeley also speaks of sensible things or ideas as existing in the mind of God. Natural things do not depend on me in the same way that the image of a unicorn depends on me. But, being ideas, they cannot subsist by themselves. Therefore 'there must be some other mind wherein they exist'.[65] Again, 'Men commonly believe that all things are known or perceived by God, because they believe the being of a God, whereas I on the other side, immediately and necessarily conclude the being of a God, because all sensible things must be perceived by Him'.[66] Berkeley was unwilling to deny all exteriority to sensible things; and he wished to give a meaning to the statement that things exist when no finite spirit is perceiving them. That is to say, he wished to give a further meaning to the statement that the horse is in the stable when nobody is perceiving it than the meaning which consists in saying that this statement is equivalent to the statement that anyone who entered the stable would or could have the experience which we call seeing a horse. And he can supply this further meaning only by saying that God is always perceiving the horse, even when no finite spirit is doing so. 'When I deny sensible things an existence out of the mind, I do not mean my mind in particular, but all minds. Now it is plain they have an existence exterior to my mind, since I find them by experience to be independent of it. There is therefore some other mind wherein they exist, during the intervals between the time of my perceiving them. . . . And as the same is true with regard to all other finite created spirits, it necessarily follows there is an *omnipresent eternal Mind*, which knows and comprehends all things, and exhibits them to our view in such a manner and according to such rules as he himself hath ordained, and are by us termed the *Laws of Nature*.'[67]

At first sight at least we are faced with two divergent views in which the statement that to exist is either to perceive or to be perceived assumes different meanings. On the first view to perceive refers to the finite subject, and to be perceived means to be perceived by this subject. On the second view to perceive refers to God and to be perceived means to be perceived by God. But Berkeley attempts to reconcile the two positions by means of a distinction between eternal and relative existence. 'All objects are eternally known by God, or which is the same thing, have an eternal existence in his mind: but when things before imperceptible to creatures are, by a decree of God, made perceptible to them; then they are said to begin a relative existence, with respect to created minds.'[68] Sensible things, therefore, have an 'archetypal and eternal' existence in the divine mind and an 'ectypal or natural' existence in created minds.[69] Creation takes place when the ideas receive 'ectypal' existence.

This distinction justifies Berkeley in saying that he does not share Malebranche's theory of the vision of ideas in God. For what we perceive are ideas as possessing relative or ectypal existence. These ideas come into being when they are imprinted on our minds by God. And they are thus distinct from the ideas as eternally present in the divine mind. But it then appears to follow that we cannot speak of the ideas which we perceive as existing in the divine mind when we are not perceiving them. For they are not the same as the ideas which are present in the divine mind. If they were the same, it would be very difficult for Berkeley to escape embracing the theory of the vision of things in God, a theory which he emphatically rejects.

It may be said that this distinction should not be pressed to the extent of supposing that Berkeley postulated multitudinous sets of ideas; one set for each human percipient, all these sets possessing ectypal existence, and one set in the divine mind, possessing archetypal existence. What Berkeley means, it may be said, is simply that the same sensible things which, as perceived by a finite subject, possess ectypal or natural existence possess, as perceived by God, archetypal existence. After all, Berkeley speaks explicitly of objects eternally known by God and having an eternal existence in His mind as being made perceptible to creatures and thus beginning a relative existence.[70]

True, Berkeley does speak in this way, and I have no wish to question the fact. But it seems to me disputable whether it will fit in with his other ways of speaking. If we perceive objects existing in the mind of God, we have that vision of things in God which, according to Berkeley, we do not enjoy. If, however, sensible things are our sensations or if they are ideas imprinted on us by God, they must presumably be distinct from the ideas in God.

Berkeley's fundamental aim is, of course, to show that sensible things have no *absolute* existence independent of mind, and thus to cut the ground from under the feet of the materialists and atheists. And this involves for him getting rid of Locke's material substrate as a useless and indeed unintelligible hypothesis and by proving that sensible things are ideas. Then two points of view seem to manifest themselves. First, sensible things are ideas in finite minds, not in the sense that they are arbitrarily constructed by the latter, but in the sense that they are imprinted on or presented to finite minds by the unceasing divine activity. To say, therefore, that the horse is in the stable when nobody is there to perceive it is simply to say that if, given the requisite conditions, anyone were to enter the stable, God would imprint certain ideas on his mind. And this is a metaphysical way of saying that the statement that the horse is in the stable when nobody is there to perceive it means that if anyone were to enter the stable, then, given the requisite conditions, he would have the experience which we call seeing a horse. But this point of view seems to raise difficulties with regard to the existence of the sensible world before the advent of man. Hence Berkeley introduces a second point of view according to which ideas (sensible things) are always perceived by God. But this cannot mean that sensible things are perceived by God because they exist. For they would then be made independent of mind. They must exist because God perceives them. And this means that they must be ideas in the divine mind. But Berkeley does not wish to say that we enjoy the vision of things in God. Hence he introduces the distinction between ectypal or natural and archetypal existence, falling back on the old theory of 'divine ideas'. But in this case sensible things as our ideas are distinct from the ideas possessing archetypal existence in the divine mind. And it is not then proper to say that the horse is in the stable, when it is not perceived by a finite spirit, because God perceives it. For God does not have my ideas when I am not having them. I should not care to state dogmatically that these various ways of speaking cannot be reconciled. But it seems to me very difficult to reconcile them.

It is sometimes said that Berkeley's position is difficult to refute because of the difficulty in showing that God could not act in the way that he describes, namely, imprinting ideas on our minds or presenting them to us. But those who say this forget that they are presupposing God's existence, whereas Berkeley argues from *esse est percipi* to God's existence. He does not presuppose theism and use it to prove phenomenalism: he proceeds the other way round, maintaining that phenomenalism entails theism. This is a point of view which those philosophers who followed him in his empiricism and developed it can scarcely be said to have shared. But, quite apart from this question, his phenomenalism itself seems to contain two elements. First, there is the view that sensible things are simply what we perceive or can perceive them to be. This is what may be called the common-sense element inasmuch as the ordinary man never thinks of Locke's inert, unchanging and unknowable material substrate. (The exclusion of Locke's material substrate does not necessarily entail the exclusion of substance in any sense, of course.) Secondly, there is the view that sensible things are ideas. And in so far as this view cannot be reduced to a mere decision to use a word in an uncommon way, it can scarcely be said to represent the view of the ordinary man, whatever Berkeley may say. It is disputable whether these two elements are, as Berkeley thought they were, inseparable.

Finally, there is one topic which should be briefly mentioned in this section. It has sometimes been maintained that Berkeley came to substitute *esse est concipi* for *esse est percipi*, moving from empiricism to rationalism. And the main foundation of this contention is constituted by a number of remarks in *Siris* where he speaks in a deprecatory way of the senses in comparison with reason. Thus he says that 'we know a thing when we understand it; and we understand it when we can interpret or tell what it signifies. Strictly, the sense knows nothing. We perceive indeed sounds by hearing, and characters (letters) by sight; but we are not therefore said to understand them.'[71] And he blames 'the Cartesians and their followers, who consider sensation as a mode of thinking'.[72]

It seems, indeed, to be true that in *Siris* we can see a Platonic influence at work, leading to frequent disparaging remarks about the cognitive value of sensation by itself. And it also seems to be true that Berkeley felt that there was some difficulty in talking about God as 'perceiving' things. Alluding to Newton's idea of space as the divine *sensorium*, he remarks that 'there is no sense nor sensory, nor anything like a sense or sensory, in God. Sense implies an impression from some other being, and denotes a dependence in the soul which hath it. Sense is a passion; and passions imply imperfection. God knoweth all things as pure mind or intellect; but nothing by sense, nor in nor through a sensory. Therefore to suppose a sensory of any kind—whether space or any other—in God, would be very wrong, and lead us into false conceptions of His nature.'[73] But though the philosophical parts of *Siris* (most of this curious work is concerned with the virtues of tar-water) manifest a rather different atmosphere or mood from that of Berkeley's earlier writings, it is questionable if the book represents any such fundamental change of view as has been suggested. The distinction between sensation and thought may have been accentuated in *Siris*, but it was implicit in Berkeley's earlier writings. As we have seen, he insisted on the distinction between observation of phenomena and reasoning or theorizing about them. Again, Berkeley had already stated in express terms in the *Dialogues* that 'God, whom no external being can affect, who perceives nothing by sense as we do . . . (cannot be affected by) any sensation at all'.[74] God knows or understands all things, but not by sense. Hence I do not think that it is correct to say that *Siris* represents any fundamental change in Berkeley's philosophy. The most we can say is that if certain lines of thought had been followed out and developed, lines of thought which were already implicit in earlier writings, a different version of his philosophy might have been produced in which, for example, difficulties arising from talk about God perceiving things and about 'ideas' existing in the divine mind when we are not perceiving them would have been cleared up.

6. We have already seen that Berkeley gives an empiricist or phenomenalistic analysis of the causal relation as far as the activity of sensible things is concerned. In fact, we cannot properly speak of them as active causes at all. If *B* regu-

larly follows A in such a way that, given A, B follows and that, in the absence of A, B does not occur, we speak of A as cause and of B as effect. But this does not mean that A acts efficiently in the production of B. The latter follows the former according to the disposition of God. Ideas, being ideas, are passive and cannot, properly speaking, exercise efficient causality. The occurrence of A is the sign of the coming occurrence of B. 'The connexion of ideas does not imply the relation of *cause* and *effect*, but only of a mark or *sign* with the thing *signified*. The fire which I see is not the cause of the pain I suffer upon my approaching it, but the mark that forewarns me of it.'[75]

There are, therefore, as one would expect, two elements in Berkeley's analysis of the causal relation as far as sensible things are concerned. There is first the empiricist element. All we observe is regular sequence. There is secondly the metaphysical element. A is a God-given prophetic sign of B; and the whole system of Nature is a system of signs, a visual divine language, speaking to our minds of God. Moreover, it is not that God established a system in the beginning and then left it to operate 'as an artist leaves a clock, to go thenceforward of itself for a certain period. But this Visual Language proves, not a Creator merely, but a provident Governor. . . .'[76] God produces each and every sign: He is constantly active, constantly speaking to finite spirits through signs. Perhaps it is not very easy to see why God should act in this way. For visual signs can be of use only to spirits with bodies; and bodies, on Berkeley's principles, are themselves congeries of ideas, and so visual signs. But this difficulty is not cleared up.

In the *Third Dialogue* Hylas objects that if God is made the immediate author of all events in Nature, He is made the author of sin and crime. But to this Philonous answers, 'I have nowhere said that God is the only agent who produces motions in bodies'.[77] Human spirits are truly active efficient causes. Further, sin does not consist in the physical action 'but in the internal deviation of the will from the laws of reason and religion'.[78] The physical action of committing murder may be similar to the physical action of executing a criminal; but from the moral point of view the two actions are unlike one another. Where there is sin or moral turpitude there is a departure of the will from the moral law, and for this the human agent is responsible.

Thus Berkeley does not say that causality is nothing but

regular sequence. What he says is that only spirits are truly
active efficient causes. Nor does he say that God is the only
true cause. What he says is that the only truly active causes
are spirits. As so often with Berkeley, empiricism and metaphysics are combined.

7. Among the continental philosophers of the early modern period the one for whom one would naturally expect
Berkeley to show most sympathy is Malebranche. But though
he had studied Malebranche and, one must suppose, learned
from him, Berkeley was at pains to draw a sharp distinction
between his own philosophy and that of the French Oratorian. Several times in the notebooks he expresses disagreement with the latter. For example 'he (Malebranche) doubts
of the existence of Bodies. I doubt not in the least of this.'[79]
Again, apropos of Malebranche's occasionalism, he remarks:
'We move our legs ourselves. 'Tis we that will their movement. Herein I differ from Malebranche.'[80] And in the
Dialogues he speaks at length about the remoteness of his
philosophy from the 'enthusiasm' of the Frenchman. 'He
builds on the most abstract general ideas, which I entirely
disclaim. He asserts an absolute eternal world, which I deny.
He maintains that we are deceived by our senses and know
not the real natures or the true forms and figures of extended
being; of all of which I hold the direct contrary. So that upon
the whole there are no principles more fundamentally opposite than his and mine.'[81] Berkeley was, of course, well
aware of the comparisons which were sometimes drawn,
and understandably drawn, between his writings and those
of Malebranche, especially with regard to the latter's theory
of the vision of all things in God. And these comparisons
irritated him. At this distance of time it may, indeed, be a
little difficult to understand this irritation, even if we allow
for the fact that in his own mind Berkeley had dissociated
himself from Malebranche from the start. But he evidently
thought of Malebranche as an 'enthusiast' who paid little
attention to strict philosophical argumentation. Thus he remarks, apropos of the existence of matter, that 'Scripture
and possibility are the only proofs with Malebranche. Add to
these what he calls a great propension to think so.'[82] Malebranche was not concerned, in Berkeley's opinion, to recall
men from metaphysics to common sense; and he made great
use of alleged general, abstract ideas. However, though
Berkeley's critical attitude towards the Oratorian was doubtless sincere and an expression of his honest opinion, his con-

cern to dissociate himself from Malebranche shows that he saw that grounds for making a comparison were not altogether wanting.

The philosophy of Descartes Berkeley found uncongenial, and he criticized it frequently. Referring to the former's view that we are not immediately certain of the existence of bodies, he exclaims: 'What a jest is it for a philosopher to question the existence of sensible things, till he hath it proved to him from the veracity of God. . . . I might as well doubt of my own being, as of the being of those things I actually see and feel.'[83] And for Spinoza and Hobbes he had little, if any, sympathy. In the *Dialogues* they are grouped with Vanini as atheists and 'abbettors of impiety',[84] while in the notebooks Berkeley declares that if his own doctrines are rightly understood 'all that philosophy of Epicurus, Hobbes, Spinoza, etc., which has been a declared enemy of religion, comes to the ground'.[85] 'Hobbes and Spinoza make God extended.'[86] And it was 'silly of Hobbes to speak of the will as if it were motion, with which it has no likeness'.[87] If Berkeley disapproved of Descartes, he disapproved much more strongly of Hobbes's materialism. Nor had he much use for the deists, as can be seen from the text of the *Theory of Vision Vindicated and Explained*.[88]

The chief influence on Berkeley as a philosopher was naturally the writings of Locke. For the latter he had a great respect. He calls him 'as clear a writer as I have met with', and goes on to remark that 'such was the candour of this great man that I persuade myself, were he alive, he would not be offended that I differ from him, seeing that in so doing I follow his advice, viz. to use my own judgment, see with my own eyes and not with another's'.[89] Again, after referring to his reiterated and vain attempts to apprehend the general idea of a triangle he remarks that 'surely if anyone were able to introduce that idea into my mind, it must be the author of the *Essay concerning Human Understanding*; he who has so far distinguished himself from the generality of writers by the clearness and significancy of what he says'.[90] But though Berkeley felt a profound respect for Locke, and though the latter had furnished him to a great extent with his point of departure, his respect was, of course, accompanied by sustained criticism. In the notebooks he remarks that Locke would have done better to begin his *Essay* with the third book.[91] In other words, if the latter had begun with an examination and critique of language, he might not have fallen into his theory of abstract general ideas, which, according to Berkeley, was largely responsible for the doctrine of material substance. In general, we can say that Berkeley considered Locke to have been insufficiently empiricist and insufficiently observant of his own declared principles.

8. It is worth remarking that Berkeley was influenced by Locke's notion that ethics could be turned into a demonstrative science like mathematics. Thus he made a memorandum to consider well what Locke meant in saying of algebra 'that it supplies intermediate ideas. Also to think of a method affording the same use in Morals, etc. that this doth in mathematics'.[92] The notion that the mathematical method could be applied to ethics, rendering it a demonstrative science was, of course, common at the time, partly because of the prestige won by mathematics through its successful application in physical science and partly because it was widely thought that ethics had formerly depended on authority and needed a new rational basis. Berkeley saw, indeed, that ethics could not in any case be a branch of pure mathematics; but he shared, at one time at least, the hope of making it analogous to a branch of applied mathematics or, as he puts it, 'mixt Mathematics'.[93] This dream he never attempted to fulfil systematically; but he made some remarks which show that he differed from Locke in his view of what form ethical demonstration would take. For Locke mathematics studies the relations between abstract ideas and can pursue demonstration by means of 'intermediate ideas'; but for Berkeley it considers the relations not between abstract ideas but between signs or symbols. Ethics, treated mathematically, would not demonstrate the relations between abstract ideas; it would concern words. It seems, he says, that all that is necessary to make ethics a demonstrative science is to make a dictionary of words and see which includes which.[94] The first important task, therefore, would be that of defining words.[95] It is clear, however, from some remarks in the notebooks that Berkeley realized even then that there is much more difficulty in attaining common agreement about the meaning of ethical terms than there is about the meaning of algebraic symbols. When one learns mathematics one learns the meaning of the symbols at the same time, without preconceptions about their meaning; but this is not the case with the terms used in ethics. This was possibly one of the reasons why Berkeley never wrote the part of the *Principles* which was to have dealt with ethics.

As it is, Berkeley's moral philosophy is fragmentary and undeveloped. In his notebooks we find the surprising assertion that 'Sensual Pleasure is the Summum Bonum. This (is) the Great Principle of Morality'.[96] This seems at first sight to be the expression of a crass hedonism. But the words which follow immediately in the same entry show that this would be a rash conclusion to draw: 'This once rightly understood all the doctrines even the severest of the Gospels may clearly be demonstrated.' For if the statement that sensual pleasure is the *summum bonum* or supreme good is to be made consistent with the severest doctrines of the Gospels, it obviously cannot be taken in its prima facie sense. Moreover, in other entries Berkeley makes a distinction between different kinds of pleasure. 'Sensual pleasure qua pleasure is good and desirable by a wise man. But if it be contemptible, 'tis not qua pleasure but qua pain or cause of pain, or (which is the same thing) of loss of greater pleasure.'[97] Again, he states that 'he that acts not in order to the obtaining of eternal happiness must be an infidel; at least he is not certain of a future judgment'.[98] These entries may seem to be inconsistent; but by 'sensual pleasure' Berkeley apparently means pleasure which is sensed or perceived (concrete pleasure) rather than the gratification of sensual appetite in an exclusive sense. If happiness is the end of human life, it must be something concrete, not a mere abstraction. 'What it is for a man to be happy, or an object good, every one may think he knows. But to frame an abstract idea of *happiness*, prescinded from all particular pleasure, or of *goodness*, from everything that is good, this is what few can pretend to. . . . And in effect, the doctrine of *abstraction* has not a little contributed towards spoiling the most useful parts of knowledge.'[99]

Berkeley came to make a distinction between 'natural' pleasures, suited to man as a rational as well as a sensitive being, and 'fantastical' pleasures, which feed desire without satisfying it. He supposed that self-love, as the desire for happiness, is the ruling motive in conduct; but he emphasized rational self-love and came to depreciate the pleasures of sense in comparison with the pleasures of reason, just as in his later writings, particularly in *Siris*, he depreciated sensation in comparison with rational knowledge.

Some of Berkeley's remarks appear to represent utilitarianism and the view that the common good, rather than private happiness, is the proper object of human endeavour. Thus he speaks of 'moral or practical truths being ever connected with universal benefit'.[100] And in the treatise on *Passive Obedience* we read that it is 'the general well-being of all men, of all nations, of all ages of the world, which God designs should be procured by the concurring actions of each individual'.[101] But insistence on the common good was not in Berkeley's opinion incompatible with insistence on the primacy of rational self-love. For the latter does not spell egoism; it includes what we call altruism. And God has so contrived things that the pursuit of happiness according to reason always contributes to the common good and welfare.

Further, being convinced that morality requires rational, moral laws, Berkeley maintained that reason can ascertain a natural moral law, implying human freedom and duty. But to assert the validity of universal standards and rules is not inconsistent with saying that everyone seeks his own interest. What the moral law commands is that we should seek our true interest according to reason, and it enables us to ascertain where our true interest lies. Thus, as Berkeley observes in *Alciphron*, 'everyone's true interest is combined with his duty' and 'wisdom and virtue are the same thing'.[102]

As Berkeley believed that rational self-love includes altruism, it is only to be expected that he would attack what he regarded as the narrow egoism of Hobbes. In *Alciphron* he also attacked Mandeville and Shaftesbury, the former in the second *Dialogue*, the latter in the third. Berkeley did not accept the theory of the moral sense, and in his view neither of these philosophers understood the function of reason in the moral life, nor did either of them provide an effective motive for altruistic conduct. The common defects of the two, and the special defects of each, illustrate the moral insufficiencies of the free-thinkers. To Shaftesbury at least Berkeley was definitely unfair, and he misrepresented his position. But his criticism of the free-thinkers is of interest because it shows his conviction that morality is not autonomous and that it must be linked with religion. 'Conscience always supposeth the being of a God.'[103] It may be that by the time he wrote *Alciphron* Berkeley had been influenced by the sermons of Bishop Butler; but it does not seem that this can be proved. However, he came to believe, as Butler believed, that rational and universal rules of morality have a real importance in the moral life and that ethics and religion are more closely connected than some writers supposed.

These remarks may suggest that Berkeley threw out a number of remarks about ethics and morality, and that he did not attempt to render them fully consistent, still less to develop them systematically. And it is indeed true that we cannot find in his writings anything which can properly be called a developed ethical system. At the same time we can find in the treatise on *Passive Obedience* what may be called perhaps prolegomena to Berkeley's ethical system. And it is perhaps worth while drawing attention, at the close of this section, to the relevant passages.

Self-love, as a principle of action, has the primacy. 'Self-love being a principle of all others the most universal, and the most deeply engraven in our hearts, it is natural for us to regard things as they are fitted to augment or impair our own happiness; and accordingly we denominate them *good* or *evil*.'[104] At first the human being is guided by the impressions of sense, and sensible pleasure and pain are taken as the infallible characteristics of good and evil. But as the human being grows up, experience shows him that present pleasure is sometimes followed by a greater pain, and that present pain may be the occasion of procuring a greater future good. Further, when the nobler faculties of the soul display their activities, we discover goods which excel those of the senses. 'Hence an alteration is wrought in our judgments; we no longer comply with the first solicitations of sense, but stay to consider the remote consequences of an action, what good may be hoped, or what evil feared from it, according to the wonted course of things.'[105]

But this is but a first step. Consideration of eternity in comparison with time shows us that every reasonable man ought so to act as to contribute most effectively to his eternal interest. Further, reason shows that there is a God who can make man eternally happy or eternally miserable. And it follows from this that the reasonable man will conform his actions to God's expressed will. But Berkeley does not keep exclusively to this theological utilitarianism. If, he says, we consider the relation which God bears to creatures, we shall have to draw the same conclusion. For God, as maker and preserver of all things, is the supreme legislator. 'And mankind are, by all the ties of duty, no less than interest, bound to obey His laws.'[106] Duty and interest point in the same direction.

But how are we to know these laws, apart from revelation? 'Laws being rules directive of our actions to the end intended by the legislator, in order to attain the knowledge of God's laws we ought first to inquire what that end is which He designs should be carried on by human actions.'[107] The end must be good, for God is infinitely good. But it cannot be God's good; for God is already perfect. Hence the end must be the good of man. Now, it is moral goodness which makes this man rather than that man more acceptable to God. And moral goodness presupposes obedience to law. Hence the end envisaged by the legislator must logically precede all differentiations between individuals. And this means that the end must be the good, not of this or that particular man or nation, but of man in general; that is, of all men.

From this it follows that 'whatsoever practical proposition doth to right reason evidently appear to have a necessary connexion with the universal well-being included in it is to be looked upon as enjoined by the will of God'.[108] These propositions are called 'laws of nature' because they are universal and derive their obligation from God, not from civil sanction. They are said to be stamped on the mind because they are well known by men and inculcated by conscience. They are termed 'eternal rules of reason' because 'they necessarily result from the nature of things, and may be demonstrated by the infallible deductions of reason'.[109]

This sketch of an ethical system is of some interest because it combines consideration of contemporary themes, such as the place of self-love in the moral life, the relation of duty to interest and the common good as the end of conduct, with traditional elements such as the idea of a natural moral law, determined not by the arbitrary will of God but by an objective end. It is also of interest as showing Berkeley's insistence on the function of reason in morality. On this matter it is possible that Berkeley was influenced, to some slight extent at least, by the Cambridge Platonists. As we have seen, he speaks of 'eternal rules of reason', and he asserts that 'in morality the eternal rules of action have the same immutable universal truth with propositions in geometry. Neither of them depend on circumstances or accidents, being at all times, and in all places, without limitations or exception, true.'[110] But though Berkeley's sketch is of some interest, he is not, as moral philosopher, of the same rank as Butler.

9. To understand Berkeley's own attitude towards his philosophy, we must bear in mind his concern to prove the existence and providential activity of God and the spirituality and immortality of the soul. He was convinced that through

his criticism of the theory of material substance he had deprived materialism of its chief support. 'How great a friend material substance hath been to *atheists* in all ages, were needless to relate. All their monstrous systems have so visible and necessary a dependence on it, that when this corner-stone is once removed, the whole fabric cannot choose but fall to the ground.'[111] In order to see Berkeley's philosophy as he saw it, it is essential to remember his religious, apologetic and moral interests.

But it can scarcely be claimed that the metaphysical elements in Berkeley's philosophy have exercised much influence. It was the empiricist element which was most influential. Hume, as will be seen in the following chapters, developed his phenomenalistic analysis. And in the nineteenth century J. S. Mill praised his 'three first rate philosophical discoveries, each sufficient to have constituted a revolution in psychology, and which by their combination have determined the whole course of subsequent philosophical speculation'.[112] These three discoveries were, according to Mill, Berkeley's theory of visual perception (that is, the theory expounded in the *Essay towards a New Theory of Vision*), his doctrine that reasoning is always about particulars, and his view that reality consists of collections or groups of sensations. (Mill himself defined a corporeal thing as a permanent possibility of sensations.)

In speaking of Berkeley's importance Mill was quite justified. He remains as one of the three outstanding classical British empiricists, and his thought, in its empiricist aspect, has influenced, directly or indirectly, the subsequent development of English philosophy in this tradition. Today, when the movement of linguistic analysis is so strong in British thought, particular interest is taken in his anticipations of the theory and practice of this analysis. And it is important that this element in his thought should be brought out. But Berkeley himself would doubtless regret that the more metaphysical elements in his philosophy are generally considered unacceptable by those who esteem him on other grounds.

Chapter Fourteen

HUME (1)

Life and writings — The science of human nature — Impressions and ideas — The association of ideas — Substance and relations — Abstract general ideas — Relations of ideas; mathematics — Matters of fact — The analysis of causality — The nature of belief.

1. Locke, as we have seen, combined an acceptance of the principle that all our ideas arise ultimately from experience with a modest metaphysics. Berkeley, though he carried empiricism further than Locke had done by rejecting the latter's conception of material substance, nevertheless utilized empiricism in the service of a spiritualist metaphysical philosophy. The task of completing the empiricist experiment and of presenting an uncompromising antithesis to continental rationalism was reserved for David Hume. It is to Hume, therefore, that modern empiricists look as the progenitor of the philosophy which they accept. I do not mean that the modern empiricist accepts all Hume's assertions or that he imitates all the latter's ways of expressing empiricist theories and analyses. But Hume remains for him the one outstanding philosopher up to the end of the eighteenth century who took empiricism seriously and who endeavoured to develop a consistent empiricist philosophy.

David Hume was born at Edinburgh in 1711. His family wished him to become a lawyer, but he tells that he was dominated by a passion for literature and felt 'an insurmountable aversion to everything but the pursuits of philosophy and general learning'. Hume's father was not, however, sufficiently wealthy to enable his son to follow his inclinations, and the latter went into business at Bristol. This was not a successful experiment, and after a few months of uncongenial work Hume went to France, resolved to devote himself to literary pursuits and to make a consistent frugality compensate for his lack of fortune. During the years which he spent in France, 1734-7, he composed his famous work, *A Treatise of Human Nature*. It was published in three volumes (1738-40) and according to its author's account it 'fell dead-born from the press', without even exciting 'a murmur among the zealots'.

After his return from France in 1737 Hume lived in Scotland with his mother and brother. In 1741-2 he published *Essays, Moral and Political*; and the success of this work stimulated him to set about re-writing the *Treatise* in the hope that in its new form it might prove more acceptable to the public. In 1745 Hume applied for the chair of ethics and pneumatic philosophy at the University of Edinburgh, but his reputation for scepticism and atheism helped to make his application unsuccessful. After a year as a private tutor he went abroad as secretary to General St. Clair, and he did not return home until 1749. In the meantime his revision of the first part of the *Treatise* had appeared in 1748 under the title of *Philosophical Essays concerning Human Understanding*. A second edition appeared in 1751, and Hume gave to the book the title which it now bears, *An Enquiry concerning Human Understanding*. In the same year he published *An Enquiry concerning the Principles of Morals*, which was more or less a recasting of the third part of the *Treatise* and which was regarded by its author as the best of his works. In 1752 he published his *Political Discourses*, which earned for him a considerable reputation.

In the same year, 1752, Hume became librarian to the Faculty of Advocates in Edinburgh and set up house with his sister in the city, his brother having married in the previous year. Helped by the use of his library, he now turned his attention to writing on the history of England. In 1756 he published a history of Great Britain from the accession of James I to the death of Charles I, and this was followed by the appearance in 1756 of a second volume which continued the history of Great Britain up to the revolution of 1688. His *History of England under the House of Tudor* was published in 1759, and in 1761 there appeared his *History of England from the Invasion of Julius Caesar to the Accession of Henry VII*. As far as philosophy is concerned, he did not publish much at this time, though his *Four Dissertations*, which included one on the natural history of religion, appeared in 1757.

In 1763 Hume went to Paris with the earl of Hertford, British Ambassador to France, and for some time he was secretary to the embassy. While in Paris he consorted with the group of French philosophers associated with the *Encyclopaedia*, and on returning to London in 1716 he brought back with him Rousseau, though the latter's suspicious character soon led to a break in their relations. For two years Hume was an Under-secretary of State, but in 1769 he returned to Edinburgh, where he died in 1776. His *Dialogues concerning Natural Religion*, which had been written before 1752, were published posthumously in 1779. His essays on suicide and immortality appeared anonymously in 1777 and under Hume's name in 1783.

Hume's autobiography, edited by his friend Adam Smith, appeared in 1777. In it he describes himself in a frequently quoted passage as 'a man of mild disposition, of command of temper, of an open, social and cheerful humour, capable of attachment, but little susceptible of enmity, and of great moderation in all my passions. Even my love of literary fame, my ruling passion, never soured my temper, notwithstanding my frequent disappointments.' To judge by the memories of the earl of Charlemont, his appearance seems to have been remote from anything which the reader of his works would be likely to attribute to him spontaneously. For according to Charlemont, Hume looked much more like 'a turtle-eating Alderman than a refined philosopher'. We are also told that he spoke English with a very broad Scottish accent and that his French was far from exemplary. However, his personal appearance and his accent, though of interest to those who like to know such details about famous men, are clearly irrelevant to his importance and influence as a philosopher.[1]

2. In his Introduction to the *Treatise of Human Nature* Hume remarks that all the sciences have some relation to human nature. This is obvious, he says, in the case of logic, morals, criticism and politics. Logic is concerned with the principles and operations of man's faculty of reasoning and with the nature of our ideas; morals and criticism (aesthetic) treat of our tastes and sentiments; politics considers the union of men in society. Mathematics, natural philosophy and natural religion appear, indeed, to be concerned with subjects quite other than man. But they are known by man,

and it is man who judges what is true and what is false in these branches of knowledge. Moreover, natural religion treats not only of the nature of the divine but also of God's disposition towards us and of our obligations towards Him. Human nature is thus the 'capital or centre' of the sciences, and it is of paramount importance that we should develop a science of man. How is this to be done? By applying the experimental method. 'As the science of man is the only solid foundation for the other sciences, so the only solid foundation we can give to this science itself must be laid on experience and observation.'[2]

Hume's *Treatise* is thus inspired by no mean ambition. 'In pretending, therefore, to explain the principles of human nature, we in effect propose a complete system of the sciences, built on a foundation almost entirely new, and the only one upon which they can stand with any security.'[3] His point is that the experimental method which has been applied with such success in natural science should be applied also in the study of man. That is to say, we ought to start with a close observation of man's psychological processes and of his moral behaviour and endeavour to ascertain their principles and causes. We cannot, indeed, make experiments in this field in precisely the same way that we can in, for example, chemistry. We have to be content with the data as they are given to us in introspection and in observation of human life and conduct. But in any case we must start with the empirical data, and not with any pretended intuition of the essence of the human mind, which is something that eludes our grasp. Our method must be inductive rather than deductive. And 'where experiments of this kind are judiciously collected and compared, we may hope to establish on them a science which will not be inferior in certainty, and will be much superior in utility, to any other of human comprehension'.[4]

It is thus the intention of Hume to extend the methods of the Newtonian science, as far as this is possible, to human nature itself, and to carry further the work begun by Locke, Shaftesbury, Hutcheson and Butler. He sees, of course, that the science of human nature is in some sense different from physical science. He makes use, for instance, of the method of introspection, and he is obviously aware that this method is inapplicable outside the psychological sphere. At the same time he shares with the other philosophers of the pre-Kantian Enlightenment an insufficient understanding of the differences between the physical sciences and the sciences of the

mind or 'spirit'. However, a better understanding was in part
a result of the experiment of extending the general concepts
of 'natural philosophy' to the science of man. And in view
of the great advance in the natural sciences since the Renaissance it is no matter for surprise that the experiment was
made.

In the *Enquiry concerning Human Understanding* Hume
says that the science of human nature can be treated in two
ways. A philosopher may consider man chiefly as born for
action and concern himself with exhibiting the beauty of virtue with a view to stimulating men to virtuous conduct. Or
he may consider man as a reasoning rather than as an active
being and concern himself with enlightening man's understanding rather than with improving his conduct. Philosophers of this second type 'regard human nature as a subject
of speculation, and with a narrow scrutiny examine it, in
order to find those principles which regulate our understanding, excite our sentiments and make us approve or blame
any particular object, action or behaviour'.[5] The first type of
philosophy is 'easy and obvious', the second 'accurate and
abstruse'. The generality of mankind naturally prefers the
first type; but the second is requisite if the first is to possess
any sure foundation. True, abstract and abstruse metaphysical speculation leads nowhere. 'But the only method of
freeing learning at once from these abstruse questions is to
inquire seriously into the nature of human understanding,
and show, from an exact analysis of its powers and capacities,
that it is by no means fitted for such remote and abstruse subjects. We must submit to this fatigue, in order to live at ease
ever after; and (we) must cultivate true metaphysics with
some care, in order to destroy the false and adulterate.'[6]
Astronomers were once content with determining the motions
and size of the heavenly bodies. But at last they succeeded
in determining the laws and forces which govern the movements of the planets. 'The like has been performed with
regard to other parts of nature. And there is no reason to
despair of equal success in our inquiries concerning the
mental powers and economy, if prosecuted with equal capacity and caution.'[7] 'True metaphysics' will drive out false
metaphysics; but it will also establish the science of man on a
sure basis. And to attain this end it is worth taking trouble
and pursuing an accurate, even comparatively abstruse,
analysis.

Hume is partly concerned in the first *Enquiry* with com-

mending to his readers the lines of thought developed in the
first part of the *Treatise*, which in his opinion failed to win
due attention on its publication because of its abstract style.
Hence his apologia for a style of philosophizing which goes
beyond moralistic edification. But he also makes it clear that
he is taking up again the original project of Locke, to determine the extent of human knowledge. He shows, indeed, that
he has in mind a purpose connected with morality, namely,
to discover the principles and forces which govern our
moral judgments. But he is also concerned with discovering
the principles which 'regulate our understanding'. To emphasize Hume's role as moral philosopher is legitimate; but
this aspect of his thought is over-emphasized if his role as
epistemologist is pushed into the background.

3. Like Locke, Hume derives all the contents of the mind
from experience. But his terminology is rather different from
that employed by the former. He uses the word 'perceptions'
to cover the mind's contents in general, and he divides perceptions into impressions and ideas. The former are the immediate data of experience, such as sensations. The latter
are described by Hume as the copies or faint images of impressions in thinking and reasoning. If I look at my room, I
receive an impression of it. 'When I shut my eyes and think
of my chamber, the ideas I form are exact representations of
the impressions I felt; nor is there any circumstance of the
one, which is not to be found in the other. . . . Ideas and
impressions appear always to correspond to each other.'[8] The
word 'idea' is obviously used here to signify image. But, passing over this point, we can see immediately the general direction of Hume's thought. Just as Locke derived all our
knowledge ultimately from 'simple ideas', so Hume wishes
to derive our knowledge ultimately from impressions, from
the immediate data of experience. But while these preliminary remarks illustrate the general direction of Hume's
thought, they give a very insufficient account of it. And
further explanation is required.

Hume describes the difference between impressions and
ideas in terms of vividness. 'The difference betwixt these
consists in the degrees of force and liveliness with which
they strike upon the mind and make their way into our
thoughts or consciousness. Those perceptions which enter
with most force and violence we may name *impressions*;
and, under this name, I comprehend all our sensations, passions and emotions, as they make their first appearance in

the soul. By *ideas* I mean the faint images of these in thinking and reasoning; such as, for instance, are all the perceptions excited by the present discourse, excepting only those
which arise from the sight and touch, and excepting the immediate pleasure or uneasiness it may occasion.'[9] Hume
proceeds to qualify this statement by adding that 'in sleep,
in a fever, in madness, or in any very violent emotions of
soul, our ideas may approach to our impressions: as, on the
other hand, it sometimes happens that our impressions are so
faint and low that we cannot distinguish them from our
ideas'.[10] But he insists that in general the distinction holds
good; and in the *Enquiry* he remarks that 'the most lively
thought is still inferior to the dullest sensation'.[11] This distinction between impressions and ideas in terms of liveliness
and force is, however, somewhat misleading. At least it can
be misleading, if, that is to say, it diverts our attention from
the fact that Hume is primarily concerned to distinguish between the immediate data of experience and our thoughts
about these data. At the same time he regards ideas as copies
of impressions or images of them, and it is perhaps natural
that he stresses the difference in vividness between original
and image.

As we have seen, Hume asserts that 'ideas and impressions appear always to correspond to each other'. But he goes
on to qualify and correct this 'first impression'. He makes
a distinction between simple and complex perceptions, a
distinction which he applies to both kinds of perceptions,
namely, both to impressions and to ideas. The perception
of a red patch is a simple impression, and the thought (or
image) of the red patch is a simple idea. But if I stand on
the hill of Montmartre and survey the city of Paris, I receive
a complex impression of the city, of roofs, chimneys, towers
and streets. And when I afterwards think of Paris and recall
this complex impression, I have a complex idea. In this case
the complex idea corresponds in some degree to the complex
impression; though it does not do so exactly and adequately.
But let us take another case. 'I can imagine to myself a city
as the New Jerusalem, whose pavement is gold, and walls are
rubies, though I never saw any such.'[12] In this case my
complex idea does not correspond to a complex impression.

We cannot say, therefore, with truth that to every idea
there is an exactly corresponding impression. But it is to be
noted that the complex idea of the New Jerusalem can be
broken down into simple ideas. And we can ask whether

every simple idea has a corresponding simple impression and every simple impression a corresponding simple idea. Hume answers, 'I venture to affirm that the rule here holds without any exception, and that every simple idea has a simple impression which resembles it, and every simple impression a correspondent idea'.[13] This cannot be proved by examining all possible cases; but anyone who denies the statement can be challenged to mention an exception to it.

Are the impressions derived from ideas or ideas from impressions? To answer this question we need only examine the order of their appearance. It is clear that impressions precede ideas. 'To give a child an idea of scarlet or orange, of sweet or bitter, I present the objects, or, in other words, convey to him these impressions; but proceed not so absurdly as to endeavour to produce the impressions by exciting the ideas.'[14] However, Hume mentions an exception to the general rule that ideas are derived from corresponding impressions. Suppose a man who is familiar with all shades of blue except one. If he is presented with a graded series of blues, running from the deepest to the lightest, and if the particular shade of blue which he has never seen is absent, he will notice a blank in the continuous series. Is it possible for him to supply this deficiency by the use of his imagination and frame the 'idea' of this particular shade, though he has never had the corresponding impression? 'I believe there are few but will be of opinion that he can.'[15] Furthermore, it is obviously possible to form ideas of ideas. For we can reason and talk about ideas, which are themselves ideas of impressions. We then frame 'secondary ideas', which are derived from previous ideas rather than immediately from impressions. But this second qualification does not, strictly speaking, involve an exception to the general rule that impressions precede ideas. And if we make allowance for the exception mentioned in the first qualification, we can safely enunciate the general proposition that our simple impressions are prior to their corresponding ideas.

The following point, however, must be added. Impressions can be divided into impressions of sensation and impressions of reflection. 'The first kind arises in the soul originally from unknown causes.'[16] What, then, of impressions of reflection? These are derived, 'in great measure', from ideas. Suppose that I have an impression of cold, accompanied by pain. A 'copy' of this impression remains in the mind after the impression has ceased. This 'copy' is called an 'idea', and it can produce new impressions of aversion, for example, which are impressions of reflection. These again can be copied by the memory and imagination and become ideas; and so on. But even though in such a case impressions of reflection are posterior to ideas of sensation, they are prior to their corresponding ideas of reflection, and they are derived ultimately from impressions of sensation. In the long run, therefore, impressions are prior to ideas.

This analysis of the relation between impressions and ideas may appear to constitute a theory of purely academic interest and of little importance, except as a restatement of empiricism which excludes the hypothesis of innate ideas. But its importance becomes manifest if we bear in mind the way in which Hume applies it. For example, he asks, as will be seen later, from what impressions the idea of substance is derived. And he comes to the conclusion that we have no idea of substance apart from a collection of particular qualities. Again, his general theory about impressions and ideas is of great importance in his analysis of causality. Further, the theory can be used to get rid of what Hume calls 'all that jargon which has so long taken possession of metaphysical reasonings and drawn disgrace upon them'.[17] Philosophers may use terms which are vacuous, in the sense that they signify no determinate ideas and possess no definite meaning. 'When we entertain, therefore, any suspicion that a philosophical term is employed without any meaning or idea (as is but too frequent), we need but to inquire, *from what impression is that supposed idea derived?* And if it be impossible to assign any, this will serve to confirm our suspicion.'[18]

Hume's position can be expressed in a rather different way from that in which he actually expresses it. If a child comes across the word 'skyscraper', he may ask his father what it means. The latter can explain its meaning by definition or description. That is to say, he can explain to the child the meaning of the word 'skyscraper' by employing words such as 'house', 'tall', 'storey', and so on. But the child cannot understand the meaning of the description unless he understands the meanings of the terms employed in the description. Some of these terms can themselves be explained by definition or description. But ultimately we come down to words, the meaning of which must be learned ostensively. That is to say, the child must be shown examples of the way in which these words are used, instances of their application. In Hume's language, the child must be given 'impressions'. It is possible, therefore, to explain Hume's point by the use of a distinction between terms, the meaning of which is learned ostensively, and terms, the meaning of which is learned by definition or by description. In other words, it is possible to substitute for Hume's psychological distinction between impressions and ideas a linguistic distinction between terms. But the main point, the priority of experience, of the immediately given, remains the same.

It is worth noting that Hume assumes that 'experience' can be broken into atomic constituents, namely, impressions or sense-data. But though this may be possible if considered as a purely abstract analysis, it is questionable whether 'experience' can profitably be described in terms of these atomic constituents. It is also worth noting that Hume uses the word 'idea' in an ambiguous way. Sometimes he is obviously referring to the image, and, given this sense of idea, it is not unreasonable to speak of ideas as copies of impressions. But at other times he is referring to the concept rather than to an image, and it is difficult to see how the relation of concept to that of which it is a concept can legitimately be described in the same terms as the relation of an image to that of which it is an image. In the first Enquiry[19] he uses the terms 'thoughts and ideas' as synonymous. And it is clear, I think, that his main distinction is between the immediately given, namely, impressions, and the derived, to which he gives the general name 'ideas'.

It has been said that Hume's theory of impressions and ideas excludes the hypothesis of innate ideas. But this statement needs some qualification in view of the way in which Hume employs the term 'innate idea'. If innate is taken as equivalent to natural, 'then all the perceptions and ideas of the mind must be allowed to be innate or natural'.[20] If by innate is meant contemporary with birth, the dispute whether there are innate ideas or not is frivolous; 'nor is it worth while to inquire at what time thinking begins, whether before, at or after our birth'.[21] But if by innate we mean copied from no precedent perception, 'then we may assert that all our impressions are innate, and our ideas not innate'.[22] Obviously, Hume did not assert that there are innate ideas in the sense in which Locke was concerned to deny that there are such things. To say that impressions are innate is merely to say that they are not themselves copies of impressions; that is, that they are not ideas in Hume's sense of the word.

4. When the mind has received impressions, they can reappear, as Hume puts it, in two ways. First, they can reappear with a degree of vividness which is intermediate between the vividness of an impression and the faintness of an idea. And the faculty by which we repeat our impressions in this way is the memory. Secondly, they can reappear as mere ideas, as faint copies or images of impressions. And the faculty by which we repeat our impressions in this second way is the imagination.

Thus, just as Hume described the difference between impressions and ideas in terms of degrees of vividness, so now he describes the difference between ideas of the memory and ideas of the imagination in a similar manner. But he goes on to give another account of this difference, which is rather more satisfactory. Memory, he says, preserves not only simple ideas but also their order and position. In other words, when we say, for example, that a person has a good memory of a cricket-match, we mean that he recalls not only the various events taken singly but also the order in which they occurred. The imagination, however, is not tied down in this way. It can, for instance, combine simple ideas arbitrarily or break down complex ideas into simple ideas and then rearrange them. This is frequently done in poems and romances. 'Nature there is totally confounded, and nothing mentioned but winged horses, fiery dragons, and monstrous giants.'[23]

But though the imagination can freely combine ideas, it generally works according to some general principles of association. In memory there is an inseparable connection between ideas. In the case of the imagination this inseparable connection is wanting; but there is nevertheless a 'uniting principle' among ideas, 'some associating quality by which one idea naturally introduces another'.[24] Hume describes it as 'a gentle force, which commonly prevails'. Its causes are 'mostly unknown and must be resolved into *original* qualities of human nature, which I pretend not to explain'.[25] In other words, there is in man an innate force or impulse which moves him, though without necessity, to combine together certain types of ideas. What this 'gentle force' is in itself, Hume does not undertake to explain: he takes it as something given. At the same time we can ascertain the qualities which bring this gentle force into play. 'The qualities from which this association arises, and by which the mind is, after this manner, conveyed from one idea to another, are three, viz. *resemblance, contiguity* in time or place, and *cause* and *effect*.'[26] The imagination runs easily from one idea to another which resembles it. Similarly, by long custom the mind acquires the habit of associating ideas which are contiguous, immediately or mediately, in space and time. 'As to the connection that is made by the relation of *cause and effect*, we shall have occasion afterwards to examine it to the bottom, and therefore shall not at present insist upon it.'[27]

5. In the *Treatise* the section on the association of ideas is followed by sections on relations and on modes and substances. These are complex ideas which are asserted to be effects of the association mentioned above. In classifying complex ideas in this way Hume is adopting one of Locke's classifications. We can take the idea of substance first.

Hume asks, as we would expect, from what impression or impressions the idea of substance is derived, supposing that there is such an idea. It cannot be derived from impressions of sensation. If it is perceived by the eyes, it must be a colour; if by the ears, a sound; if by the palate, a taste. But nobody would say that substance is a colour, or a sound or a taste. If, therefore, there is an idea of substance, it must be derived from impressions of reflection. But these can be resolved into our passions and emotions. And those who speak of substances do not mean by the word passions or emotions. The idea of substance is derived, therefore, neither from impressions of sensation nor from impressions of reflection. It follows that there is, properly speaking, no idea of substance at all. The word 'substance' connotes a collection of 'simple ideas'. As Hume puts it, 'the idea of a substance . . . is nothing but a collection of simple ideas that are united by the imagination and have a particular name assigned them, by which we are able to recall, either to ourselves or others, that collection'.[28] Sometimes the particular qualities which form a substance are referred to an unknown something in which they are thought to inhere; but even when this 'fiction' is avoided, the qualities are at least supposed to be closely related with one another by 'contiguity and causation'. Thus an association of ideas is set up in the mind, and when we perform the activity which we describe as discovering a new quality of a given substance, the new idea enters into the cluster of associated ideas.

Hume dismisses the subject of substance in a summary manner. It is clear that he accepts the general line of Berkeley's criticism of Locke's notion of material substance, and that he does not consider that the theory of an unknown substratum needs further refutation. What is peculiar to him is that he also rejects Berkeley's theory of spiritual substance. That is to say, he extends the phenomenalistic interpretation of things from bodies to souls or minds. True, he evidently does not feel very happy about the resolution of minds into psychic events, united with the aid of the principle of association. But his general empiricist position obviously points to a consistent phenomenalism, to an analysis of all complex ideas into impressions, and he is involved in the attempt to treat spiritual substance in the same way as material substance. If he feels that his analysis leaves something out and suspects that his explanation of minds is an instance of explaining by explaining away, his doubts indicate either the insufficiency of phenomenalism in general or, at least, the inadequacy of his statement of phenomenalism. However, it is only in a later section of the *Treatise* that he deals with the mind or soul, under the heading of 'personal identity', and we may leave aside this problem for the moment, though it is useful to note at once that he does not confine himself, as Berkeley did, to a phenomenalistic analysis of the idea of material substance.

When discussing relations in the *Treatise* Hume distinguishes two senses of the word 'relation'. First, the word may be used to signify the quality or qualities 'by which two ideas are connected together in the imagination, and the one naturally introduces the other, after the manner above explained'.[29] These 'qualities' are resemblance, contiguity and the causal relation, and Hume calls them natural relations. In the case of natural relations, therefore, ideas are connected with one another by the natural force of association, so that the one tends naturally or by custom to recall the other. Secondly, there are what Hume calls philosophical relations. We can compare at will any objects, provided that there is at least some similarity of quality between them. In such comparison the mind is not impelled by a natural force of association to pass from one idea to another: it does so simply because it has chosen to institute a certain comparison.

Hume enumerates seven types of philosophical relation: resemblance, identity, relations of time and place, proportion in quantity or number, degrees in any quality, contrariety and causation.[30] It will be noted at once that there is a certain over-lapping between natural and philosophical relations. In fact, all three natural relations occur in the list of philosophical relations, though not, of course, as natural relations.

But this over-lapping is not due to any oversight on Hume's part. He explains, for example, that no objects can be compared unless there is some resemblance between them. Resemblance is, therefore, a relation without which no philosophical relation can exist. But it does not follow that every resemblance produces an association of ideas. If a quality is very general and is found in a very great number of objects or in all objects, it does not lead the mind from one particular member of the class to any other particular member. For instance, all material things resemble one another in being material, and we can compare any material thing with any other material thing. But the idea of a material thing *as such* does not lead the mind by the force of association to any other particular material thing. Again, greenness is common to a great many things. And we can freely compare or group together two or more green things. But the imagination is not impelled, as it were, by natural force of association to move from the idea of green thing X to the idea of green thing Y. Again, we can compare any two things according to spatio-temporal relations, but it does not necessarily follow that the mind is impelled to do this by the force of association. In some cases it is (for example, when we have always experienced two things as spatially and immediately contiguous or as always succeeding one another immediately); but in very many cases there is no force of association at work. It may be that I am naturally, if not inevitably, impelled to think of St. Peter's when I think of the Vatican palace; but the idea of New York does not naturally recall the idea of Canton, though I can, of course, compare these two cities from a spatial point of view, asserting, for instance, that the one is so far distant from the other.

As for causation, Hume again postpones discussion of it. But it may be as well to remark here that in his view causation, considered as a philosophical relation, is reducible to such relations of space and time as contiguity, temporal succession and constant conjunction or togetherness. There is here no necessary connection between ideas; there are only factual spatio-temporal relations. Hence causation as a philosophical relation affords no ground for proceeding beyond experience by inferring transcendent causes from observed effects. In causation considered as a natural relation there is, indeed, an inseparable connection between ideas; but this element must be explained subjectively, with the aid of the principles of association.

6. Hume treats of general abstract ideas in the first part of the *Treatise*, in close connection, therefore, with his analysis of ideas and impressions. He begins by remarking that 'a great philosopher', namely, Berkeley, has asserted that all general ideas are 'nothing but particular ones annexed to a certain term, which gives them a more extensive signification, and makes them recall upon occasion other individuals, which are similar to them'.[31] This is not perhaps a very happy statement of Berkeley's position; but in any case Hume regards it as of one of the greatest and most valuable of recent discoveries and proposes to confirm it by some further arguments.

In the first place, abstract ideas are individual or particular in themselves. What Hume means can be illustrated by his arguments in favour of this proposition. First, 'the mind cannot form any notion of quantity or quality without forming a precise notion of degrees of each'.[32] For instance, the precise length of a line is not distinguishable from the line itself. We cannot form a general idea of a line without any length at all. Nor can we form the general idea of a line possessing all possible lengths. Secondly, every impression is determinate and definite. Since, therefore, an idea is an image or copy of an impression, it must itself be determinate and definite, even though it is fainter than the impression from which it is derived. Thirdly, everything which exists must be individual. No triangle, for instance, can exist, which is not a particular triangle with its particular characteristics. To postulate an existent triangle which is at the same time all and none of the possible kinds and sizes of triangle would be an absurdity. But what is absurd in fact and reality is absurd also in idea.

It is clear that Hume's view follows from his conception of ideas and of their relation to impressions. If the idea is an image or copy, it must be particular. He thus agrees with Berkeley that there are no *abstract* general ideas. At the same time he admits that what are called abstract ideas, though they are in themselves particular images, 'may become general in their representation'.[33] And what he tries to do is to define the way in which this extension of signification occurs.

When we have found a resemblance between things which we often observe, we are accustomed to apply the same name to them all, whatever the differences between them may be. For instance, having frequently observed what we call trees and having noticed resemblances between them, we apply the same word 'tree' to them all, in spite of the differences between oaks, elms, larches, tall trees, short trees, deciduous trees, evergreens, and so on. And after we have acquired the custom of applying the same word to these objects, the hearing of the word revives the idea of one of these objects, and makes the imagination conceive it. The hearing of the word or name cannot call up ideas of all the objects to which the name is applied: it calls up one of them. But at the same time it calls into play 'a certain custom', a readiness to produce any other individual resembling this idea, if occasion should demand it. For example, suppose that I hear the word 'triangle' and that this word calls up in my mind the idea of a particular equilateral triangle. If I then assert that the three angles of a triangle are equal to each other, 'custom' or 'association' calls up the idea of some other triangle which shows the falsity of this universal statement. To be sure, this custom is mysterious; and 'to explain the ultimate causes of our mental actions is impossible'.[34] But analogous cases can be cited to confirm the existence of such a custom. For example, if we have learned by heart a long poem, we do not recollect it all at once; but remembrance or hearing of the first line, possibly of the first word, puts the mind in readiness to recall all that follows as occasion demands; that is, in due order. We may not be able to explain how this association works, but there is no doubt about the empirical facts. Again, when we make use of terms such as *government* or *church*, we seldom conceive distinctly in our minds all the simple ideas of which these complex ideas are composed. But we can very well avoid talking nonsense about these complex ideas, and if someone makes a statement which is incompatible with some element of the full content of such an idea, we may recognize at once the absurdity of the statement. For 'custom' calls up the distinct component idea as occasion requires. Again, we may not be able to give any adequate causal explanation of the process; but none the less it occurs.

7. In the first *Enquiry* Hume asserts that 'all the objects of human reason or inquiry may naturally be divided into two kinds, to wit, *relations of ideas* and *matters of fact*. Of the first kind are the sciences of geometry, algebra and arithmetic, and, in short, every affirmation which is either intuitively or demonstratively certain. . . . Matters of fact, which are the second objects of human reason, are not ascertained in the

same manner; nor is our evidence of their truth, however great, of a like nature with the foregoing.'[35] Hume means that all our reasoning concerns the relations between things. These relations are, as Locke stated, of two kinds, relations of ideas or matters of fact. An arithmetical proposition is an example of the former, while the statement that the sun will rise tomorrow is an example of the latter. In this section we are concerned with relations of ideas.

Of the seven philosophical relations only four, says Hume, depend solely on ideas; namely, resemblance, contrariety, degrees in quality and proportions in quantity or number. The first three of these are 'discoverable at first sight and fall more properly under the province of intuition than demonstration'.[36] As we are concerned with demonstrative reasoning, we are left, therefore, with proportions in quantity or number, namely, with mathematics. Mathematical propositions assert relations between ideas, and ideas only. In algebra, for example, it makes no difference to the certainty of the demonstrations and the truth of the propositions whether or not there are objects corresponding to the symbols employed. The truth of a mathematical proposition is independent of questions about existence.

Hume's account of mathematics is, therefore, rationalist and non-empiricist, in the sense that he maintains that the relations asserted are necessary. The truth of a mathematical proposition depends simply and solely on the relations between ideas, or, as we might say, on the meanings of certain symbols; and it requires no confirmation from experience. We should not, of course, understand Hume as meaning that mathematical ideas are innate in Locke's sense of the word. He was quite well aware of the ways in which we come to know the meanings of arithmetical and algebraic symbols. His point is that the truth of the propositions is quite independent of the ways in which we come to know the meanings of the symbols. Their truth cannot possibly be refuted by experience; for nothing is said about matters of fact. They are formal propositions, not empirical hypotheses. And though, of course, mathematics can be applied, the truth of the propositions is independent of this application. In this sense they can be called *a priori* propositions, though Hume does not use the term.

In the nineteenth century J. S. Mill tried to show that mathematical propositions are empirical hypotheses. But in the characteristic empiricism of the twentieth century it is the view of Hume rather than that of Mill which is accepted. The neo-positivists, for instance, interpret mathematical propositions as *a priori* and analytic propositions. At the same time, while not, of course, denying their applicability in science, they insist that in themselves they are void of factual, empirical content. To say that four plus three equals seven is not in itself to say anything about existent things: the truth of the proposition depends simply on the meanings of the terms. And this is the view maintained by Hume.

There is a further point to be noticed. In the *Treatise* Hume asserts that 'geometry falls short of that perfect precision and certainty which are peculiar to arithmetic and algebra, yet it excels the imperfect judgments of our senses and imagination'.[37] The reason he gives is that the first principles of geometry are drawn from the general appearances of things; and that appearances cannot give us certainty. 'Our ideas seem to give a perfect assurance that no two right lines can have a common segment; but if we consider these ideas, we shall find that they always suppose a sensible inclination of the two lines, and that where the angle they form is extremely small, we have no standard of a right line so precise as to assure us of the truth of this proposition.'[38] And the conclusion Hume draws is that 'there remain therefore algebra and arithmetic as the only sciences in which we can carry on a chain of reasoning to any degree of intricacy and yet preserve a perfect exactness and certainty'.[39] But there does not appear to be any adequate reason for treating geometry as an exception to a general interpretation of mathematics. If the truth of algebraic and arithmetical propositions depends solely on 'ideas' or on definitions, the same can be said of geometry, and sensible 'appearances' are irrelevant. Hume seems to have felt this himself; for in the first *Enquiry* geometry is placed on the same footing as algebra and arithmetic. And he remarks that 'though there never were a circle or triangle in nature, the truths demonstrated by Euclid would for ever retain their certainty and evidence'.[40]

8. Philosophical relations are divided by Hume into invariable and variable relations. Invariable relations cannot be changed without a change in the objects related or in the ideas of them. Conversely, if the latter remain unchanged, the relation between them remains unchanged. Mathematical relations are of this type. Given certain ideas or meaningful symbols, the relations between them are invariable. In order to make an arithmetical or an algebraic proposition untrue,

we should have to change the meanings of the symbols; if we
do not do this, the propositions are necessarily true; that is,
the relations between the ideas are invariable. Variable relations, however, can change without any change in the related objects or in their ideas being necessarily involved. For
example, the spatial relation of distance between two bodies
can vary, though the bodies and our ideas of them remain
the same.

It follows that we cannot come to have certain knowledge
of variable relations by pure reasoning; that is, simply by
analysis of ideas and *a priori* demonstration: we become acquainted with them by experience and observation, or, rather,
we depend upon experience and observation, even in those
cases where inference is involved. We are here concerned with
matters of fact, and not with purely ideal relations. And, as
we have seen, we cannot attain the same degree of evidence
about matters of fact which we attain about relations of ideas.
A proposition which states a relation of ideas, in Hume's
sense of the term, cannot be denied without contradiction.
Given, for example, the meanings of the symbols 2 and 4,
we cannot deny that $2 + 2 = 4$ without being involved
in contradiction: the opposite is inconceivable. But 'the contrary of every matter of fact is still possible, because it can
never imply a contradiction. . . . That the sun will not rise
tomorrow is no less intelligible a proposition and implies no
more contradiction than the affirmation that it will rise.'[41]
Hume does not mean that it is untrue to say that the sun
will rise tomorrow: he means that no logical contradiction is
involved in saying that the sun will not rise tomorrow. Nor
does he intend to deny that we may feel certain that the sun
will rise tomorrow. He is maintaining, however, that we do
not and cannot have the same grounds for assurance that the
sun will rise tomorrow that we have for the truth of a proposition in pure mathematics. It may be highly probable that
the sun will rise tomorrow, but it is not certain if we mean
by a certain proposition one which is logically necessary and
the opposite of which is contradictory and impossible.

Hume's position on this matter is of considerable importance. Propositions asserting what he calls relations of ideas
are now generally called analytic propositions. And propositions which assert matters of fact are called synthetic propositions. It is the contention of modern empiricists that all *a
priori* propositions, the truth of which is known independently of experience and observation and the opposites of

which are self-contradictory, are analytic propositions, their truth depending simply on the meanings of symbols. No synthetic proposition, therefore, is an *a priori* proposition; it is an empirical hypothesis, enjoying a greater or lesser degree of probability. The existence of synthetic *a priori* propositions, propositions, that is to say, which assert matters of fact but which at the same time are absolutely certain, is excluded. This general position represents a development of Hume's views.

A further point. We can make the following distinction between different kinds of variable or 'inconsistent' relations. According to Hume, 'we ought not to receive as reasoning any of the observations we may make concerning identity and relations of time and place; since in none of them the mind can go beyond what is immediately present to the senses, either to discover the real existence or the relations of objects'.[42] Thus I see immediately that this piece of paper is contiguous with the surface of the table. Here we have a case of perception rather than of reasoning. And I do not go beyond the actual perception by inferring the existence or activity of anything which transcends the actual perception. I can do so, of course; but in this case I introduce causal inference. In Hume's view, therefore, any 'conclusion (about matters of fact) beyond the impressions of our senses can be founded only on the connection of cause and effect'.[43] 'All reasonings concerning matter of fact seem to be founded on the relation of cause and effect. By means of that relation alone we can go beyond the evidence of our memory and senses.'[44] In other words, all reasoning in matters of fact, as contrasted with relations of ideas, is causal inference. Or, to put the matter more concretely, in mathematics we have demonstration, and in the empirical sciences we have causal inference. In view, therefore, of the important role played by causal inference in human knowledge we must inquire into the nature of the causal relation and the grounds which we have for proceeding by means of causal inference beyond the immediate testimony of the senses.

9. Hume approaches his examination of the causal relation by asking from what impression or impressions the idea of causation is derived. In the first place no quality of those things which we call 'causes' can be the origin of the idea of causation. For we cannot discover any quality which is common to them all. 'The idea then of causation must be derived

from some *relation* among objects; and that relation we must now endeavour to discover.'⁴⁵

The first relation which Hume mentions is contiguity. 'I find in the first place that whatever objects are considered as causes or effects are contiguous.'⁴⁶ He does not mean, of course, that the things which we consider to be causes and effects are always immediately contiguous; for there may be a chain or series of causes between thing A, which we call a cause, and thing Z, which we call an effect. But it will be found that A and B are contiguous, B and C, and so on, even though A and Z are not themselves immediately contiguous. What Hume rules out is action at a distance in the proper sense of the term. It must be added, however, that he is speaking of the popular idea of causation. It is popularly believed, he thinks, that cause and effect are always contiguous, either immediately or mediately. But he does not commit himself definitely in the third part of the *Treatise* to the statement that the relation of contiguity is essential to the causal relation. He says that we can take it that this is the case 'till we can find a more proper occasion to clear up this matter, by examining what objects are or are not susceptible of juxtaposition and conjunction'.⁴⁷ And later on he makes it clear that he does not regard spatial contiguity as essential to the idea of causation. For he maintains that an object can exist and yet be nowhere. 'A moral reflection cannot be placed on the right or on the left hand of a passion; nor can a smell or sound be either of a circular or a square figure. These objects and perceptions, so far from requiring any particular place, are absolutely incompatible with it, and even the imagination cannot attribute it to them.'⁴⁸ We certainly think of passions, for example, as entering into causal relations; but they cannot be said to be spatially contiguous with other things. Hume does not, therefore, regard spatial contiguity as an indispensable element in the causal relation.

The second relation which Hume discusses is that of temporal priority. He argues that the cause must be temporally prior to the effect. Experience confirms this. Further, if in any instance an effect could be perfectly contemporary with its cause, this would be so in all instances of true causation. For in any instance in which it was not the case, the so-called cause would remain for some time in inactivity and would need some other factor to push it into activity. It would not then be a true or proper cause. But if all effects were perfectly contemporary with their causes, 'it is plain there would be no such thing as succession, and all objects must be co-existent'.[49] This is, however, patently absurd. We can take it, therefore, that an effect cannot be perfectly contemporary with its cause, and that a cause must be temporally prior to its effect.

But Hume is evidently not altogether sure of the cogency of this argument. For he goes on to say: 'If this argument appear satisfactory, it is well. If not, I beg the reader to allow me the same liberty which I have used in the preceding case, of supposing it such. For he shall find that the affair is of no great importance.'[50] It is thus untrue to say that Hume lays great emphasis on contiguity and on temporal succession as essential elements of the causal relation. He decided, indeed, to treat them as though they were essential elements, but there is another element of greater importance. 'Shall we then rest contented with these two relations of contiguity and succession, as affording a complete idea of causation? By no means. An object may be contiguous and prior to another, without being considered as its cause. There is a *necessary connection* to be taken into consideration; and that relation is of much greater importance than any of the other two above mentioned.'[51]

The question arises, therefore, from what impression or impressions is the idea of necessary connection derived. But in the *Treatise* Hume finds that he has to approach this question indirectly, by, as he says, beating about all the neighbouring fields in the hope that he may light on his quarry. This means that he finds it necessary to discuss first of all two important questions. 'First, for what reason (do) we pronounce it *necessary* that everything whose existence has a beginning, should also have a cause? Secondly, why (do) we conclude that such particular causes must *necessarily* have such particular effects; and what is the nature of that inference we draw from the one to the other, and of the belief we repose in it?'[52]

The maxim that whatever begins to exist must have a cause of its existence is, Hume maintains, neither intuitively certain nor demonstrable. He does not say much about the first point and to all intents and purposes contents himself with challenging anyone who thinks that it is intuitively certain to show that it is. As for the non-demonstrability of the maxim or principle, Hume argues first of all that we conceive an object as non-existent at one moment and as existent at the next moment without having any distinct idea of a cause or productive principle. And if we can conceive a beginning of existence in separation from the idea of a cause, 'the actual separation of these objects is so far possible, that it implies no contradiction nor absurdity; and is therefore incapable of being refuted by any reasoning from mere ideas, without which it is impossible to demonstrate the necessity of a cause'.[53] After this argument, which is connected with his theory of ideas as copies or images of impressions and with his nominalism, he proceeds to refute certain formulations of the pretended demonstration of the principle that everything which begins to be does so through the productive agency of a cause. For example, Clarke and others argued that if anything began to exist without a cause, it would cause itself; and this is obviously impossible, because to do so it would have to exist before itself. Again, Locke argued that a thing which came into being without a cause would be caused by nothing; and nothing cannot be the cause of anything. Hume's main criticism of arguments of this sort is that they all beg the question by presupposing the validity of the very principle which they are supposed to demonstrate, namely, that anything which begins to exist must have a cause.

If this principle is neither intuitively certain nor demonstrable, our belief in it must arise from experience and observation. But at this point Hume drops the subject, saying that he proposes to pass to his second question, why we believe that this particular cause must have this particular effect. Perhaps the answer to the second question will be found to answer the first as well.

In the first place, causal inference is not the fruit of intuitive knowledge of essences. 'There is no object which implies the existence of any other, if we consider these objects in themselves and never look beyond the ideas which we form of them. Such an inference would amount to knowledge, and would imply the absolute contradiction and impossibility of conceiving anything different. But as all distinct ideas are separable, it is evident there can be no impossibility of that kind.'[54] For example, we do not, according to Hume, intuit the essence of flame and see its effect or effects as logically necessary consequences.

'It is therefore by *experience* only that we can infer the existence of one object from another.'[55] What does this mean in the concrete? It means that we frequently experience the conjunction of two objects, say, flame and the sensation which we call heat, and we remember that these objects have appeared in a regular recurrent order of contiguity and succession. Then, 'without any further ceremony we call the one *cause* and the other *effect* and infer the existence of the one from that of the other'.[56] The last remark shows that Hume is thinking of the ordinary man's idea of causality, and not simply of that of the philosopher. The ordinary man observes the 'constant conjunction' of A and B in repeated instances, where A is contiguous with B and is prior to B, and he calls A the cause and B the effect. 'When one particular species of events has always, in all instances, been conjoined with another, we make no longer any scruple of foretelling one upon the appearance of the other, and of employing that reasoning (causal inference) which can alone assure us of any matter of fact or existence. We then call the one object *cause*, the other *effect*.'[57] 'Suitably to this experience, therefore, we may define a cause to be *an object, followed by another, and where all the objects similar to the first are followed by objects similar to the second. Or, in other words, where, if the first object had not been, the second never had existed.*'[58]

In saying that we 'remember' past instances Hume obviously goes beyond what common experience warrants him saying. For we may very well infer cause from effect or effect from cause without recalling any past instances. But Hume corrects this error presently, by means of the principle of association.

If our belief in regular particular causal connections rests on memory of past instances of constant conjunction, it appears that we are assuming the principle or at least acting as though we assumed the principle that 'instances of which we have had no experience must resemble those of which we have had experience, and that the course of nature continues always uniformly the same'.[59] But this principle is neither intuitively certain nor demonstrable. For the notion of a change in the course of nature is not self-contradictory. Nor can the principle be established by probable reasoning from experience. For it lies at the basis of our probable reasoning. We always tacitly presuppose the uniformity. Hume does not mean that we ought not to assume the principle. To do this would be to adopt a scepticism which he considered incapable of being put into practice. He simply wishes to observe that we cannot prove the validity of our belief in causal inference by means of a principle which cannot itself be proved and which is not intuitively certain. At the same time we do in fact presuppose the principle, and we could neither act nor reason (outside pure mathematics) unless we tacitly presupposed it. This *'supposition that the future resembles the past* is not founded on arguments of any kind, but is derived entirely from habit, by which we are determined to expect for the future the same train of objects to which we have been accustomed.'[60] Again, ' 'Tis not, therefore, reason which is the guide of life, but custom. That alone determines the mind, in all instances, to suppose the future conformable to the past. However easy this step may seem, reason would never, to all eternity, be able to make it.'[61] The idea of habit or custom plays a great part in Hume's final analysis of causality.

To return to the idea of constant conjunction. The statement that it is experience of constant conjunction which leads us to assert particular causal connections does not answer Hume's question, from what impression or impressions the idea of necessary connection is derived. For the idea of constant conjunction is the idea of the regular recurrence of two kinds of similar events according to a constant pattern of contiguity and succession, and this idea does not comprise that of necessary connection. 'From the mere repetition of any past impression, even to infinity, there never will arise any new original idea, such as that of a necessary connection; and the number of impressions has in this case no more effect than if we confined ourselves to one only.'[62] But we cannot, in Hume's opinion, derive the idea of necessary connection from observation of regular sequences or causal connections. We must say, therefore, either that there is no such idea or that it must be derived from some subjective source. Hume cannot adopt the first of these alternatives; for he has already laid stress on the importance of the idea of necessary connection. He must therefore adopt the second alternative; and this is in fact what he does.

To say that the idea of necessary connection is derived from a subjective source is to say, within the framework of Hume's philosophy, that it is derived from some impression of reflection. But it does not follow that the idea is derived from the relation of the will to its effects, and that it is then extrapolated. 'The will, being here considered as a cause, has no more a discoverable connection with its effects than any material thing has with its proper effect. . . . In short, the actions of the mind are, in this respect, the same with those of matter. We perceive only their constant conjunction. . . .'[63] We must look, therefore, for another solution. Suppose that we observe several instances of constant conjunction. This repetition cannot, by itself alone, give rise to the idea of necessary connection. This point has been already admitted. To give rise to this idea, the repetition of similar instances of constant conjunction 'must either *discover* or *produce* something new, which is the source of that idea'.[64] But repetition does not make us discover anything new in the conjoined objects. Nor does it produce any new quality in the objects themselves. Observation of the repetition does, however, produce a new impression in the mind. 'For after we have observed the resemblance in a sufficient number of instances, we immediately feel a determination of the mind to pass from one object to its usual attendant. . . . Necessity, then, is the effect of this observation, and is nothing but an internal impression of the mind, or a determination to carry our thoughts from one object to another. . . . There is no internal impression which has any relation to the present business, but that propensity, which custom produces, to pass from an object to its usual attendant.'[65] The propensity, therefore, caused by custom or association, to pass from one of the things which have been observed to be constantly conjoined to the other is the impression from which the idea of necessary connection is derived. That is to say, the propensity, produced by custom, is something given, an impression, and the idea of necessary connection is its reflection or image in consciousness. This explanation of the idea of necessary connection is applicable both to external causal relations and to internal causal relations, such as the relation between the will and its effects.

We are now in a position to define the notion of cause more accurately. Causation, as was seen above, can be considered either as a philosophical or as a natural relation. Considered as a philosophical relation, it can be defined thus. A cause is 'an object precedent and contiguous to another, and where all the objects resembling the former are placed in like relations of precedency and contiguity to those objects that resemble the latter'.[66] Considered as a natural relation, 'a *cause* is an object precedent and contiguous to another, and so united with it that the idea of the one determines the mind to form the idea of the other, and the impression of the one to form a more lively idea of the other'.[67] It is to be noted that 'though causation be a *philosophical* relation, as implying contiguity, succession and constant conjunction, yet it is only so far as it is a *natural* relation and produces a union among our ideas, that we are able to reason upon it or draw any inference from it'.[68]

Hume has thus given an answer to his question 'why we conclude that such particular causes must necessarily have such particular effects, and why we form an inference from one to another'.[69] The answer is couched in psychological terms, referring to the psychological effect of observation of instances of constant conjunction. This observation produces a custom or propensity of the mind, an associative link, whereby the mind passes naturally from, say, the idea of flame to the idea of heat or from an impression of flame to the lively idea of heat. This enables us to pass beyond experience or observation. From the observation of smoke we naturally infer fire, even though the fire is not observed. If it is asked what guarantee we have of the objective validity of such an inference, the only ultimate answer which Hume can give is empirical verification. And in an empiricist philosophy this is the only answer which is really required.

Has Hume also answered the question, how experience gives rise to the principle that whatever begins to exist must have a cause of existence? His answer to the question why we conclude that this particular cause must have this particular effect suggests that it is custom which makes us expect every event to have some cause and which prevents us from maintaining that there can be absolutely uncaused events. And this is, I think, what he must say, given his premisses. After giving his analysis of causality he remarks that in view of the resulting definitions of *cause* 'we may easily conceive that there is no absolute nor metaphysical necessity that every beginning of existence should be attended with such an object'.[70] We cannot demonstrate the truth of the principle in question. Yet he says in the first *Enquiry* that 'it is universally allowed that nothing exists without a cause of its existence'.[71] Our belief in this principle must, then, be due to custom. It is worth noting, however, that the sentence just quoted from the *Enquiry* goes on in this way: 'and that chance, when strictly examined, is a mere negative word, and means not any real power which has anywhere a being in nature'.[72] Now, 'chance' means for Hume a fortuitous or uncaused event. And not to believe in chance is to believe that every event has a cause. And to believe this is, for Hume, to believe that every cause is a necessary or determining cause. True, events may occur contrary to expectation. And this may lead the vulgar to believe in chance. But 'philosophers' (including, of course, scientists), finding on close examination in several instances that the unexpected event was due to the counteracting effect of a hitherto unknown cause, 'form a maxim that the connection betwixt all causes and effects is equally necessary, and that its seeming uncertainty in some instances proceeds from the secret opposition of contrary causes'.[73] Here the principle that every event has a cause is described as a maxim 'formed' by philosophers. But our belief in the maxim would seem to be the result of custom or habit.

Hume remarks that there can be only one kind of cause. 'For as our idea of efficiency is derived from the constant conjunction of two objects, wherever this is observed, the cause is efficient; and where it is not, there can never be a cause of any kind.'[74] The Scholastic distinction between formal, material, efficient and final causes is rejected. So is the distinction between cause and occasion, so far as these terms are used with different meanings. Further, just as there is only one kind of cause, so there is only one kind of necessity. The distinction between physical and moral necessity lacks any real foundation. 'It is the constant conjunction of objects, along with the determination of the mind, which constitutes a physical necessity: and the removal of these is the same thing with *chance*.'[75]

The foregoing sketch of Hume's analysis of causality indicates, I hope, the fact that he devoted considerable attention to the subject. It occupies a much more prominent position in the *Treatise* than is occupied by his treatment of substance. No doubt, he considered that the theory of material substance had already been refuted by Berkeley. But the main reason why he devotes so much attention to causality is his understanding of the all-important role played by causal influence in the sciences and in human life in general. And the great merit of his analysis, which one can recognize whether one agrees with it or not, is his attempt to combine a consistent empiricism with a recognition of the meaning which we ordinarily attribute to causation. Thus he recognizes that when we say that X caused Y we mean something more than that X preceded Y temporally and was spatially contiguous with it. He faces up to the difficulty and tries to solve it on empiricist lines. This attempt to develop a consistent empiricist philosophy is his chief title to fame. What he said was by no means so novel as has been sometimes supposed. To take one example, Nicholas of Autrecourt[76] in the fourteenth century maintained that from the existence of one thing we cannot infer with certainty the existence of another thing, since, in the case of two distinct things, it is always possible without logical contradiction to affirm the existence of the one and deny the existence of the other. It is only analytic propositions, 'reducible' to the principle of non-contradiction, which are certain. Furthermore, Nicholas appears to have explained our belief in regular causal connections in terms of our experience of repeated sequences which gives rise to the expectation that if B has followed A in the past it will do so in the future. I am not suggesting, of course, that Hume knew anything at all about Nicholas of Autrecourt or similar thinkers of the fourteenth century. I am simply drawing attention to the historical fact that a number of Hume's positions had been anticipated in the fourteenth century, even though Hume was unaware of the fact. Nevertheless, it remains true that it is Hume, and not his early predecessors, who is the patron and father of modern empiricism. Terminology has changed since the eighteenth century, and the modern empiricist tries to avoid Hume's tendency to muddle up logic and psychology. But of the modern empiricist's direct or indirect debt to Hume there can be no doubt.

To emphasize Hume's historical importance is not necessarily to accept his analysis of causality. To take one example of a possible line of criticism, it seems to me that in spite of what Hume says on the matter we are conscious of interior causal production of a kind which cannot be explained simply in terms of his analysis. He seems to suppose that the notorious difficulty in explaining how our wills influence our bodily movements, or even how we perform at will certain interior operations, shows that even here causality, on the objective side, is simply constant conjunction, or at least that we perceive only constant conjunction. But this way of arguing appears to presuppose the validity of the position which had been maintained by the occasionalists that there is no productive causal efficacy or power unless we know not only that we act causally but also how we do so. And the validity of this contention is open to question. Again, it is important to distinguish between the question whether the scientist can get along with Hume's idea of causality and the question whether this idea represents an analysis that is adequate from the philosophical point of view. The physicist is not concerned, for instance, with the problem of the logical and ontological status of the principle that everything which begins to be does so through the agency of an extrinsic cause. It is not necessary for him to concern himself with such a problem. But the philosopher does ask this question. And Hume's treatment of it is open to criticism. For instance, even if one can imagine first a blank, as it were, and then X existing, it by no means follows necessarily that X can begin to exist without an extrinsic cause. Nor, from the fact that there is no verbal contradiction between the statements 'X began to exist' and 'X had no cause' does it necessarily follow that the statements are compatible when examined from the point of view of 'metaphysical analysis'. We have on the one hand analytic and 'formal' propositions and on the other empirical hypotheses: there is, in his scheme, no room for synthetic *a priori* propositions. And this is, indeed, the problem, whether or not there are propositions which are certain and yet informative about reality. But to discuss this matter adequately would mean discussing the nature and status of metaphysics. Once given Hume's premises and his conception of 'reason', something resembling his analysis of causality must follow. We cannot accept his premises and then add on a metaphysical doctrine of causality.

In criticizing Hume it is, however, important to remember that he does not deny that there are causal relations. That is to say, he does not deny the truth of the statement that flame causes heat. Nor does he deny even the truth of the statement that flame necessarily causes heat. What he does is to inquire into the meaning of these statements. And the question, in a discussion with Hume, is not whether there are causal relations, but what it means to say that there are causal relations. Again, the question is not whether there are any necessary connections, but what it means to say that there are necessary connections.

10. As we have seen, the uniformity of nature is not demonstrable by reason. It is the object of belief rather than of intuition or demonstration. We can say, indeed, as the ordinary man would say, that we know it, if the word *know* is used with the wide range of meaning that it has in common discourse. But if the word is used in a strict sense, to mean our apprehension of those propositions in the case of which all other alternatives are excluded, we cannot be said to have knowledge of the uniformity of nature. For Hume, we have analytic propositions on the one hand, which express relations between ideas, and synthetic propositions, which are based in some way on experience. But experience by itself gives us only

factual data: it cannot tell us about the future. Nor can we prove by reason that our beliefs and expectations about the future are justified. Yet belief plays a very important part in human life. If we were confined to analytic propositions on the one hand and immediate empirical data, present or re-membered, on the other, human life would be impossible. Every day we perform actions which are based on belief. It becomes necessary, therefore, to investigate the nature of belief.

Hume's account of belief illustrates his tendency to con-fuse logic and psychology. For he gives a psychological an-swer to the logical question about the grounds of that assur-ance which he calls belief. But he is perhaps bound to do this. For on his premisses there can be no logical grounds for our beliefs about the future course of events. He must, therefore, content himself with showing how we come to have these be-liefs.

According to Hume, believing a proposition cannot be ex-plained in terms of the operations of joining ideas. If, to take one of his examples, someone tells me that Julius Caesar died in his bed, I understand his statement and I join the same ideas as he does, but I do not assent to the proposition. We must look elsewhere for the difference between belief and in-credulity. In Hume's view belief 'does nothing but vary the manner in which we conceive any object, it can only bestow on our ideas an additional force and vivacity. An opinion, therefore, or belief, may be most accurately defined, *a lively idea related to or associated with a present impression*.'[77] For example, when we infer the existence of one thing from that of another (that is to say, when we believe as the result of inference that something exists), we pass from the im-pression of one object to the 'lively' idea of another; and it is this liveliness or vivacity of the idea which is characteristic of belief. In passing from the impression to the idea 'we are not determined by reason, but by custom, or a principle of as-sociation. But belief is something more than a simple idea. It is a particular manner of forming an idea; and as the same idea can only be varied by a variation of its degrees of force and vivacity, it follows upon the whole that belief is a lively idea produced by a relation to a present impression, according to the foregoing definition.'[78]

We can distinguish, therefore, between belief and fancies by referring to the manner in which we conceive the relevant ideas. 'An idea assented to *feels* different from a fictitious idea that the fancy alone presents to us: and this different feeling I endeavour to explain by calling it a superior *force*, or *vivacity*, or *solidity*, or *firmness*, or *steadiness*.'[79] Belief is 'a term that everyone sufficiently understands in common life';[80] but in philosophy we can describe it only in terms of feeling.

However, even if words like 'vivacity' and 'liveliness' suffice to distinguish propositions in which we believe from fancies which are known to be fancies, is it not true that we have many beliefs about which we have no strong feelings at all? We believe that the earth is not flat and that the moon is a satellite of the earth, but most of us have no strong *feelings* on these matters. It seems that in answer Hume must refer to the attributes of steadiness and firmness rather than to those of vivacity and liveliness. In Hume's view our assent to a proposition must be conditioned by the exclusion of alternatives. In the cases of an analytic proposition any contrary proposition is excluded because the denial of an analytic proposition is seen to be self-contradictory. In the case of a synthetic proposition the alternatives are excluded in proportion to the regularity with which the situation asserted in the proposition has occurred in the past, observation of this repetition having set up a custom and brought into play the principles of association. In the case of the statement that the moon is a satellite of the earth, we have always been told that it is true, nothing has occurred to make us doubt the truth of the statement, and any observations we may have made are compatible with its truth. We have, therefore, a firm and steady belief in the truth of the statement, even though we may not feel so strongly about it as we might feel, for example, about the honesty of an intimate friend when it has been maliciously impugned.

I have said that we have always been told that the moon is a satellite of the earth. This means that belief can be generated by education, and so by ideas. This Hume admits. 'All those opinions and notions of things, to which we have been accustomed from our infancy, take such deep root, that it is impossible for us, by all the powers of reason and experience, to eradicate them; and this habit not only approaches in its influence, but even on many occasions prevails over that which arises from the constant and inseparable union of causes and effects. Here we must not be contented with saying that the vividness of the idea produces the belief: we must maintain that they are individually the same. . . . I

am persuaded that, upon examination, we shall find more
than one half of those opinions which prevail among mankind
to be owing to education, and that the principles which are
thus implicitly embraced overbalance those which are owing
either to abstract reasoning or experience. . . . Education is
an artificial and not a natural cause.'[81]

According to Hume, therefore, 'when I am convinced of
any principle, it is only an idea which strikes more strongly
upon me. When I give the preference to one set of arguments
above another, I do nothing but decide from my feeling concerning the superiority of their influence.'[82] Again, 'all our
reasonings concerning causes and effects are derived from
nothing but custom, and belief is more properly an act of the
sensitive than of the cogitative part of our natures'.[83] How,
then, can we decide between rational and irrational beliefs?
Hume does not appear to give any very clear and explicit answer to this question; and when he is dealing with irrational
beliefs, he tends to indicate how, in his opinion, the mind
works rather than to make it clear how we are to distinguish
between beliefs which are rational and those which are not.
But his general answer to the problem seems to be more or
less this. Many beliefs are the result of 'education', and
some of them are irrational. The way to cure ourselves
of them is to have recourse to experience or, rather, to
test those beliefs by experience. Does the belief which is the
result of our having been constantly told that it is true fit in
with the beliefs which are founded on experience of causal relations? If the former is incompatible or inconsistent with
the latter, it should be discarded. Education is an 'artificial
cause', and we should prefer the 'natural' cause of beliefs,
causal relations in the philosophical sense, that is, constant or
invariable conjunctions. Of course, we can form irrational beliefs, based on experience. Hume gives the example of generalizations about the members of some foreign nation which
are the result of one or two encounters with foreigners. But
the way to correct prejudices of this kind is obvious: it is the
way by which such prejudices are in fact corrected, if they
are corrected. Further, irrational beliefs can be generated by
experience of uniformities or of constant conjunctions. But
these can be corrected by reflection in the light of wider experience which reveals contrary instances or brings other factors to light. Tolstoy speaks somewhere of the belief of some
peasants that the budding of the oak trees in the spring is
due to a certain wind. And if the wind was contiguous with

the trees and prior to their budding, the belief can be explained. But if experience reveals instances where the oaks bud even when this particular wind is not blowing, we do not entertain the peasants' belief. Again, even if in all instances oak trees budded only when the particular wind was blowing, the belief that the budding is caused by the wind might still be incompatible with our experience and observation of other cases of budding. The mind would not, then, form a habit or custom supplying, so to speak, the element of necessary connection; and we would not believe that the wind caused the budding of the oak trees.

If these remarks represent Hume's mind, a further difficulty arises. Hume often speaks as though custom not only does dominate but also ought to dominate in human life. At the same time he also speaks as though experience ought to be our guide. Thus he says that 'the experienced train of events is the great standard by which we all regulate our conduct. Nothing else can be appealed to in the field, or in the senate. Nothing else ought ever to be heard of in the school or in the closet.'[84] But perhaps the difficulty can be answered to some extent in this way. According to Hume, there are certain fundamental customary beliefs which are essential to human life; belief in the continuous and independent existence of bodies, and the belief that everything which begins to be has a cause. These fundamental customary beliefs dominate and ought to dominate, if, that is to say, human life is to be possible. And they condition our more specific beliefs. But these latter are not inevitable and necessary: we are capable of testing and altering them. The test is the experienced course of events and consistency with beliefs which are themselves compatible with the experienced course of events.

Chapter Fifteen

HUME (2)

Our belief in the existence of bodies — Minds and the problem of personal identity — The existence and nature of God — Scepticism.

1. At the close of the last chapter we saw that belief in the continuing existence of bodies independently of the mind or of perception is for Hume a fundamental natural belief. But we must examine rather more closely what he has to say on this matter.

The main difficulty, Hume says, which arises in connection with our notion of a world of permanently existing objects independent of our perception, is that we are confined to the world of perceptions and enjoy no access to a world of objects existing independently of these perceptions. 'Now since nothing is ever present to the mind but perceptions, and since all ideas are derived from something antecedently present to the mind, it follows that it is impossible for us so much as to conceive or form an idea of anything specifically different from ideas and impressions. Let us fix our attention out of ourselves as much as possible; let us chase our imagination to the heavens, or to the utmost limits of the universe; we never really advance a step beyond ourselves, nor can conceive any kind of existence, but those perceptions which have appeared in that narrow compass. This is the universe of the imagination, nor have we any idea but what is there produced.'[1] Ideas are ultimately reducible to impressions, and impressions are subjective, pertaining to the percipient subject. We cannot, therefore, ever conceive what objects would be like, or are like, apart from our perceptions.

It is important to understand that Hume does not intend to deny the existence of body or bodies independently of our perceptions. He maintains, indeed, that we are unable to prove that body exists; but at the same time he insists that we cannot help assenting to the proposition. 'Nature has not left this to his (the sceptic's) choice, and has doubtless esteemed it an affair of too great importance to be trusted to our uncertain reasonings and speculations. We may well ask, *What causes induce us to believe in the existence of body?*, but it is in vain to ask *whether there be body or not*. That is a point which we must take for granted in all our reasonings.'[2] The sceptic, as well as the non-sceptic, consistently acts as though body really exists; he cannot help believing in this, whatever academic doubts he may air in his study. We can only inquire, therefore, what is the cause or what are the causes which induce us to believe in the continued existence of bodies distinct from our minds and perceptions.

In the first place the senses cannot be the source of the notion that things continue to exist when they are unperceived. For in order for this to be the case, the senses would have to operate when they have ceased to operate. And this would involve a contradiction. Nor do the senses reveal to us bodies which are distinct from our perceptions; that is, from the sensible appearances of bodies. They do not reveal to us both a copy and the original. It may, indeed, seem that I perceive my own body. But 'properly speaking, it is not our body we perceive, when we regard our limbs and members, but certain impressions, which enter by the senses; so that the ascribing a real and corporeal existence to these impressions, or to their objects, is an act of the mind as difficult to explain as that which we examine at present'.[3] It is true that among the classes of impressions we ascribe a distinct and continuous existence to some and not to others. Nobody attributes distinct and continuous existence to pains and pleasures. The 'vulgar', though not 'philosophers', suppose that colours, tastes, sounds and, in general, the so-called secondary qualities possess such existence. Both philosophers and the vulgar alike suppose figure, bulk, motion and solidity to exist continuously and independently of perception. But it cannot be the senses themselves which lead us to make these distinctions; for, as far as the senses are concerned, all these impressions are on the same footing.

In the second place it is not reason which induces us to believe in the continuous and distinct existence of bodies. 'Whatever convincing arguments philosophers may fancy they can produce to establish the belief of objects independent of the mind, it is obvious these arguments are known but to very few; and that it is not by them that children, peasants, and the greatest part of mankind are induced to attribute objects to some impressions and deny them to others.'[4] Nor can we rationally justify our belief, once we have it. 'Philosophy informs us that everything which appears to the mind is nothing but a perception, and is interrupted and dependent on the mind.'[5] And we cannot infer the existence of objects from perceptions. Such an inference would be a causal inference. And for it to be valid we should have to be able to observe the constant conjunction of those objects with these perceptions. And this we cannot do. For we cannot get outside the series of our perceptions to compare them with anything apart from them.

Our belief in the continued and independent existence of bodies, and our habit of supposing that objective and independent counterparts of certain impressions exist, must be due, therefore, neither to the senses nor to the reason or understanding but to the imagination. The question thus arises, which are the features of certain impressions that work on the imagination and produce our persuasion of the continued and distinct existence of bodies? It is useless to refer this belief or persuasion to the superior force or violence of certain impressions as compared with others. For it is obvious that the majority of people suppose that the heat of a fire, placed at a convenient distance, is in the fire itself, whereas they do not suppose that the intense pain caused by too great proximity to the fire is anywhere else but in the impressions of the percipient subject. Hence we have to look elsewhere for the peculiar features of certain impressions, which work upon the imagination.

Hume mentions two such peculiar features, namely, constancy and coherence. 'Those mountains and houses and trees which lie at present under my eye have always appeared to me in the same order; and when I lose sight of them by shutting my eyes or turning my head, I soon after find them return upon me without the least alteration.'[6] Here we have constantly recurring similar impressions. But, obviously, bodies often change not only their positions but also their qualities. However, even in their changes there is a coherence. 'When I return to my chamber after an hour's absence, I find not my fire in the same situation in which I left it; but then I am accustomed, in other instances, to see a like alteration produced in a like time, whether I am present or absent, near or remote. This coherence, therefore, in their changes, is one of the characteristics of external objects, as well as their constancy.'[7] Hume's meaning is, I think, sufficiently clear. My impressions of the mountain which I can see through the window are constant, in the sense that, given the requisite conditions, they are similar. From the point of view of perception the mountain remains more or less the same. But the impression which I receive of the fire in my room at 9 p.m. is not the same as the impression which I receive when I return to the room at 10 30 p.m. The fire, as we say, has died down in the meantime. On the other hand, these two separate impressions agree with the two separate impressions which I receive at the same interval of time on another evening. And if I watch the fire for a stretch of time on two or more occasions, there is a regular pattern of coherence between the different series of impressions.

Hume is not, however, satisfied with an explanation of our belief in the continuous and independent existence of bodies, which rests simply and solely on the actual course of our impressions. On the one hand our impressions are in fact interrupted, while on the other hand we habitually believe in the continuous existence of bodies. And the mere repetition of interrupted, though similar, impressions cannot by itself produce this belief. We must look there for 'some other principles', and Hume, as we would expect, has recourse to psychological considerations. 'The imagination, when set into any train of thinking, is apt to continue even when its object fails it, and, like a galley put in motion by the oars, carries on its course without any new impulse.'[8] Once the mind begins to observe a uniformity or coherence among impressions, it tends to render this uniformity as complete as possible. The supposition of the continued existence of bodies suffices for this purpose and affords us a notion of greater regularity and coherence than is provided by the senses. But though coherence may give rise to the supposition of the continuous existence of objects, the idea of constancy is needed to explain our supposition of their distinct existence; that is, of their independence of our perceptions. When we have been accustomed to find, for example, that the perception of the sun recurs constantly in the same form as on its first appearance, we are inclined to regard these different and interrupted perceptions as being the same. Reflection, however, shows us that the perceptions are not the same. Therefore, to free ourselves from this contradiction, we disguise or remove the interruption 'by supposing that these interrupted perceptions are connected by a real existence, of which we are insensible'.[9]

These observations are not, it is true, very enlightening. And Hume endeavours to make his position more precise and clear. To do this, he distinguishes between the opinion of the vulgar and what he calls the 'philosophical system'. The vulgar are 'all the unthinking and unphilosophical part of mankind, that is, all of us at one time or other'.[10] These people suppose, says Hume, that their perceptions are the only objects. 'The very image which is present to the senses is with us the real body; and it is to these interrupted images we ascribe a perfect identity.'[11] In other words, the vulgar know nothing of Locke's material substance; material objects are for them simply what they perceive them to be. And to say this is, for Hume, to say that for the vulgar objects and perceptions are the same. This presupposed, we are then faced by a difficulty. On the one hand, 'The smooth passage of the imagination along the ideas of the resembling perceptions makes us ascribe to them a perfect identity'.[12] On the other hand, the interrupted manner of their occurrence or, as Hume says, appearance, leads us to consider them as distinct entities. But this contradiction gives rise to an uneasiness, and it must therefore be resolved. As we cannot bring ourselves to sacrifice the propensity produced by the smooth passage of the imagination, we sacrifice the second principle. It is true that the interruptions in the appearance of similar perceptions are often so long and frequent that we cannot overlook them; but at the same time 'an interrupted appearance to the senses implies not necessarily an interruption in the existence'.[13] Hence we can 'feign' a continued existence of objects. Yet we do not merely feign this; we *believe* it. And, according to Hume, this belief can be explained by reference to memory. Memory presents us with a great number of instances of similar perceptions which recur at different times after considerable interruptions. And this resemblance produces a propensity to look upon these interrupted perceptions as the same. At the same time it also produces a propensity to connect the perceptions by means of the hypothesis of a continued existence, in order to justify our ascription of identity to them and in order to avoid the contradiction in which the interrupted character of our perceptions seems to involve us. We have, therefore, a propensity

to feign the continuous existence of bodies. Further, since
this propensity arises from lively impressions of the memory,
it bestows vivacity on this fiction, 'or, in other words, makes
us believe the continued existence of body'.[14] For belief
consists in the vivacity of an idea.

But though we are led in this way to believe in the continued existence of 'sensible objects or perceptions', philosophy makes us see the fallacy of the supposition. For reason
shows us that our perceptions do not exist independently of
our perceiving. And they have no more a continued than an
independent existence. Philosophers, therefore, have made a
distinction between perceptions and objects. The former are
interrupted and dependent on the percipient subject: the
latter exist continuously and independently. But this theory
is arrived at by first embracing and then discarding the vulgar
opinion, and it contains not only all the difficulties attaching
to the latter but also some which are peculiar to itself. For
instance, the theory involves postulating a new set of perceptions. We cannot, as has been seen earlier, conceive of
objects except in terms of perceptions. Hence, if we postulate
objects as well as perceptions, we merely reduplicate the
latter and at the same time ascribe to them attributes,
namely, uninterruptedness and independence, which do not
belong to perceptions.

The upshot of Hume's examination of our belief in the
continued and independent existence of bodies is, therefore,
that there is no rational justification for it. At the same time
we cannot eradicate the belief. We can take it for granted,
'whatever may be the reader's opinion at this present moment, that an hour hence he will be persuaded there is both
an external and internal world'.[15] It is only in the actual
course of philosophical reflection that scepticism on this
point is possible, and even there it is only theoretical. It is
to be noted that Hume does not recommend the theory that
certain qualities (the so-called secondary qualities) are subjective, while others (the primary qualities) are objective.
On the contrary, he maintains that 'if colours, sounds, tastes
and smells be merely perceptions, nothing we can conceive
is possessed of a real, continued and independent existence;
not even motion, extension and solidity, which are the primary qualities chiefly insisted on'.[16] True, he agrees that
'when we reason from cause to effect, we conclude that neither colour, sound, taste nor smell have a continued and
independent existence'.[17] But 'when we exclude these sensi-

ble qualities, there remains nothing in the universe which has such an existence'.[18] Hume certainly accepted the main lines of Berkeley's criticism of Locke, but he did not follow him further. For though Berkeley intended to refute the sceptics, as well as the atheists and materialists, his arguments, according to Hume, lead to scepticism in that 'they admit of no answer and produce no conviction. Their only effect is to cause that momentary amazement and irresolution and confusion, which is the result of scepticism.'[19] The retort can be made, of course, that Hume's position is more sceptical than Berkeley's, since he consciously underlines a fundamental and irreconcilable contradiction between the conclusions of philosophical reasoning and our natural belief. It is also arguable that he tends to misrepresent Berkeley to the extent that he depicts him as wishing to correct the opinions of 'the vulgar'. But, though all this may well be true, we must remember that Hume ultimately takes the side of the vulgar. His point is that we have an inevitable and ineradicable propensity to believe in the continuous and independent existence of bodies. This propensity produces belief, and this belief operates in the vulgar and the philosophical alike. All attempts to give a rational justification of this belief are failures. There may be something apart from our perceptions, but we cannot prove that this is the case. At the same time nobody does or can live his life on sceptical principles. Natural belief inevitably, and rightly, prevails.

It is clear, I think, that a good deal of the force of Hume's arguments depends on the premiss that it is our perceptions with which we are immediately acquainted. Moreover, he seems to use the word 'perception' in two senses, to signify, that is, the act of perceiving and the object perceived. It is obvious that our perceptions, in the first sense of the word 'perception', are interrupted and discrete. But the ordinary man is aware of this, and he does not identify, for example, two interrupted perceptions of the sun. If he can be said to identify his perceptions, he identifies them in the second sense of the word 'perception'. Hume might retort, of course, that to make this distinction is to beg the whole question; for it is the distinction itself which is the subject of dispute. At the same time the discussion cannot be profitably carried on unless linguistic distinctions are carefully sorted out. And Hume's discussion of the problem seems to me to suffer from the defect common to Locke's 'way of ideas' and its derivatives, namely, that a term such as 'idea' or 'perception' is used in an unusual sense without sufficient care being taken to discriminate between the unusual and the usual senses. And this point is of considerable importance. For momentous philosophical conclusions follow if these words are taken in the unusual sense. It is, indeed, arguable that it is the empiricists who beg the whole question and that Hume's sceptical conclusions follow from his linguistic usage.

At the same time Hume's general position, that it is natural belief, analogous to animal 'belief', which does and should prevail in human life and that reason is powerless to justify these beliefs, if 'justify' is taken to mean something more than giving a psychological account of the genesis of the beliefs, is of great historical importance. It is probably this position which is characteristic of Hume and which sets him apart from both Locke and Berkeley. There are, indeed, some anticipations of the position in Locke; but Locke's philosophy had, as we have seen, a markedly rationalist element. It is Hume, above all other classical empiricists, who embodies the anti-rationalist current of thought. And it is a mistake to dwell so exclusively on his scepticism as to pass over or minimize the great emphasis which he places on the role of natural belief.

2. According to Hume, the problem of minds is not so complicated and difficult as the problem of bodies. 'The intellectual world, though involved in infinite obscurities, is not perplexed with any such contradictions as those we have discovered in the natural. What is known concerning it, agrees with itself; and what is unknown, we must be contented to leave so.'[20] Further reflection, as we shall see, led Hume to a less optimistic conclusion; but this is what he begins by saying.

Tackling first of all the subject of the immateriality of the soul, Hume suggests that the question whether perceptions inhere in a material or an immaterial substance is a meaningless question, in the sense that we can attach no clear meaning to it and cannot, therefore, answer it. In the first place, have we any idea of substance? If so, what is the impression which produces this idea? It may be said that we have an idea of substance because we can define it as 'something which may exist by itself'. But this definition will fit everything conceivable. For whatever is clearly and distinctly conceivable can exist by itself, as far as possibility is concerned. Hence the definition will not serve to distinguish substance from accident or soul from perceptions. In the second place, what is meant by 'inhesion'? 'Inhesion in something is supposed to be requisite to support the existence of our perceptions. Nothing appears requisite to support the existence of a perception. We have, therefore, no idea of inhesion.'[21] Perceptions cannot inhere in a body. For in order to do so they would have to be present locally. But it is absurd to speak of a passion, for example, being situated locally in relation to a moral reflection, as being above or below it, to the right or left of it. It does not follow, however, that perceptions can inhere in an immaterial substance. 'That table, which just now appears to me, is only a perception, and all its qualities are qualities of a perception. Now the most obvious of all its qualities is extension. The perception consists of parts.'[22] But what does it mean to say that an extended perception inheres in an immaterial substance? The supposed relation is inexplicable. If it is said that perceptions must inhere in something, to say this is to beg the question. In truth an object can exist and yet exist nowhere. 'And I assert that this is not only possible but that the greatest part of beings do and must exist after this manner.'[23]

Hume's remarks about the table evidently presupposes that what I know, when I know the table, is a perception. There may be things other than perceptions; but, if so, we cannot know what they are. We are confined to the world of perceptions. This presupposition is present also, I think, in his argument to show that the theory of the soul as an immaterial substance is indistinguishable in the long run from what he calls, perhaps ironically, the 'hideous hypothesis' of Spinoza. There is, first, the universe of objects or bodies. All these, according to Spinoza, are modifications of one substance or subject. There is, secondly, the universe of thought, the universe of my impressions and ideas. These, we are told by the 'theologians', are modifications of a simple, unextended substance, the soul. But we cannot distinguish between perceptions and objects, and we can find no relation, whether of connection or repugnance, which affects the one and does not affect the other. If, therefore, we object against Spinoza that his substance must be identical with its modifications and, further, that it must be identical with incompatible modifications, exactly the same line of objection can be urged against the hypothesis of the theologians. The immaterial soul must be identical, for instance, with tables and chairs. And if we have an idea of the soul, this idea will itself be a perception and a modification. We shall thus end up with Spinoza's theory of one substance. In fine, any argument to show the absurdity of saying that all so-called natural objects are modifications of one substance will also serve to show the absurdity of saying that all impressions and ideas, that is, all perceptions, are modifications of an immaterial substance, the soul. And all arguments to establish that perceptions are modifications of the soul will also tend to establish the hypothesis of Spinoza. For we cannot distinguish between perceptions and objects and make statements about the one which will not apply to the other.

Of course, it is not Hume's intention to argue in favour of Spinoza's monism. He is engaged in an *argumentum ad hominem*, trying to show that the theological view of the soul is as open to criticism as is the theory of Spinoza. The conclusion which he draws is that 'the question concerning the substance of the soul is absolutely unintelligible. All our perceptions are not susceptible of a local union, either with what is extended or unextended; there being some of them of the one kind, and some of the other.'[24] The problem about the substance of the soul had, therefore, better be dismissed. For we can make no sense of it.

But if there is no substance, whether extended or unextended, which can be called the 'soul', what of personal identity? Hume is obviously compelled to deny that we have any idea of the self as distinct from our perceptions. Some philosophers, he tells us, imagine that we are always conscious of the self as something which remains in a permanent state of self-identity. But if we have any clear and intelligible idea of the self, it must be derived from an impression. Yet 'self or person is not any one impression, but that to which our several impressions and ideas are supposed to have a reference. If any impression gives rise to the idea of self, that impression must continue invariably the same, through the whole course of our lives; since self is supposed to exist after that manner. But there is no impression constant and invariable . . . and consequently there is no such idea.'[25] All our perceptions are distinguishable and separable, and we can discover no self apart from or underlying these perceptions. 'For my part, when I enter most intimately into what I call *myself*, I always stumble on some particular perception or other, of heat or cold, light or shade, love or hatred, pain or pleasure. I never catch *myself* at any time without a perception, and never can observe anything but the perception. . . . If anyone upon serious and unprejudiced reflection thinks he has a different notion of *himself*, I must confess I can reason no longer with him. All I can allow him is that he may be in the right as well as I, and that we are essentially different in this particular. He may perhaps perceive something simple and continued, which he calls *himself*, though I am certain there is no such principle in me.'[26] Hume's conclusion is, therefore, that 'the mind is a kind of theatre where several perceptions successively make their appearance; pass, re-pass, glide away and mingle in an infinite variety of postures and situations. There is properly no *simplicity* in it at one time, nor *identity* in different; whatever natural propension we have to imagine that simplicity and identity. The comparison of the theatre must not mislead us. They are the successive perceptions only that constitute the mind; nor have we the most distant notion of the place where these scenes are represented or of the materials of which it is composed.'[27]

What, then, causes our propensity to attribute identity and simplicity to the mind? According to Hume, we tend to confuse the two ideas of identity and of a succession of related objects. For example, an animal body is an aggregate, and its component parts are constantly changing: in the strict sense it does not remain self-identical. But the changes are normally gradual and cannot be perceived from moment to moment. Further, the parts are related to one another, enjoying a mutual dependence on and connection with one another. The mind thus tends to neglect, as it were, the interruptions and to ascribe persistent self-identity to the aggregate. Now, in the case of the human mind there is a succession of related perceptions. Memory, by raising up images of past perceptions, produces a relation of resemblance among our perceptions: and the imagination is thus carried more easily along the chain, so that the chain appears to be a continued and persistent object. Further, our perceptions are mutually related by means of the causal relation. 'Our impressions give rise to their correspondent ideas: and these ideas in their turn produce other impressions. One thought chases another and draws after it a third, by which it is expelled in its turn.'[28] Here again memory is of primary importance. For it is only by memory that we are able to be aware of the causal relations between our perceptions. Hence memory is to be accounted the chief source of the idea of personal identity. Once given memory, our perceptions are linked by association in the imagination, and we attribute identity to what is in fact an interrupted succession of related perceptions. Indeed, unless corrected by philosophy, we may 'feign' a uniting principle, a permanent self distinct from our perceptions. If we rule out this 'fiction', all questions about personal identity 'are to be regarded rather as grammatical than as philosophical difficulties'.[29] That is to say, the question whether in any given instance it is proper to speak of a thing as identical or not, is a linguistic problem.

Given Hume's phenomenalistic analysis of the self, it is hardly worth discussing whether he believed in immortality. True he did not explicitly deny the possibility of survival. James Boswell records that in his last interview with Hume, on July 7th, 1776, he asked the philosopher whether he did not think it possible that there might be a future state. Hume replied that it was possible that a piece of coal put upon the fire would not burn. In other words, if Hume meant his remark to be taken seriously, survival is a logical possibility. He added, however, that it was a most unreasonable fancy that he should exist for ever. And it seems clear enough from what he has to say on the subject elsewhere not only that he did not think that immortality could be proved, either by metaphysical or moral arguments, but also that he himself did not believe in it. And this, it seems to me, is only what we would expect, if we bear in mind his account of the self.

It is important to add, however, that Hume realized that his account of the self presented difficulties. In his Appendix to the *Treatise* he admits that when it comes to explaining what binds together our distinct perceptions and makes us attribute to them a real simplicity and identity, 'I am sensible that my account is very defective, and that nothing but the seeming evidence of the precedent reasonings could have induced me to receive it. If perceptions are distinct existences, they form a whole only by being connected together. . . . But all my hopes vanish when I come to explain the principles that unite our successive perceptions in our thought or consciousness. I cannot discover any theory which gives me satisfaction on this head. In short, there are two principles which I cannot render consistent; nor is it in my power to renounce either of them, viz. *that all our distinct perceptions are distinct existences*, and *that the mind never perceives any real connection among distinct existences.* . . . For my part, I must plead the privilege of a sceptic and confess that this difficulty is too hard for my understanding.'[30] Hume might well feel some doubts about his account of the self and personal identity. Apart from objections which might be levelled against, for example, his ambiguous use of the word 'identity',[31] he gives no real explanation of the functioning of memory, though he emphasizes its importance. And some explanation is required. For it is not easy to see how memory is possible on his theory. Further, as he admits, if the mind can be said in some sense to collect the collection, how can it do this when it is identified with a collection, each member of which is a distinct thing? Does one perception enjoy awareness of others? If so, how? The difficulties do not seem to me to be in any way diminished if we adopt the modern empiricist device of talking about the mind as a 'logical construction' out of psychic events. In fact, precisely the same difficulties recur; and they must recur in any phenomenalistic account of the self.

3. Before outlining Hume's views about the existence of God, it may be appropriate to say something about his general personal attitude towards religion. He was brought up as a Calvinist, but at a fairly early age he discarded the doctrines which he had been taught in boyhood. In spite, however, of his undoubted dislike for Calvinism, it would be a mistake to think of his attitude towards religion as being no more than the expression of a hostile reaction towards a theology and a religious discipline which had overshadowed his early years. The truth seems to be that, once he had shed his initial Calvinism, religion was for him a purely external phenomenon which aroused little or no response within himself. In this sense he was an 'irreligious' man. Conscious of the part played by religion in the life of humanity, he was interested in its nature and power; but he was interested in it from the outside, as it were. Furthermore, he came to the conclusion that the influence of religion was far from beneficial. For instance, he thought that religion impairs morality by encouraging people to act for motives other than love of virtue for its own sake. In his essay on *The Natural History of Religion* he traces the development from polytheism to monotheism. The multiple gods and goddesses of polytheism, who were simply magnified human beings, were progressively attributed with different perfections as by a species of flattery, until infinity was at length attributed to the divine, and this involved monotheism. But though in the course of religious development a lessening of superstition has been observable, the transition from polytheism to theism has also been accompanied by a growth of fanaticism, bigotry and

intemperate zeal, as the behaviour of Mohammedans and Christians shows. Again, the idea of the greatness and majesty of the infinite God has encouraged emphasis on attitudes of abasement and on practices of asceticism and mortification which were foreign to the pagan mentality. Further, whereas in ancient Greece, for example, there was no dogma, as Christians understand it, and philosophy was free and unencumbered by dogmatic theology, in the Christian world philosophy has been misused in the service of theological doctrines. Hume does not, indeed, reject all religion explicitly and in so many words: he distinguishes between true religion on the one hand and superstition and fanaticism on the other. But when we come to look in his writings for an account of what he understands by true religion we find that its content is tenuous in the extreme.

In the *Enquiry concerning Human Understanding* the eleventh section is devoted, according to its title, to the subject of a particular providence and of a future state. In order to give himself a free hand Hume puts what he has to say into the mouth of an Epicurean friend who, at Hume's request, delivers an imaginary speech to the Athenians. The speaker observes that the religious philosophers, instead of resting content with tradition, 'indulge a rash curiosity, in trying how far they can establish religion upon the principles of reason; and they thereby excite, instead of satisfying, the doubts which naturally arise from a diligent and scrutinous enquiry'.[32] He then remarks that 'the chief or sole argument for a divine existence is derived from the order of nature. . . . You allow that this is an argument drawn from effects to causes. From the order of the work you infer that there must have been project and forethought in the workman. If you cannot make out this point, you allow that your conclusion fails: and you pretend not to establish the conclusion in a greater latitude than the phenomena of nature will justify. These are your concessions. I desire to mark the consequences.'[33]

What are these 'consequences'? First, it is not permissible, when inferring a particular cause from an effect, to ascribe to the cause any qualities other than those which are required and which are sufficient to produce the effect. Secondly, it is not permissible to start with the inferred cause and infer other effects besides those already known. In the case of a human invention or work of art we can, indeed, argue that the author possesses certain attributes other than those immediately manifested in the effect. But we can do this only because we are already acquainted with human beings and with their attributes and capacities and ordinary ways of acting. In the case of God, however, this condition does not obtain. If I think that the world as I know it postulates an intelligent cause, I can infer the existence of such a cause. But I cannot legitimately infer that the cause possesses other attributes, moral qualities, for example, or that it can or will produce other effects than those already known to me. It may, of course, possess other attributes; but I do not know this. And even though conjecture may be permissible, it should be recognized as being mere conjecture, an assertion not of known fact but of mere possibility. Hume's 'friend' does not say that he regards the inference from the natural order to an intelligent designer and cause as valid and certain. On the contrary, 'it is uncertain; because the subject lies entirely beyond the reach of human experience'.[34] We can establish a causal relation only when we observe, and in so far as we observe, constant conjunction. But we cannot observe God at all, and natural phenomena remain what they are whatever explanatory hypothesis we adopt. 'I much doubt whether it be possible for a cause to be known only by its effect.'[35] The religious hypothesis is, indeed, one way of accounting for the visible phenomena of the universe; and it may be true, even though its truth is uncertain. At the same time it is not a hypothesis from which we can deduce any facts other than those which we already know. Nor can we derive from it principles and maxims of conduct. In this sense it is a 'useless' hypothesis. 'It is useless because our knowledge of this cause being derived from the course of nature, we can never, according to the rules of just reasoning, return back from the cause with any new inference, or, making additions to the common and experienced course of nature, establish any new principles of conduct and behaviour.'[36]

Substantially the same outlook is expressed at greater length in the *Dialogues concerning Natural Religion* which were published, according to Hume's wish, after his death. The participants in the *Dialogues* are named Cleanthes, Philo and Demea, and their conversation is reported by Pamphilus to Hermippus. Hume does not appear in his own person; nor does he state which of the particular views expressed is his own. Pamphilus alludes to 'the accurate philosophical turn of Cleanthes', the 'careless scepticism of Philo' and 'the rigid inflexible orthodoxy of Demea'.[37] It has not infrequently been held, therefore, that Hume identifies himself with Cleanthes. Those who support this view can appeal to the concluding words of the *Dialogues* when Pamphilus remarks that 'upon a serious review of the whole I cannot but think that Philo's principles are more probable than Demea's, but that those of Cleanthes approach still nearer to the truth'.[38] Furthermore, writing to Sir Gilbert Elliot in 1751 Hume remarks that Cleanthes is 'the hero of the Dialogue' and that anything which Elliot can think of as strengthening Cleanthes' position will be 'most acceptable' to him. But if Hume is to be identified with Cleanthes, we must ascribe to him a firm belief in the argument from design. 'By this argument *a posteriori*, and by this argument alone, we do prove at once the existence of a Deity and his similarity to human mind and intelligence.'[39] But though Hume doubtless agreed with Cleanthes' rejection of what he calls *a priori* arguments and with the latter's contention that 'the words *necessary being* have no meaning, or, which is the same thing, none that is consistent',[40] it seems to me most improbable that he regarded the argument from design as conclusive. For this would hardly have been compatible with his general philosophical principles. Nor would it be consistent with the section of the first *Enquiry*, to which reference has been made above. For though in this section Hume produces an imaginary friend as speaker, it is in his own person that he remarks that 'I much doubt whether it be possible for a cause to be known only by its effect, as you have all along supposed'.[41] It seems to me that in the *Dialogues* it is Philo, not Cleanthes, who represents Hume, so far as any particular participant in the conversation can be said to represent him. Hume set out to develop a discussion of the problems of our knowledge of God's existence and nature, and it is unnecessary to suppose that he wished to identify himself exclusively either with Philo or with Cleanthes. But in so far as their views are opposed to one another, it seems to me only reasonable to associate Hume with the views of the former rather than with those of the latter. It would appear that Cleanthes is the hero of the *Dialogues* for Pamphilus rather than for Hume; and though when the latter showed Elliot an incomplete version of the work he could quite well invite Elliot to contribute ideas which would strengthen Cleanthes' position, in order to maintain the dramatic interest of the dialogue, this does not

alter the fact that the tendency of Part XII, the final section
of the work, tends to strengthen Philo's position rather than
that of Cleanthes, in spite of Pamphilus's concluding remarks.

If we assume, then, that where Philo and Cleanthes are
really opposed to one another, it is the former who expresses
Hume's mind more nearly than the latter, what conclusion
do we arrive at concerning Hume's attitude towards our
knowledge of God's existence and nature? The answer can
be given in Philo's oft-quoted words. 'If the whole of natural theology, as some people seem to maintain, resolves itself
into one simple, though somewhat ambiguous, at least un-
defined proposition, *that the cause or causes of order in the
universe probably bear some remote analogy to human intelligence:* If this proposition be not capable of extension,
variation or more particular explication: If it afford no inference that affects human life or can be the source of any
action or forbearance: And if the analogy, imperfect as it is,
can be carried no farther than to the human intelligence,
and cannot be transferred, with any appearance of probability, to the other qualities of the mind: If this really be the
case, what can the most inquisitive, contemplative and religious man do more than give a plain, philosophical assent
to the proposition as often as it occurs; and believe that the
arguments on which it is established exceed the objections
which lie against it?'[42] Here we are reduced to the simple
proposition that the cause or causes of order in the world
probably bear a remote analogy to human intelligence. No
more can be said. No affirmation is made about the moral
qualities of the 'cause or causes'. The proposition, moreover,
is purely theoretical, in the sense that no conclusion can be
legitimately drawn from it affecting human conduct, religious
or moral. 'True religion' is reduced, therefore, to the recognition of a purely theoretical statement of probability. This
is the position which fits the eleventh section of the first
Enquiry, and it is as far as Hume is prepared to go.

Boswell records Hume's statement at the end of his life
that he had never entertained any belief in religion since he
began to read Locke and Clarke. Presumably he meant that
when he began to study the rational defence of natural theology and of religion in the works of these philosophers he
found their arguments so weak that he ceased to believe in
the conclusions. It was Hume's view that religion originated
in such passions as fear of disaster and hope of advantage or

betterment when these passions are directed towards some invisible and intelligent power. In the course of time men attempted to rationalize religion and to find arguments in favour of belief; but most of these arguments will not stand up to critical analysis. This he thought to be true of the arguments adduced by Locke and Clarke and other metaphysicians. There is, however, a quasi-spontaneous tendency to regard the world as showing evidence of design; and, provided that we say no more, it is not unreasonable to say that it is probable that the cause or causes of phenomena, whatever these causes may be, bear some sort of an analogy with what we call intelligence. But in the long run, the world is an inscrutable mystery, and we cannot have any certain knowledge of ultimate causes.

The reader may expect a plain answer to the question whether Hume is to be regarded as an atheist, an agnostic or a theist. But it is not easy to give a 'plain answer' to this question. As already mentioned, he refused to recognize the validity of metaphysical arguments for God's existence; that is to say, he refused to allow that the existence of God is demonstrable. What he does is to examine the argument from design which he treats as leading to the 'religious hypothesis'. It is plain from the *Dialogues* that he disliked any form of the argument which is based principally on an analogy between human artificial constructions and the world. He admitted, however, that there are certain principles which operate in the world, namely, 'organization' or animal and vegetable life, instinct and intelligence. These principles are productive of order and pattern, and we know their effects by experience. But the principles themselves and their modes of operation are mysteries and inscrutable. However, there are points of analogy between them, to judge by their effects. And if by affirming God's existence we mean merely to affirm that the ultimate cause of order in the universe probably bears some remote analogy to intelligence, Hume is prepared to agree. This is not atheism in the sense of a categorical denial that there is anything besides phenomena; and Hume did not profess himself an atheist. Yet it is hardly to be called theism, not at least unless we read far more into Hume's admissions than he intended them to express. It might possibly be called agnosticism; but it must be remembered that Hume was not in a state of agnosticism about the existence of a personal God with moral attributes, as described by Christians in particular. The fact of the matter seems to be that Hume set out, as a detached observer, to examine the rational credentials of theism, maintaining in the meantime that religion rests on revelation, a revelation in which he personally certainly did not believe. The result of his investigation was, as we have seen, to reduce the 'religious hypothesis' to so meagre a content that it is difficult to know what to call it. It is a residuum which, as Hume was well aware, might be accepted by anyone who was not a dogmatic atheist. Its content is ambiguous, and Hume meant it to be ambiguous.

Emphasis is sometimes laid on the fact that Hume devoted his attention principally to theistic arguments as found in English writers such as Clarke and Butler. This is true enough; but if the implication is intended that Hume would have changed his mind, had he been acquainted with more satisfactory formulations of the arguments for the existence of God, it must be remembered that, given Hume's philosophical principles, especially his analysis of causality, he could not admit any cogent proofs of theism in a recognizable sense. In conclusion, it may be noted that Hume's analysis of the argument from design influenced Kant's final treatment of the matter, though the latter's attitude to theism was, of course, much more positive than that adopted by the former. Hume's thought was dissolvent of contemporary theological argument and apologetic, whereas Kant attempted to set belief in God on a new footing.

4. Some remarks on Hume's attitude towards scepticism may perhaps form a suitable conclusion to this chapter. And I shall begin by outlining the distinction which Hume draws in the *Enquiry concerning Human Understanding* between 'antecedent' and 'consequent' scepticism.

By antecedent scepticism Hume understands a scepticism which is 'antecedent to all study and philosophy'.[43] As an example he cites Cartesian doubt, taking this to involve doubt not only of all our particular previously held beliefs and opinions but also of the power of our faculties to attain truth. The definition of antecedent scepticism might suggest the sceptical attitude which may arise in the minds of non-philosophers rather than the Cartesian doubt which is part of a deliberately chosen philosophical method. However, it is, indeed, antecedent to the positive building-up of the Cartesian system; and in any case it is the example selected by Hume. According to Descartes, he says, we should entertain a universal doubt until we have reassured ourselves by means of a chain of reasoning deduced from some original principle which cannot itself be doubtful or fallacious. There is, however, no such original principle. And even if there were, we could not advance beyond it except by the use of the very faculties whose trustworthiness we have placed in doubt. Scepticism of this sort is not really possible; and, if it were, it would be incurable. But there is a more moderate and reasonable form of antecedent scepticism. That is to say, before pursuing philosophical inquiry we ought to free ourselves, so far as we can, from all prejudice and attain a state of impartiality. We ought to begin with clear and evident principles and advance carefully, examining all the steps of our reasoning. But this is a matter of common sense. Without such care and accuracy we cannot hope to make any sure progress in knowledge.

Consequent scepticism is scepticism which is 'consequent to science and enquiry'.[44] In other words, it is the result of the discovery, or supposed discovery, by philosophers either of the untrustworthy character of our mental faculties or, at least, of their unfitness for reaching any reliable conclusion 'in all those curious subjects of speculation about which they are commonly employed'.[45] And it may be divided into scepticism about the senses and scepticism about reason. In the *Treatise*[46] Hume discussed scepticism about the senses first, but in the first *Enquiry* the order of treatment is reversed.

What Hume calls the 'more trite topics' adduced by sceptics in all ages to show that the evidence of the senses is untrustworthy are dismissed in a rather summary manner. He refers to the familiar example of the oar which appears to be bent or crooked when partly immersed in water and to the double images which result from exerting pressure on one eye. All that such examples show, however, is that we may need to correct the immediate evidence of the senses by reason and by considerations based on the nature of the medium, the distance of the object, the disposition of the sense-organ, and so on. This is what we do in practice, and it is quite sufficient. 'There are other more profound arguments against the senses, which admit not of so easy a solution.'[47]

Men are led by a natural impulse to put faith in their senses, and from the start we suppose that there exists an external universe which is independent of the senses. Further, led by this 'blind and powerful instinct of nature',[48] men instinctively take the images presented by the senses to be the external objects themselves. 'But this universal and primary opinion of all men is soon destroyed by the slightest philosophy. And no man, who reflects, ever doubted that the existences which we consider when we say *this house* and *that tree* are nothing but perceptions in the mind and fleeting copies or representations of other existences which remain uniform and independent.'[49] To this extent, therefore, philosophy leads us to contradict or depart from our natural instincts. At the same time philosophy finds itself in an embarrassing situation when asked to give a rational defence of its position. For how can we prove that images or perceptions are representations of objects which are not themselves images or perceptions? 'The mind has never anything present to it but the perceptions and cannot possibly reach any experience of their connection with objects. The supposition of such a connection is, therefore, without any foundation in reasoning.'[50] To have recourse with Descartes to the divine veracity is useless. If the divine veracity were really involved, our senses would be always and entirely infallible. Moreover, if we once question the existence of an external world, how can we prove the existence of God or any of His attributes? We are faced, therefore, with a dilemma. If we follow the propensity of nature, we believe that perceptions or images are the external objects themselves; and this is a belief which reason refutes. If, however, we say that perceptions or images are caused by and represent objects, we cannot find any convincing argument, based on experience, to prove that the former are in fact connected with external objects. 'This is a topic, therefore, in which the profounder and more philosophical sceptics will always triumph, when they endeavour to introduce an universal doubt into all subjects of human knowledge and enquiry.'[51]

Scepticism about reason may concern either abstract reasoning or matters of fact. The chief sceptical objection to the validity of abstract reasoning is derived, according to Hume in the *Enquiry*, from examination of our ideas of space and time. Let us suppose that extension is infinitely divisible. A given quantity X contains within itself a quantity Y which is infinitely less than X. Similarly, Y contains within itself a quantity Z which is infinitely less than Y. And so on indefinitely. A supposition of this kind 'shocks the clearest and most natural principles of human reason'.[52] Again, 'an infinite number of real parts of time, passing in succession and exhausted one after another, appears so evident a contradiction that no man, one should think, whose judgment is not corrupted, instead of being improved, by the sciences, would ever be able to admit it'.[53]

As for sceptical objections to 'moral evidence' or to reasonings concerning matters of fact, these may be either popular or philosophical. Under the former heading can be grouped objections derived from the variety of mutually incompatible opinions held by different men, the different opinions held by the same man at different times, the contradictory beliefs of different societies and nations, and so on. According to Hume, however, popular objections of this sort are ineffective. 'The great subverter of *Pyrrhonism* or the excessive principle of scepticism is action and employment and the occupations of common life.'[54] It may not be possible to refute these objections in the classroom, but in ordinary life they 'vanish like smoke and leave the most determined sceptic in the same condition as other mortals'.[55] More important are the philosophical objections. And chief among these is the objection deriving from Hume's own analysis of causality; for, given this analysis, we have no argument to prove that because *a* and *b* have always been conjoined in our past experience they will be similarly conjoined in the future.

Now, given Hume's view about mathematics and abstract reasoning, which concerns relations between ideas, he could not admit real grounds for scepticism in this field. Hence we find him saying 'how any clear, distinct idea can contain circumstances contradictory to itself or to any other clear, distinct idea is absolutely incomprehensible; and is, perhaps, as absurd as any proposition which can be formed. So that nothing can be more sceptical, or more full of doubt and hesitation, than this scepticism itself, which arises from some of the paradoxical conclusions of geometry or the science of quantity.'[56] He tried to avoid the antinomies which seemed to him to give rise to scepticism by denying that space and time are infinitely divisible in the sense alleged.[57] But whereas he felt bound to indicate a theoretical answer to scepticism about abstract reasoning, he pursued a different method with regard to thorough-going scepticism about the senses and about reasoning concerning matters of fact. As we have already seen when considering the problem of the existence of bodies, Hume remarked that scepticism on this point cannot be maintained in ordinary life. 'Carelessness and inattention alone can afford us any remedy. For this reason I rely entirely upon them.'[58] His remark that action and em-

ployment and the occupations of common life constitute the
great subverter of Pyrrhonism has been quoted above in connection with popular objections to reasonings concerning
matters of fact. Similarly, after speaking in the *Enquiry*
about the principal philosophical objection against reasoning
concerning matters of fact he observes that 'here is the chief
and most confounding objection to *excessive* scepticism, that
no durable good can ever result from it, while it remains in
its full force and vigour. We need only ask such a sceptic,
*What his meaning is? And what he proposes by all these
curious researches?* He is immediately at a loss and knows
not what to answer. A Copernican or Ptolemaic, who supports each his different system of astronomy, may hope to
produce a conviction, which will remain constant and durable, with his audience. A Stoic or Epicurean displays principles which may not be durable but which have an effect
on conduct and behaviour. But a Pyrrhonian cannot expect
that his philosophy will have any constant influence on the
mind; or if it had, that its influence would be beneficial to
society. On the contrary, he must acknowledge, if he will
acknowledge anything, that all human life must perish, were
his principles universally and steadily to prevail. All discourse, all action would immediately cease; and men remain
in a total lethargy, till the necessities of nature, unsatisfied,
put an end to their miserable existence. It is true; so fatal an
event is little to be dreaded. Nature is always too strong for
principle.'[59] In the *Treatise*, after speaking of the intense
realization of the manifold antinomies in which human reason is involved, he says: 'Most fortunately it happens that
since reason is incapable of dispelling these clouds, nature
herself suffices to that purpose. . . . I dine, I play a game
of backgammon, I converse and am merry with my friends;
and when after three or four hours' amusement, I would return to these speculations, they appear so cold and strained
and ridiculous that I cannot find in my heart to enter into
them any farther. Here then I find myself absolutely and
necessarily determined to live and talk and act like other
people in the common affairs of life.'[60]

Though Hume rejects, we may say, what he calls 'excessive' scepticism, he admits as 'both durable and useful' a
'mitigated' or 'academical' scepticism, which may be in part a
result of Pyrrhonism (or excessive scepticism) when this has
been 'corrected by common sense and reflection'.[61] This
mitigated scepticism involves, for example, limiting our in-

quiries to those subjects for the consideration of which our mental capacities are adapted. 'It seems to me that the only objects of the abstract science or of demonstration are quantity and number, and that all attempts to extend this more perfect species of knowledge beyond these bounds are mere sophistry and illusion.'[62] As for inquiries about matters of fact and existence, we are here outside the sphere of demonstration. 'Whatever *is* may *not be*. No negation of a fact can involve a contradiction. . . . The existence, therefore, of any being can only be proved by arguments from its cause or its effect; and these arguments are founded entirely on experience. If we reason *a priori*, anything may appear able to produce anything.'[63]

Divinity or theology has a rational foundation in so far as it is supported by experience. 'But its best and most solid foundation is faith and divine revelation.'[64] What we are to think of this last proposition is made clear enough, I think, by the *Dialogues*. As for morals and aesthetics (which Hume calls 'criticism'), these are objects of taste and sentiment more than of the understanding. 'Beauty, whether moral or natural, is felt, more properly than perceived.'[65] We may, indeed, try to fix some standard, but then we have to consider some empirical fact, such as the general tastes of mankind.

Hume's famous conclusion deserves quotation here. 'When we run over libraries, persuaded of these principles, what havoc must we make? If we take in hand any volume; of divinity or school metaphysics, for instance; let us ask, *Does it contain any abstract reasoning concerning quantity or number?* No. *Does it contain any experimental reasoning concerning matter of fact and existence?* No. Commit it then to the flames: for it can contain nothing but sophistry and illusion.'[66]

Hume's remarks about scepticism, including 'Pyrrhonism', and about carelessness and inattention as the remedy for scepticism should not be understood in a purely ironical sense or as indicating that the philosopher had his tongue in his cheek. Scepticism was a matter of importance in his eyes, partly because it was a living issue at the time, though more in France than in England, and partly because he was well aware of the sceptical conclusions which followed from the application of his own principles. For one thing, it was, he thought, a healthy antidote to dogmatism and fanaticism. Indeed, 'a true sceptic will be diffident of his philosophical doubts, as well as of his philosophical conviction'.[67] He will refrain from showing dogmatism and fanaticism in his scepticism. At the same time a thorough-going scepticism is untenable in practice. This fact does not prove its falsity; but it shows that in ordinary life we have inevitably to act according to natural belief or the propensities of our human nature. And this is how things should be. Reason is dissolvent; at least, there is very little that it leaves unshaken and unquestionable. And the philosophical spirit is the spirit of free inquiry. But human nature is very far from being governed and directed by reason alone. Morality, for example, is grounded on feeling rather than on the analytic understanding. And though the philosopher in his study may arrive at sceptical conclusions, in the sense that he sees how little reason can prove, he is at the same time a man; and in his ordinary life he is governed, and ought to allow himself to be governed if he wishes to live at all, by the natural beliefs which common human nature imposes on him as on others. In other words, Hume had little sympathy for any attempt to turn philosophy into a creed, a dogmatically propounded standard for belief and conduct. It is, if you like, a game; a game of which Hume was fond, and one which has its uses. But in the long run 'Nature is always too strong for principle'.[68] 'Be a philosopher; but, amidst all your philosophy, be still a man.'[69]

Chapter Sixteen

HUME (3)

Introductory — The passions, direct and indirect — Sympathy — The will and liberty — The passions and the reason — Moral distinctions and the moral sense — Benevolence and utility — Justice — General remarks.

1. Hume is chiefly famous for his epistemological analyses and for his examinations of causality and of the notions of the self and of personal identity; in other words, for the contents of the first book of the *Treatise*. But the *Treatise of Human Nature* was described by him as an attempt to introduce the experimental method of reasoning into moral subjects. In the Introduction he says that in the four sciences of logic, morals, criticism and politics 'is comprehended almost everything which it can any way import us to be acquainted with, or which can tend either to the improvement or ornament of the human mind'.[1] And he makes it clear that he hopes to lay the foundation of moral science. Towards the close of the first book he speaks of having been led into several topics which will 'prepare the way for our following opinions',[2] and he alludes to 'those immense depths of philosophy which lie before me'.[3] At the beginning of the third book he declares that 'morality is a subject that interests us above all others'.[4] It is true that he uses the term 'moral philosophy' to mean the science of human nature, and that he divides this into the study of man as 'a reasonable rather than as an active being' and the study of man 'chiefly as born for action'.[5] But there can be no doubt of the importance which Hume attached to moral philosophy in the ordinary sense. He thought of himself as carrying on the work of Shaftesbury, Hutcheson, Butler and so on, and as doing for morals and politics what others, such as Galileo and New-

ton, had accomplished for natural science. 'Moral philosophy is in the same condition as natural, with regard to astronomy before the time of Copernicus.'[6] The ancient astronomers invented intricate systems which were overloaded with unnecessary hypotheses. But these systems have at last given place to 'something more simple and natural'.[7] So Hume wishes to discover the fundamental or elementary principles which operate in man's ethical life.

We have seen that according to Hume the basic assumptions on which we act, those fundamental beliefs, that is to say, which are necessary for practical life, are not conclusions drawn by the understanding from rational argument. This is not to say, of course, that people do not reason about their practical affairs: it is to say that the ordinary man's reflections and reasoning presuppose beliefs which are not themselves the fruit of reasoning. It is not surprising, therefore, that Hume should also minimize the part played by reason in morals. He is well aware, of course, that we do in fact reflect and reason and argue about moral problems and decisions; but he maintains that moral distinctions are derived ultimately, not from reasoning, but from feeling, from the moral sentiment. Reason alone is not capable of being the sole immediate cause of our actions. Indeed, Hume goes so far as to say that 'reason is, and ought to be the slave of the passions, and can never pretend to any other office than to serve and obey them'.[8]

I shall return later to the subject of the moral sentiment and to Hume's view of the part played by reason in morals. But if we bear in mind the general fact that he emphasizes the role of what we may call the emotional aspect of human nature in man's moral life, we can understand more easily why, before coming to ethics proper in the third book of the *Treatise*, he devotes the long second book to a discussion of the passions. I do not propose to enter in a detailed manner into his treatment of this subject; but something at least ought to be said about it. Before doing so, however, it may be as well to remark that the word 'passion' is not used by Hume to signify simply a burst of unregulated emotion, as when we speak of someone flying into a passion. The word is used by him, as by other philosophers of the period, to include emotions and affects in general. He is concerned with analysing the emotional aspect of human nature, considered as a source of action, not with moralizing about inordinate passions.

2. As we saw in Chapter Fourteen, Hume distinguished between impressions of sensation and impressions of reflection. This is the same as distinguishing between original and secondary impressions. 'Original impressions or impressions of sensation are such as without any antecedent perception arise in the soul, from the constitution of the body, from the animal spirits, or from the application of objects to the external organs. Secondary, or reflective impressions are such as proceed from some of these original ones, either immediately or by the interposition of its idea. Of the first kind are all impressions of the senses, and all bodily pains and pleasure: of the second are the passions, and other emotions resembling them.'[9] Thus a bodily pain, such as the pain of gout, can produce passions like grief, hope and fear. Then we have passions, secondary impressions, derived from an original or primary impression, namely, a certain bodily pain.

I have said that Hume used the word 'passion' to cover all emotions and affects without confining it to unregulated bursts of emotion. But a qualification is needed. For he distinguishes between calm and violent reflective or secondary impressions. The sense of beauty and deformity in actions, in works of art and in natural objects belongs to the first class, while love and hatred, joy and grief, belong to the second. Hume admits, indeed, that 'this division is far from being exact,'[10] on the ground that the raptures of poetry and music may be very intense whereas 'those other impressions, properly called *passions*, may decay into so soft an emotion as to become, in a manner, imperceptible'.[11] But my point is that here he seems to restrict the word 'passion' to what he calls violent reflective impressions. And this is one reason why I said that my former statement stands in need of qualification. At the same time these 'violent' emotions, or passions in a restricted sense, are not necessarily disordered. Hume is thinking of intensity: he is not passing a moral judgment.

The passions are divided by Hume into direct and indirect passions. The former are those which arise immediately from the experience of pleasure or pain; and Hume mentions desire, aversion, grief, joy, hope, fear, despair and security. The pain of gout, for instance, produces direct passions. Hume also mentions direct passions which arise 'from a natural impulse or instinct, which is perfectly unaccountable. Of this kind is the desire of punishment to our enemies and of happiness to our friends; hunger, lust, and a few other bodily

appetites'.[12] These passions are said to produce good and
evil (that is, pleasure and pain) rather than to proceed
from them as other direct passions do. Indirect passions do
not arise simply from feelings of pleasure or pain; they arise
from what Hume calls 'a double relation of impressions and
ideas'.[13] His meaning can best be explained by using examples, such as pride and humility, love and hatred.

In the first place we must distinguish between the object
and the cause of a passion. The object of pride and humility
is the self, 'that succession of related ideas and impressions,
of which we have an intimate memory and consciousness'.[14]
Whatever other objects we may have in mind when we feel
pride or humility, they are always considered in relation to
the self. And when self does not enter into consideration,
there can be neither pride nor humility. But though the
self is the object of these two passions, it cannot be their
sufficient cause. If it were, a certain degree of pride would
always be accompanied by a corresponding degree of humility, and conversely. Again, the object of love and hatred is
some person other than the self. According to Hume, 'when
we talk of *self-love*, it is not in a proper sense, nor has the
sensation it produces anything in common with that tender
emotion which is excited by a friend or mistress'.[15] But the
other person is not the sole and sufficient cause of these passions. If it were, production of the one passion would involve production of the other.

In the second place we must distinguish, within the cause
of a passion, between the quality which operates and the
subject in which it is placed. To take an example given by
Hume, when a man is vain of a beautiful house which belongs to him we can distinguish between the beauty and the
house. Both are necessary component parts of the cause of
the passion of vanity, but they are none the less distinguishable.

In the third place we must make the following distinction.
The passions of pride and humility are 'determined to have
self for their *object*, not only by a natural but also by an
original property'.[16] The constancy and steadiness of the
determination shows its 'natural' character. The self-regarding
direction of pride and humility is 'original' in the sense that
it is primary and cannot be further resolved into other elements. Similarly, the other-regarding determination of the
passions of love and hatred is both natural and original. But
when we turn from 'object' to 'cause', in the sense indicated

above, we find a somewhat different situation. The causes of these passions are, according to Hume, natural, in the sense that the same sort of objects tend to give rise to the passions. Material possessions and physical qualities tend to give rise, for example, to pride and vanity, in whatever epoch men may live. But the causes of pride and humility are not original in the sense of being 'adapted to these passions by a particular provision and primary constitution of nature'.[17] There is a vast number of causes, and many of them depend on human artifice and invention (houses, furniture and clothes, for instance); and it would be absurd to suppose that nature foresaw and provided for each possible cause of a passion. Hence, although it is from natural principles that a great variety of causes excites pride and humility, it is not true that each different cause is adapted to its passion by a different principle. The problem, therefore, is to discover among the various causes a common element on which their influence depends.

In his solution of this problem Hume invokes the principles of association of ideas and association of impressions. When one idea is present to the imagination, any other idea which is related to it by resemblance, contiguity or causality tends to follow. Again, 'all resembling impressions are connected together, and no sooner one arises than the rest immediately follow'.[18] (Impressions, unlike ideas, are associated only by resemblance.) Now, these two kinds of association assist one another and, 'both uniting in one action, bestow on the mind a double impulse'.[19] The cause of the passion produces in us a sensation. In the case of pride this is a sensation of pleasure, in the case of 'humility' or self-depreciation it is a sensation of pain. And this sensation or impression has a natural and original reference to the self as object or to the idea of the self. There is, therefore, a natural relation between impression and idea. And this permits a concurrent working of the two kinds of association—association of impressions and association of ideas. When a passion has been aroused it tends to call forth a succession of resembling passions by force of the principle of association of resembling impressions. Again, by force of the principle of association of ideas the mind passes easily from one idea (say, the idea of one aspect of the causes and object of pride) to another idea. And these two movements reinforce one another, the mind easily passing from one set to the other in virtue of the correlation between them. Suppose that a man has suffered an in-

jury from another and that this has produced in him a passion. This passion (an impression) tends to call forth in him
resembling passions. And this movement is facilitated by the
fact that the man's idea of the causes and objects of the
passion tend to call forth other ideas, which in turn are corre-
lated with impressions. 'When an idea produces an impression, related to an impression, which is connected with an
idea, related to the first idea, these two impressions must be
in a manner inseparable, nor will the one in any case be un-
attended with the other.'[20]

Hume's intention is obviously that of explaining the complex emotional life of mankind with the aid of as few principles as possible. In treating of the indirect passions and of
the transition from one passion to another he makes use of
the principles of association. I say 'principles' rather than
'principle' because it is his view that the association of ideas
by itself is not sufficient to give rise to a passion. He therefore speaks of indirect passions as arising from 'a double
relation of impressions and ideas', and he explains the transition from one such passion to another as the effect of the
concurrent operation of associated ideas and impressions.
But he also emphasizes the influence of sympathy in our
emotional life; and something must be said about this topic.

3. Our knowledge of the passions of others is gained by
observation of the effects of these passions. 'When any affection is infused by sympathy, it is at first known only by its
effects and by those external signs in the countenance and
conversation which convey an idea of it.'[21] Now, the difference between ideas and impressions has been defined in
terms of force and vivacity. A lively idea can, therefore, be
converted into an impression. And this is what happens in
the case of sympathy. The idea of a passion which is produced by observation of the latter's effects 'is presently converted into an impression and acquires such a degree of force
and vivacity as to become the very passion itself'.[22] How does
this conversion take place? Hume presupposes that 'nature
has preserved a great resemblance among all human creatures, and that we never remark any passion or principle in
others, of which, in some degree or other, we may not find a
parallel in ourselves'.[23] Besides this general relation of resemblance there are other more specific relationships, such
as blood-relationship, common membership of one nation,
use of the same language, and so on. And 'all these relations,
when united together, convey the impression or conscious-

ness of our own person to the idea of the sentiments or passions of others and makes us conceive them in the strongest
and most lively manner'.[24] To each one of us his own self is,
so to speak, intimately and always present. And when we
observe the effects of the passions of others and so form ideas
of these passions, these ideas tend to become converted into
impressions; that is, into similar passions, to the degree that
we associate ourselves with them in virtue of some relation-
ship or relationships. 'In sympathy there is an evident conversion of an idea into an impression. This conversion arises
from the relation of objects to oneself. Ourself is always intimately present to us.'[25]

Again, we may perceive the causes of a passion or emotion.
Hume gives the example of seeing the preparations for a
'terrible' surgical operation (without anaesthetic, of course).
These may excite in the beholder's mind, even though he is
not the patient, a strong emotion of terror. 'No passion of
another discovers itself immediately to the mind. We are
only sensible of its causes or effects. From *these* we infer the
passion: And consequently *these* give rise to our sympathy.'[26]

Whether all this fits in with Hume's phenomenalism is
disputable. For he appears to postulate more than is war-
ranted by his phenomenalistic analysis of mind. But it is
clear at least that he was well aware of the intimate links
between human beings. And he tries to explain the contagious
character of the passions and emotions. In point of fact
Hume's world is not a world of mutually sundered human
atoms, but the world of ordinary experience in which human
beings stand to one another in varying degrees of mutual
relationships. This he takes for granted. It is the psychological
mechanism of sympathy with which he is concerned. And he
is sure that sympathetic communication is one important
cause in the generation of passions.

4. Something having been said about the causes and mechanism of the passions, we can now turn to consider the relations between the will, the passions and the reason. And in
the first place we can ask what Hume understands by will,
and whether he recognizes free-will.

Hume speaks of the will as one of the immediate effects
of pleasure and pain. It is not, however, properly speaking,
a passion. He describes it as 'the internal impression we feel
and are conscious of, when we knowingly give rise to any new
motion of our body, or new perception of our mind'.[27] It
cannot be defined, since it cannot be further resolved, and it

is needless to describe it any further. We can, therefore, turn immediately to the problem of freedom.

According to Hume, the union between motive and action possesses the same constancy which we observe between cause and effect in physical operations. Further, this constancy influences the understanding in the same way that constant conjunction in physical operations influences the understanding, namely, by 'determining us to infer the existence of one from that of another'.[28] In fact, there is no known circumstance which enters into the production of purely material operations which is not also found in volition. Hence we have no good reason for attributing necessity to the former and denying it of the latter. True, human action often appears uncertain. Yet the more our knowledge is increased, the clearer become the connections between character, motive and choice. In any case we have no adequate reason for supposing that there is a privileged sphere of freedom, where necessary connection is wanting.

It is important to note that for Hume, as for some modern empiricists, absence of necessity spells chance, so that to assert liberty of indifference is to say that human choices are uncaused and are due simply to chance. 'According to my definitions, necessity makes an essential part of causation; and consequently liberty, by removing necessity, removes also causes, and is the very same thing with chance. As chance is commonly thought to imply a contradiction, and is at least directly contrary to experience, there are always the same arguments against liberty or free-will.'[29] It will be remembered that Hume recognized only one type of causal relation, in which constant conjunction forms the objective element and necessary connection the subjectively contributed element. Once given this restricted view of causality, it follows, of course, that free action would be uncaused action; if, that is to say, assertion of freedom involves denial of necessity. Hume admits, however, that the problem of freedom is to a certain extent a linguistic problem, in the sense that though freedom must be denied if it is defined in such a way as to exclude necessity, it can be asserted if it is defined in another way. For instance, if freedom is identified with spontaneity, there is freedom. For it is clear that a great number of actions proceed from a man as a rational agent without any external coercion. Indeed, spontaneity is the only form of liberty which we should have any interest in asserting. For, Hume maintains, if so-called free actions are due to chance and are not caused by the agent, it would be unjust for God or man to hold human beings responsible for bad and vicious actions and to pass moral condemnation on the agents. For the agents would not in fact be agents at all in any proper sense. Obviously the validity of Hume's point of view on this matter depends on the validity of his notion of causality.

5. Having disposed of freedom, except when it is reduced to spontaneity, Hume attempts to prove the truth of two propositions. The first proposition is that 'reason alone can never be a motive to any action of the will', and the second is that reason 'can never oppose passion in the direction of the will'.[30] His defence of these two propositions arises out of the fact that 'nothing is more usual in philosophy, and even in common life, than to talk of the combat of passion and reason, to give the preference to reason and to assert that men are only so far virtuous as they conform themselves to its dictates'.[31]

In the first place, reason in the sense of the abstract understanding concerned with relations between ideas or with matters of demonstration is never the cause of any action. 'Mathematics, indeed, are useful in all mechanical operations, and arithmetic in almost every art and profession: but it is not of themselves they have any influence.'[32] They do not influence action unless we have a purpose or end which is not dictated or determined by mathematics.

The second operation of the understanding concerns probability, the sphere not of abstract ideas but of things related causally to one another, of matters of fact. Here it is obvious that when any object causes pleasure or pain we feel a consequent emotion of attraction or aversion and are impelled to embrace or avoid the object in question. But we are also impelled by the emotion or passion to reason concerning the objects which are or may be causally related with the original object. And 'according as our reasoning varies, our actions receive a subsequent variation'.[33] But the impulse which governs our actions is only directed by reason; it does not arise from it. 'It is from the prospect of pain or pleasure that the aversion or propensity arises towards any object.'[34]

Reason alone, therefore, can never produce any action. And Hume concludes from this to the truth of his second proposition. 'Since reason alone can never produce any action, or give rise to volition, I infer that the same faculty is as incapable of preventing volition, or of disputing the preference with any passion or emotion. This consequence is necessary.'[35] Reason could prevent volition only by giving an impulse in a contrary direction; but this is excluded by what has been already said. And if reason has no immediate influence of its own, it cannot withstand any principle, such as passion, which does possess efficacy. Hence 'we speak not strictly and philosophically when we talk of the combat of passion and of reason. Reason is, and ought only to be the slave of the passions, and can never pretend to any other office than to serve and obey them.'[36]

Now, this appears to be a paradoxical and strange position to adopt. For, as Hume admits, it is not only philosophers who speak of the combat between reason and passion. But the words quoted above, 'we speak not strictly and philosophically', ought to be noticed. Hume does not deny that there is something which is called the combat between reason and passion: what he maintains is that it is not accurately described when it is so called. And his analysis of the situation must be briefly explained.

Reason, Hume says, exerts itself without producing any sensible emotion. Now, there are also 'calm desires and tendencies which, though they be real passions, produce little emotion[37] in the mind and are more known by their effects than by the immediate feeling or sensation'.[38] These may be of two kinds. There are, according to Hume, certain instincts, such as benevolence and resentment, love of life and kindness to children, which are originally implanted in our nature. There are also the desire for good and aversion to evil, considered merely as such. When any of these passions are calm, they are easily taken as being operations of reason 'and are supposed to proceed from the same faculty, with that which judges of truth and falsehood'.[39] The calm passions do not prevail in everyone, it is true. And whether calm or violent passions prevail, depends on the general character and present disposition of a man. However, 'what we call strength of mind implies the prevalence of the calm passions above the violent'.[40]

In asserting this view of the subordination of the reason to the passions Hume was obviously adopting an anti-rationalist position. Not reason but propensity and aversion, following experiences of pleasure and pain, are the fundamental springs of human action. Reason plays a part in man's active life, but as an instrument of passion, not as a sole sufficient cause. Of course, if we consider simply the theory that natural inclinations rather than the conclusions of the abstract reason are the influential factor in human conduct, we can scarcely call it a revolutionary or extravagant theory. It is opposed to Socratic intellectualism, but it is this intellectualism which is extravagant and which has always been attacked by its opponents as contrary to experience. Hume realized very clearly not only that man is not a kind of calculating machine but also that without the appetitive and emotional aspects of his nature he would not be man. At the same time it is arguable that his denial of liberty of indifference and his assertion of psychological determinism encouraged him to minimize in an exaggerated way the part played by the practical reason in human conduct.

6. That there are no moral distinctions whatsoever is not an opinion which is consonant with experience, common sense and reason. 'Let a man's insensibility be ever so great, he must often be touched with the images of Right and Wrong: and let his prejudices be ever so obstinate, he must observe that others are susceptible of like impressions.'[41] But though everyone makes some moral distinctions, the foundation of such distinctions is matter for dispute. Are they founded, as some claim, on reason, so that they are the same for every rational being? Or are they founded, as others claim, on a moral sense or sentiment, resting 'on the particular fabric and constitution of the human species'?[42] Arguments can be produced in favour of each theory. It may be said, on the one hand, that both in ordinary life and in philosophy disputes about good and evil, right and wrong, frequently occur. And the disputants produce reasons in favour of their several views. And how could such discussions take place and be accepted as a normal and sensible proceeding unless moral distinctions are derived from reason? On the other hand, it can be argued that the essence of virtue is to be amiable or lovable and of vice to be odious. And the attribution of such epithets must be the expression of affections or sentiments which are themselves grounded in the original constitution of man. Further, the end or purpose of moral reasoning is action, the performance of duty. But reason alone cannot move to action. It is the passions or affections which constitute the springs of conduct.

We have already seen in the preceding section that according to Hume reason alone cannot affect conduct and that it is the passions or affections which are the fundamental springs of action. He is, therefore, committed, to this extent, to the second theory; that is, to the theory of a moral sense or senti-ment. At the same time, however, he has no intention of denying that reason plays a part in morality. Hence he is willing to say that 'reason and sentiment concur in almost all moral determinations and conclusions. The final sentence, it is probable, which pronounces characters and actions amiable or odious, praiseworthy or blameable; that which stamps on them the mark of honour or infamy, approbation or censure; that which renders morality an active principle and constitutes virtue our happiness and vice our misery: it is probable, I say, that this final sentence depends on some internal sense or feeling, which nature has made universal in the whole species. For what else can have an influence of this nature? But in order to pave the way for such a senti-ment, and give a proper discernment of its object, it is often necessary, we find, that much reasoning should precede, that nice distinctions be made, just conclusions drawn, dis-tant comparisons formed, complicated relations examined, and general facts fixed and ascertained.'[43] We examine, for instance, an action under its various aspects and in relation to various circumstances, and compare it with actions to which it bears a *prima facie* resemblance. But when we have, as it were, a clear view of the action, what ultimately in-fluences our conduct is the feeling which we have towards the actions.

Examining the matter a little more closely, we find that Hume gives detailed arguments, both in the *Treatise* and in his first appendix to the *Enquiry concerning the Principles of Morals*, for saying that moral distinctions are not derived from reason. 'Reason judges either of *matter of fact* or of *relations*.'[44] 'As the operations of human understanding divide themselves into two kinds, the comparing of ideas, and the inferring of matter of fact, were virtue discovered by the understanding it must be an object of one of these operations, nor is there any third operation of the understand-ing which can discover it.'[45]

In the first place, moral distinctions are not derived from reason as concerned with matters of fact. 'Take an action allowed to be vicious: wilful murder, for instance. Examine it in all lights, and see if you can find that matter of fact, or real existence, which you call *vice*. In whichever way you take it, you find only certain passions, motives, volitions and thoughts. There is no other matter of fact in the case. . . . You can never find it, till you turn your reflection into your own breast and find a sentiment of disapprobation which arises in you towards this action. Here is a matter of fact; but it is the object of feeling, not of reason. It lies in yourself, not in the object.'[46] What Hume means is that the physical action of killing is or may be the same in a case of murder as it is in a case of justifiable homicide or of execution after judicial sentence.

In the second place, moral distinctions are not derived from reason as concerned with relations. 'There has been an opinion very industriously propagated by certain philosophers, that morality is susceptible of demonstration.'[47] In this case vice and virtue must consist in some relations. If it does, it must consist in resemblance, contrariety, degrees in quality or proportions in quantity and number. But these relations are found just as much in material things as in our actions, passions and volitions. Why is incest among human beings considered a criminal act, while we do not regard it as morally wrong when performed by animals? The relations, after all, are the same in both cases. The answer may be made that incest is not considered to be morally wrong if performed by animals because they lack the reason which is capable of discerning its wrongness, whereas man can do so. This answer, according to Hume, is patently useless. For before reason can perceive the wrongness, the wrongness must be there to perceive. Want of the reasoning faculty may prevent animals from perceiving duties and obligations, but it cannot hinder the duties and obligations from existing, 'since they must antecedently exist, in order to their being perceived. Reason must find them, and can never produce them. This argument deserves to be weighed, as being, in my opinion, entirely decisive.'[48] The same sort of argument appears in the second *Enquiry*. 'No, say you, the morality consists in the relation of actions to the rule of right, and they are denominated good or ill, according as they agree or disagree with it. What then is this rule of right? In what does it consist? How is it determined? By reason, you say, which examines the moral relations of actions. So that moral relations are determined by the comparison of action to a rule. And that rule is determined by considering the moral relations of objects. Is not this fine reasoning?'[49]

If we make moral distinctions, and if they are not derived from reason, they must be derived from or founded on feeling. 'Morality, therefore, is more properly felt than judged of.'[50] Virtue arouses an 'agreeable' impression, vice an 'un-

easy' impression. 'An action or sentiment or character is virtuous or vicious; why? because its view causes a pleasure or
uneasiness of a particular kind.'[51] But, Hume insists, the
pleasure caused by virtue and the pain caused by vice are
pleasure and pain of a special kind. The term 'pleasure'
covers many different types of sensation. 'A good composi-
tion of music and a bottle of good wine equally produce
pleasure; and what is more, their goodness is determined
merely by the pleasure. But shall we say upon that account
that the wine is harmonious or the music of a good flavour?
. . . Nor is every sentiment of pleasure or pain which arises
from characters and actions of that *peculiar* kind which makes
us praise or condemn.'[52] The moral sentiment is a feeling of
approbation or disapprobation towards actions or qualities or
characters. And it is disinterested. 'It is only when a character is considered in general, without reference to our particular interest, that it causes such a feeling or sentiment as
denominates it morally good or evil.'[53] Aesthetic pleasure is,
it is true, also disinterested. But though moral and natural
beauty closely resemble one another, it is not precisely moral
approbation which we feel, for example, for a beautiful building or a beautiful body.

Hume's 'hypothesis', therefore, 'defines virtue to be *whatever mental action or quality gives to a spectator the pleasing sentiment of approbation*; and vice the contrary'.[54] Does
this view involve sheer relativism, on the principle that there
is no dispute about tastes? It is evident that there are often
differences between different people's moral judgments. But
Hume seems to have thought that the general sentiments of
morality are common to all men, not only in the sense that
all normal human beings have moral feeling but also in the
sense that there is a certain fundamental agreement in the
operation of these feelings. When speaking of the legitimacy
of rebelling against a tyrant, he remarks that only the most
violent perversion of common sense can ever lead us to condemn resistance to oppression. He then adds: 'The general
opinion of mankind has some authority in all cases; but in
this of morals it is perfectly infallible. Nor is it less infallible
because men cannot distinctly explain the principles on which
it is founded.'[55] If the moral sentiments are due to the original constitution of men's minds, it is only natural that there
should be some fundamental agreement. And if moral distinctions are founded on feelings rather than reason, we can-

not go beyond an agreement in feeling and invoke a further criterion.

In the *Treatise* Hume raises the question 'why any action or sentiment upon the general view or survey gives a certain satisfaction or uneasiness'.[56] But the answer to this question is left for a discussion of the different virtues. For it may be that the reason why one type of action arouses the moral sentiment may not be precisely the same as the reason why another type of action does so. In any case, as Hume says in the second *Enquiry*, 'we can only expect success by following the experimental method and deducing general maxims from a comparison of particular instances'.[57] He holds, as we have seen, that what we call a moral judgment simply expresses the feeling of approval or disapproval which the man who makes the judgment has for the action or quality or character in question. And in this sense he maintains an emotive theory of ethics. But it still makes sense to ask what causes the feeling which is expressed in the judgment, even though the latter is not a statement that an action or quality or character causes the feeling. For though the judgment expresses feeling and does not make a statement about the cause of the feeling, we can very well make such statements, though they will be empirical rather than moral propositions.

It is not, however, possible to give a rational explanation of the ultimate ends of human action, if by rational explanation we mean an explanation in terms of higher or more remote principles. If we ask a man why he takes exercise, he may answer that he desires to preserve his health. And if he is asked why he desires this, he may answer that sickness is painful. But if we ask him why he dislikes pain, no answer can be given. 'This is an ultimate end, and is never referred to any other object.'[58] Similarly, if an answer to a question is given in terms of pleasure, it is useless to ask why pleasure is desired. 'It is impossible there can be a progress *in infinitum*; and that one thing can always be a reason why another is desired. Something must be desirable on its own account, and because of its immediate accord or agreement with human sentiment and affection.'[59] This consideration can be applied to virtue. 'Now as virtue is an end and is desirable on its own account, without fee or reward, merely for the immediate satisfaction which it conveys, it is requisite that there should be some sentiment which it touches . . . which distinguishes moral good and evil. . . .'[60] But we can ask why this or that particular line of action causes moral satisfaction and is therefore esteemed virtuous. Hume stresses the importance of utility, and in this respect is a forerunner of the utilitarians. But he does not make utility the sole source of moral approbation. However, the meaning which he gives to utility and the degree of importance which he attributes to it are best illustrated by considering some particular virtues.

7. Let us take first the virtue of benevolence. Benevolence and generosity everywhere excite the approbation and goodwill of mankind. 'The epithets *sociable, good-natured, humane, merciful, grateful, friendly, generous, beneficent,* or their equivalents, are known in all languages and universally express the highest merit which *human nature* is capable of attaining.'[61] Further, when people praise the benevolent and humane man, 'there is one circumstance which never fails to be amply insisted on, namely, the happiness and satisfaction derived to society from his intercourse and good offices'.[62] This suggests that the utility of the social virtues 'forms at least a *part* of their merit, and is one source of that approbation and regard so universally paid to them. . . . In general, what praise is implied in the simple epithet *useful!* What reproach in the contrary!'[63]

It is to be noted that Hume does not say that benevolence is esteemed as a virtue simply because of its utility. Some qualities, such as courtesy, are immediately agreeable, without any reference to utility (which means with Hume a tendency to produce some further or ulterior good); and benevolence itself is immediately pleasing and agreeable. But the moral approbation which benevolence arouses is caused in part by its usefulness.

Before proceeding further with the subject of utility, we should note that Hume devotes an appendix to the second *Enquiry* to showing that there is such a thing as benevolence or, rather, that so-called benevolence is not merely a disguised form of self-love. The view that benevolence is really a form of self-love may range from cheap cynicism to a philosophical attempt to preserve the realities of the moral life while providing an analysis of the way in which self-love takes that particular form which we call benevolence. But Hume rejects this view in all its shapes. For one thing, 'the simplest and most obvious cause which can be assigned for any phenomenon is probably the true one'.[64] And there are certainly cases in which it is far simpler to believe that a man is animated by disinterested benevolence and humanity than that he is prompted to act in a benevolent way by some tortuous considerations of self-interest. For another thing, even animals sometimes show a kindness when there is no suspicion of disguise or artifice. And 'if we admit a disinterested benevolence in the inferior species, by what rule of analogy can we refuse it in the superior?'[65] Further, in gratitude and friendship and maternal tenderness we can often find marks of disinterested sentiments and actions. In general 'the hypothesis which allows of a disinterested benevolence, distinct from self-love, has really more *simplicity* in it, and is more conformable to the analogy of nature than that which pretends to resolve all friendship and humanity into this latter principle'.[66]

As there is such a thing as disinterested benevolence, it is obvious that when Hume finds in utility or usefulness a part-cause of the moral approbation accorded to benevolence, he is not thinking exclusively of usefulness to oneself. Perhaps we show more alacrity in praising benevolence when it benefits us personally; but we certainly praise it often enough when it does not do so. For instance, we feel moral approbation of benevolent actions performed by historic personages in other lands. And it is a 'weak subterfuge' to argue that when we do this we transport ourselves in imagination into that other land and period and imagine ourselves to be contemporaries benefiting from the actions in question. 'Usefulness is agreeable, and engages our approbation. This is a matter of fact, confirmed by daily observation. But, *useful?* For what? For somebody's interest, surely. Whose interest, then? Not our own only; for our approbation frequently extends farther. It must, therefore, be the interest of those who are served by the character or action approved of; and these we may conclude, however remote, are not totally indifferent to us.'[67] Again, 'If usefulness, therefore, be a source of moral sentiment, and if this usefulness be not always considered with a reference to self, it follows that everything which contributes to the happiness of society recommends itself directly to our approbation and goodwill. Here is a principle which accounts, in great part, for the origin of morality.'[68] It is unnecessary to ask why we have humanity or a fellow-feeling with others. 'It is sufficient that this is experienced to be a principle in human nature. We must stop somewhere in our examination of causes.'[69]

In maintaining that usefulness for others can be directly

agreeable to us, indeed that 'everything which contributes to the happiness of society recommends itself directly to our approbation and goodwill', Hume seems to have modified, or rather changed, the view which he put forward in the *Treatise*. For there he said that 'there is no such passion in human minds as the love of mankind, merely as such, independent of personal qualities, of services, or of relation to oneself'.[70] The happiness or misery of another affects us, indeed, when it is not too far off and is represented in lively colours; 'but this proceeds merely from sympathy'.[71] And sympathy is explained, as we saw in the last chapter, with the aid of the principles of association. But in the second *Enquiry* the idea of association of ideas drops into the background, and Hume maintains the view that the thought of the pleasures and pains of other people arouses directly in us the sentiments of humanity and benevolence. In other words, the pleasures of others and that which is 'useful' to them, producing pleasure in them, is or can be directly agreeable to us. And it is unnecessary to have recourse to an elaborate associative mechanism to explain altruistic sentiments. In general, Hume tends, in the second *Enquiry*, to emphasize natural propensities, and the propensity to benevolence is one of them. It is probably not a derivative of self-love.

8. We have seen that according to Hume its utility is one of the reasons why benevolence wins our moral approbation. But it is not the only reason. He maintains, however, that 'public utility is the *sole* origin of justice, and that reflections on the beneficial consequences of this virtue are the *sole* foundation of its merit'.[72]

Society is naturally advantageous to man. Left to himself, the individual cannot provide adequately for his needs as a human being. Self-interest, therefore, drives men into society. But this alone is not sufficient. For disturbances inevitably arise in society if there are no conventions establishing and regulating the rights of property. There is need of 'a convention entered into by all the members of the society to bestow stability on the possession of those external goods, and leave everyone in the peaceable enjoyment of what he may acquire by his fortune and industry . . . it is by that means we maintain society, which is so necessary to their well-being and subsistence, as well as to our own'.[73] This convention should not be conceived as a promise. 'For even promises . . . arise from human conventions. It is only a general sense of common interest; which sense all the members of the society express to one another, and which induces them to regulate their conduct by certain rules.'[74] Once this convention about abstaining from the external goods of other people has been entered into, 'there immediately arise the ideas of justice and injustice'.[75] Hume does not mean, however, that there is a right of property which is antecedent to the idea of justice. He explicitly denies this. A 'general sense of common interest' expresses itself in the general principles of justice and equity, in fundamental laws of justice; and 'our property is nothing but those goods whose constant possession is established by the laws of society; that is, by the laws of justice. . . . The origin of justice explains that of property. The same artifice gives rise to both.'[76]

Justice, therefore, is founded on self-interest, on a sense of utility. And it is self-interest which gives rise to what Hume calls the 'natural obligation' of justice. But what gives rise to the '*moral* obligation, or the sentiment of right and wrong'?[77] Or why do we 'annex the idea of virtue to justice, and of vice to injustice'?[78] The explanation is to be found in sympathy. Even when injustice does not affect us personally as victims, it still displeases us, because we consider it as prejudicial to society. We share the 'uneasiness' of other people by sympathy. And since that which in human actions produces uneasiness arouses disapprobation and is called vice, while that which produces satisfaction is called virtue, we regard justice as a moral virtue and injustice as a moral vice. 'Thus self-interest is the original motive to the establishment of justice: but a sympathy with public interest is the source of the moral approbation which attends that virtue.'[79] Education and the words of statesmen and politicians contribute to consolidate this moral approbation; but sympathy is the basis.

Hume does not give any clear definition of justice, nor even, as it seems to me, any really clear indication of what he understands by the term. In the second *Enquiry* he asserts that 'general peace and order are the attendants of justice or a general abstinence from the possessions of others';[80] and in the *Treatise*, under the general heading of justice and injustice, he considers first of all matters relating to property. He tells us that the three fundamental 'laws of nature' are those relating to stable possession of property, the transference of property by consent, and the performance of promises.[81] What is clear, however, is that in his opinion all the laws of justice, general and particular, are grounded on public utility.

We can now understand what Hume means by calling justice an 'artificial' virtue. It presupposes a human convention, based on self-interest. Justice produces pleasure and approbation 'by means of an artifice or contrivance which arises from the circumstances and necessity of mankind'.[82] The sense of justice arises from a convention which is a remedy for certain 'inconveniences' in human life. 'The remedy, then, is not derived from nature, but from *artifice*; or more properly speaking, nature provides a remedy in the judgment and understanding for what is irregular and incommodious in the affections.'[83] By using the word 'artifice' Hume does not mean that, given human beings as they are, it is a mere matter of taste or of arbitrary choice whether we regard justice as a virtue and institute laws of justice or not. 'The sense of justice and injustice is not derived from nature, but arises artificially, *though necessarily* (my italics), from education and human conventions.'[84] Justice is 'artificial' in the sense that it is an invention of man, invented as a remedy for human selfishness and rapacity combined with the scanty provision which nature has made for his wants. If these conditions did not obtain, there would be no virtue of justice. 'By rendering justice totally *useless*, you thereby totally destroy its essence and suspend its obligation upon mankind.'[85] But the conditions do obtain, and the 'invention' is required for man's benefit. 'And where an invention is obvious and absolutely necessary, it may as properly be said to be natural as anything that proceeds immediately from original principles, without the intervention of thought or reflexion. Though the rules of justice be *artificial*, they are not arbitrary. Nor is the expression improper to call them *Laws of Nature*; if by natural we understand what is common to any species, or even if we confine it to mean what is inseparable from the species.'[86]

The particular laws of justice and equity may, of course, operate in a manner prejudicial to the public benefit if we concentrate our attention on some one particular instance. For instance, an unworthy son may inherit a fortune from a wealthy father and use it for bad ends. But it is the general scheme or system of justice which is of public utility. And here we find a difference between a virtue such as benevolence and a virtue such as justice. 'The social virtues of humanity and benevolence exert their influence immediately

by a direct tendency or instinct, which chiefly keeps in view
the simple object, moving the affections, and comprehends
not any scheme or system, nor the consequences resulting from the concurrence, imitation, or example of others.
. . . The case is not the same with the social virtues of
justice and fidelity. They are highly useful, or indeed absolutely necessary to the well-being of mankind: but the benefit
resulting from them is not the consequence of every individual single act, but arises from the whole scheme or system
concurred in by the whole, or the greater part of the
society.'[87]

Hume, therefore, will not allow that there are eternal laws
of justice, independent of man's conditions and of public
utility. Justice is an artifice, an invention. At the same time
it does not depend on a social contract, on a promise. For it
is justice itself which gives rise to contracts and binding
promises. It depends on felt utility, and this utility is real.
Men establish the laws of justice out of a concern for their
own and the public interest. But this concern is derived not
from reasoning about the eternal and necessary relations of
ideas but from our impressions and feelings. 'The sense of
justice, therefore, is not founded on our ideas, but on our
impressions.'[88] Men feel their interest in establishing a
scheme of justice, and they feel approval for customary conventions which remedy the 'inconveniences' that accompany
human life. But in elaborating particular rules reason is, of
course, employed. Hume thus brings the virtue of justice
within the general pattern of his moral theory. Feeling is
fundamental; but this does not mean that reason has no
part to play in morality.

9. Hume set out to understand the moral life of mankind by studying the empirical data. That men make moral
judgments is clear: it is an empirical fact which stands in
need of no proof. But it is not immediately evident what
men are doing when they make these judgments and what
is the ultimate foundation of the judgments in question.
Some philosophers have represented judgments of value as
being the result of reasoning, as being conclusions of a logical
process. They have tried to reconstruct the system of morals
as a rational system akin to mathematics. But an interpretation of this sort bears little resemblance to the facts. Where
there is a general agreement about values and moral principles, we can argue whether, for instance, a particular case falls
under a given principle or not. And after we have made a

moral judgment, we can look for reasons to support it. But
the suggestion that moral judgments are in the first place a
conclusion of reason, the conclusion of a deductive process
akin to mathematics, does not fit the available data. In
practice, of course, men's moral judgments are influenced by
education and other external factors. But, if we leave aside
the question what factors influence a man to make a particular moral judgment, it is clear, if we keep an eye on concrete
moral experience, that when a man makes a moral judgment
there is an element of immediacy which is not accounted for
on the rationalist interpretation of ethics. Morality is more
akin to aesthetics than to mathematics. It is truer to say that
we 'feel' values than that we deduce values or arrive at our
moral judgments by a process of logical reasoning from abstract principles.

In calling attention to the element of immediacy in the
moral judgment Hume was emphasizing a valuable point.
But in his further account of the matter he was hampered by
his general psychology. Inasmuch as he refused to allow that
moral distinctions are derived from either of the operations
of reason which he recognized, he had to say that morality is
more properly a matter of feeling than of judging and to
reduce the judgment to an expression of feeling. But terms
such as 'feeling' and 'moral sense', when used in this context,
are analogical terms which may be useful for drawing attention to an aspect of man's moral life which was neglected by
the rationalists but which need further examination than
Hume accorded them. The elements of utilitarianism in his
theory seem to me to suggest the desirability of revising
Hume's conception of 'reason' rather than of resting content with terms such as 'feeling'. In other words, Hume's
philosophy lacks a conception of the practical reason and of
its mode of operation.

Hume was also hampered, I think, by his theory of relations. He refused to allow that reason can discern a relation
between human acts and a rule of morality promulgated by
reason. In fact, he thought that any such view of the matter
involves one in circular reasoning. But his own insistence on
the original constitution or fabric of human nature suggests that this nature is in some sense the foundation of
morality or, in other words, that there is a natural law which
is promulgated by reason apprehending human nature in its
teleological and dynamic aspect. And an interpretation of
morality on these lines can be developed without implying

that men in general consciously 'reason' to general moral rules. Hume thought, of course, that if it is said that reason discerns relations which give rise to moral judgment, we shall also have to say that inanimate objects, for instance, are capable of morality. But it is difficult to see how this follows. For, after all, human acts are human acts; and it is these alone which are relevant. Hume, it is true, tended to say that acts are relevant to the moral judgment only as indicating motive and character. But this seems to be a way of saying that it is only human acts, acts which are deliberate, that are morally relevant. And the relation of such acts to a moral law are *sui generis*.

Perhaps it was only natural, given his interpretation of liberty, that Hume stressed above all character and qualities of character. For if liberty is reduced to spontaneity, an act has value either as a revelation of character or because of its 'utility'. Now, we are accustomed to regard characters and personal qualities as admirable or the reverse rather than as right or wrong, words which we reserve for acts. Hence, if we stress personal qualities rather than acts we shall probably be apt to assimilate the moral judgment or judgment of value to the aesthetic judgment. And in point of fact we find Hume slurring over the difference between moral qualities or virtues and natural gifts and talents. If, however, we look on acts as having value because of their utility, we shall tend to develop a utilitarian theory. And we find both lines of thought in Hume's analysis of morality.

It seems to me, therefore, that Hume's ethics is conditioned very largely by positions previously adopted, and that it contains different lines of thought. The utilitarian element was later developed by Bentham and the two Mills, while the insistence on feeling has found fresh life in modern empiricism in the emotive theories of ethics.

Chapter Seventeen

HUME (4)

*Politics as a science — The origin of society — The origin
of government — The nature and limits of allegiance —
The laws of nations — General remarks.*

1. Hume regarded politics as being in some sense of the word
a science. As we have already seen, politics, which is described
as considering men as united in society and dependent on
each other, is classed with logic, morals and criticism as
part of the science of man.[1] In an essay entitled *That
Politics may be reduced to a Science* Hume remarks that 'so
great is the force of laws and of particular forms of government, and so little dependence have they on the humours
and tempers of men, that consequences almost as general and
certain may sometimes be deduced from them as any which
the mathematical sciences afford us'. At the end of the first
Enquiry politics is separated from morals and criticism.
'Moral reasonings are either concerning particular or general facts'; and 'the sciences which treat of general facts are
politics, natural philosophy, physic, chemistry, etc., where
the qualities, causes and effects of a whole species of objects
are enquired into.'[2] 'Morals and criticism,' however, 'are
not so properly objects of the understanding as of taste and
sentiment'.[3] Here, then, we have a different grouping from
that in the introduction to the *Treatise*. Whatever Hume
may have come to think about morals, he tries to conserve
politics as a science, and he groups it with natural philosophy
and chemistry. In the *Dialogues concerning Natural Religion*,
however, politics is mentioned along with morals and criticism. 'So long as we confine our speculations to trade, or
morals, or politics, or criticism, we make appeals, every moment, to common sense and experience, which strengthen our

philosophical conclusions and remove (at least in part) the suspicion which we so justly entertain with regard to every reasoning that is very subtle and refined.'[4] Here economics, morals, politics and criticism or aesthetics are being contrasted with 'theological reasonings' in which we cannot, according to the speaker, the sceptically-minded Philo, confirm philosophical conclusions by appeals to common sense and experience.

Even if Hume's utterances about the relation of politics to morals differ on different occasions, it is none the less clear that he regards the former as a science or as capable of forming a science. We can form general maxims and explanatory hypotheses, and it is possible, within limits, to predict. But the unexpected may happen, even though after the event we may be able to explain it on the basis of already known principles. Thus in his essay *Of some Remarkable Customs* Hume observes that 'all general maxims in politics ought to be established with great caution', and that 'irregular and extraordinary appearances are frequently discovered in the moral as well as in the physical world. The former, perhaps we can better account for after they happen, from springs and principles of which everyone has, within himself or from observation, the strongest assurance and conviction: but it is often fully impossible for human prudence, beforehand, to foresee and foretell them.' We cannot attain in politics the certainty which is attainable in mathematics; for we are dealing mainly with matters of fact. This is doubtless the reason why, when he assimilates politics or mathematics in the passage quoted at the beginning of this section, he inserts the saving word 'almost'.

2. As we have seen when considering the virtue of justice, organized society came into existence because of its utility to man. It is a remedy for the inconveniences of life without society. 'Society provides a remedy for these *three* inconveniences. By the conjunction of forces, our power is augmented: By the partition of employment, our ability increases: And by mutual succour we are less exposed to fortune and accidents. It is by this additional *force, ability* and *security* that society becomes advantageous.'[5]

It is important to understand, however, that Hume does not imagine primitive human beings as thinking over the disadvantages of their lot without organized society, excogitating a remedy and entering upon any explicit social contract or covenant. Apart from the fact that he does not admit that

promises and contracts have binding force apart from society
and the rules of justice, he insists that the utility of society is
originally felt rather than made the subject of a reflective
judgment. There can be a convention or agreement between
people although no explicit promises are made. Speaking of
the convention from which the ideas of justice, property
and right arise, he uses a famous illustration which illustrates
what he calls a 'common sense of interest', which is expressed in action rather than in word. 'Two men who pull
the oars of a boat do it by an agreement or convention,
though they have never given promises to each other. . . .
In like manner are languages gradually established by human
conventions without any promise.'[6]

In order that society should be formed, says Hume, it is
necessary not only that it should be in fact advantageous to
men but also that they should 'be sensible of these advantages'. And if we are not to picture primitive men arriving at
this knowledge by reflection and study, how did they arrive at
it? Hume's answer is that society arose through the family.
Natural appetite draws members of the two sexes together
and preserves their union until a new bond arises, their common concern for their offspring. 'In a little time, custom and
habit operating on the tender minds of the children makes
them sensible of the advantages which they may reap from
society, as well as fashions them by degrees for it, by rub-
bing off those rough corners and untoward affections which
prevent their coalition.'[7] The family, therefore (or, more
accurately, the natural appetite between the sexes), is 'the
first and original principle of human society'.[8] The transition
to a wider society is effected principally by the felt need for
stabilizing the possession of external goods.

As there is question of feeling a need rather than of consciously studying man's situation and arriving at a common
and reflective judgment concerning the appropriate way of
meeting it, and as this need is present practically from the
beginning of human life on earth, it is understandable that
Hume felt no more sympathy for the theory of a state of nature than for that of a social contract. He concludes that 'it is
utterly impossible for men to remain any considerable time
in that savage condition which precedes society, but that his
very first state and situation may justly be esteemed social.
This, however, hinders not but that philosophers may, if
they please, extend their reasoning to the supposed *state of
nature*; provided they allow it to be a mere philosophical

fiction, which never had, and never could have any reality.
. . . This *state of nature*, therefore, is to be regarded as a
mere fiction.'[9] The same point is made in the second *Enquiry*.
There, too, Hume speaks of the state of nature as a philosophical fiction and remarks that 'whether such a condition of
human nature could ever exist or, if it did, could continue
so long as to merit the appellation of a *state*, may justly be
doubted. Men are necessarily born in a family-society at
least'.[10]

3. Similar statements may be made about the origin of
government. If natural justice were sufficient to govern human
conduct, if no disorder or wickedness ever arose, there would
be no need for curtailing individual liberty by establishing
governments to which we owe allegiance. 'It is evident that, if
government were totally useless, it never could take place, and
that the sole foundation of the duty of allegiance is the *advantage* which it procures to society by preserving peace and
order among mankind.'[11] Its usefulness, therefore, is the
foundation of the institution of government. And the principal
advantage which it secures for mankind is the establishment
and maintenance of justice. Thus in his essay *Of the Origin
of Government* Hume begins by saying that 'Man, born in a
family, is compelled to maintain society from necessity, from
natural inclination and from habit. The same creature, in his
further progress, is engaged to establish political society in
order to administer justice, without which there can be no
peace among them, nor safety, nor mutual intercourse. We
are, therefore, to look upon all the vast apparatus of our government as having ultimately no other object or purpose
but the distribution of justice.' In the *Treatise*, however,
where Hume speaks more precisely, he observes that though
the administration of justice and the settlement of controversies relating to matters of justice and equity are the principal advantages derived from government, they are not the
only ones. Without government men would find it very difficult to agree about schemes and projects for the common
good and to carry out such projects harmoniously. Organized
society remedies such inconveniences. 'Thus bridges are built;
harbours opened; ramparts raised; canals formed; fleets
equipped; and armies disciplined; everywhere by the care of
government.'[12]

Government, therefore, is an 'invention' of great advantage to men. But how does it arise? Is it so essential to society
that there cannot be a society without government? In the

Treatise Hume expressly says that he disagrees with those philosophers who declare that men are incapable of social unity without government. 'The state of society without government is one of the most natural states of men, and must subsist with the conjunction of many families, and long after the first generation. Nothing but an increase of riches and possessions could oblige men to quit it.'[13] According to Hume, the existence of societies without regular government is empirically verified in the American tribes. And he seems, at first sight at least, to imply that primitive men, perceiving after a time the necessity of government, met together to choose magistrates, determine their power and promise them obedience. This would be because the 'laws of nature' (the fundamental principles of justice) and the binding character of promises are presupposed. They are antecedent to the establishment of government, though they are not antecedent to the establishment of the convention which lies at the root of society.

If it were really Hume's view that government owes its origin to an explicit compact or agreement, this would scarcely be consistent with his general outlook. For, as we have seen in connection with the origin of society, he lays stress on 'felt' utility and mistrusts the rationalistic theory of social contracts. But, however he may speak on occasion, I do not think that Hume intends to say that government originated through explicit agreements. In his view government probably originated, not through a simple development and enlargement of paternal authority or of patriarchal government, but through wars between different societies. Foreign war necessarily produces civil war in the case of societies without government. The first rudiments of government, then, as can be seen among the American tribes, is the authority enjoyed by the captain or tribal chieftain during a campaign. 'I assert the first rudiments of government to arise from quarrels, not among men of the same society, but among those of different societies.'[14] Thus in his essay *Of the Original Contract* Hume remarks that 'the chieftain, who had probably acquired his influence during the continuance of war, ruled more by persuasion than command; and till he could employ force to reduce the refractory and disobedient, the society could scarcely be said to have attained a state of civil government. No compact or agreement, it is evident, was expressly formed for general submission; an idea far beyond the comprehension of savages: each exertion of authority in the chieftain must have been particular, and called forth by the present exigencies of the case: the sensible utility resulting from his interposition made these exertions become daily more frequent; and their frequency gradually produced an habitual, and, if you please to call it so, a voluntary, and therefore precarious, acquiescence in the people.' Inasmuch, therefore, as government probably first arose through a gradual process, implying a progressive realization of its utility, it can be said to have been founded on a 'contract'. But if by 'contract' is meant an explicit agreement by which civil government was established all at once in a form which would be immediately recognized by us as civil government, there is no cogent evidence that any explicit agreement or contract of this kind was ever made. I think that this represents Hume's view of the matter, the hypothesis which he puts forward, though not dogmatically.

But though Hume seems to be willing to allow that in prehistoric times government probably originated in some sense through consent, and though he suggests that observation of the American tribes affords some empirical confirmation of this hypothesis, he has no use at all for the contract theory when its assertions go further than these modest admissions. In the essay *Of the Original Contract* he observes that some philosophers are not content with saying that government in its first beginnings 'arose from consent, or rather the voluntary acquiescence of the people'; they assert, too, that government always rests on consent, on promises, on a contract. 'But would these reasoners look abroad in the world, they would meet with nothing that in the least corresponds to their ideas or can warrant so refined and philosophical a system.' Indeed, 'almost all the governments which exist at present, or of which there remains any record in story, have been founded originally, either on usurpation or conquest or both, without any pretence of a fair consent or voluntary subjection of the people. . . . The face of the earth is continually changing, by the increase of small kingdoms into great empires, by the dissolution of great empires into smaller kingdoms, by the planting of colonies, by the migration of tribes. Is there anything discoverable in all these events but force and violence? Where is the mutual agreement or voluntary association so much talked of?' Even when elections take the place of force, what does it amount to? It may be election by a few powerful and influential men. Or it may take the form of popular sedition, the people following a ringleader who owes his advancement to his own impudence or to the momentary caprice of the crowd, most of whom have little or no knowledge of him and his capacities. In neither case is there a real rational agreement by the people.

Whatever, then, may be the case with regard to the authority in war of really primitive tribal chieftains and leaders, whom the people may be said to have followed voluntarily, the contract theory of the origin of government gains very little empirical support from the available data in historic times. The theory is a mere fiction, which is invalidated by the facts. This being the case, it is necessary to inquire into the foundations of the duty of political allegiance.

4. Granted that there is a duty of political allegiance, it is obviously idle to look for its foundation in popular consent and in promises if there is little or no evidence that popular consent was ever asked or given. As for Locke's idea of tacit consent, 'it may be answered that such an implied consent can only have place where a man imagines that the matter depends on his choice'.[15] But anyone who is born under an established government thinks that he owes allegiance to the sovereign by the very fact that he is by birth a citizen of the political society in question. And to suggest with Locke that every man is free to leave the society to which he belongs by birth is unreal. 'Can we seriously say that a poor peasant or artisan has a free choice to leave his country, when he knows no foreign language or manners and lives from day to day by the small wages which he acquires?'[16]

The obligation of allegiance to civil government, therefore, 'is not derived from any promise of the subjects'.[17] Even if promises were made at some time in the remote past, the present duty of allegiance cannot rest on them. 'It being certain that there is a moral obligation to submit to government, because everyone thinks so, it must be as certain that this obligation arises not from a promise, since no one whose judgment has not been led astray by too strict adherence to a system of philosophy has ever yet dreamt of ascribing it to that origin.'[18] The real foundation of the duty of allegiance is utility or interest. 'This interest I find to consist in the security and protection which we can enjoy in political society, and which we can never attain when perfectly free and independent.'[19] This holds good both of natural and of moral obligation. 'It is evident that, if government were totally useless, it never could have place, and that the sole foundation of the duty of allegiance is the *advantage* which it procures to society by preserving peace and order among mankind.'[20] Similarly, in the essay *Of the Original Contract* Hume observes: 'If the reason be asked of that obedience which we are bound to pay to government, I readily answer, *Because society could not otherwise subsist*; and this answer is clear and intelligible to all mankind.'

The obvious conclusion to be drawn from this view is that when the advantage ceases, the obligation to allegiance ceases. 'As interest, therefore, is the immediate sanction of government, the one can have no longer being than the other, and whenever the civil magistrate carries his oppression so far as to render his authority perfectly intolerable, we are no longer bound to submit to it. The cause ceases; the effect must cease also.'[21] It is obvious, however, that the evils and dangers attending rebellion are such that it can be legitimately attempted only in cases of real tyranny and oppression and when the advantages of acting in this way are judged to outweigh the disadvantages.

But to whom is allegiance due? In other words, whom are we to regard as legitimate rulers? Originally, Hume thought or inclined to think, government was established by voluntary convention. 'The same promise, then, which binds them (the subjects) to obedience, ties them down to a particular person and makes him the object of their allegiance.'[22] But once government has been established and allegiance no longer rests upon a promise but upon advantage or utility, we cannot have recourse to the original promise to determine who is the legitimate ruler. The fact that some tribe in remote times voluntarily subjected itself to a leader is no guide to determining whether William of Orange or James II is the legitimate monarch.

One foundation of legitimate authority is long possession of the sovereign power: 'I mean, *long possession* in any one form of government, or succession of princes'.[23] Generally speaking, there are no governments or royal houses which do not owe the origin of their power to usurpation or rebellion and whose original title to authority was not 'worse than doubtful and uncertain'.[24] In this case 'time alone gives solidity to their right and, operating gradually on the minds of men, reconciles them to any authority and makes it seem just and reasonable'.[25] The second source of public authority is present possession, which can legitimize the possession of power even when there is no question of its having been acquired a long time ago. 'Right to authority is nothing but the constant possession of authority, maintained by the laws of society and the interests of mankind.'[26] A third source of legitimate political authority is the right of conquest. As fourth and fifth sources can be added the right of succession and positive laws, when the legislature establishes a certain form of government. When all these titles to authority are found together, we have the surest sign of legitimate sovereignty, unless the public good clearly demands a change. But if, says Hume, we consider the actual course of history, we shall soon learn to treat lightly all disputes about the rights of princes. We cannot decide all disputes in accordance with fixed, general rules. Speaking of this matter in the essay *Of the Original Contract*, Hume remarks that 'though an appeal to general opinion may justly, in the speculative sciences of metaphysics, natural philosophy or astronomy, be deemed unfair and inconclusive, yet in all questions with regard to morals, as well as criticism, there is really no other standard by which any controversy can ever be decided'. To say, for example, with Locke that absolute government is not really civil government at all is pointless if absolute government is in fact accepted as a recognized political institution. Again, it is useless to dispute whether the succession of the Prince of Orange to the throne was legitimate or not. It may not have been legitimate at the time. And Locke, who wished to justify the revolution of 1688, could not possibly do so on his theory of legitimate government being founded on the consent of the subjects. For the people of England were not asked for their opinion. But in point of fact William of Orange was accepted, and the doubts about the legitimacy of his accession are nullified by the fact that his successors have been accepted. It may perhaps seem to be an unreasonable way of thinking, but 'princes often *seem* to acquire a right from their successors as well as from their ancestors'.[27]

5. Inasmuch as it is to the interest of different political societies to carry on trade and commerce with one another and, in general, to enter into mutual relations, there arises a set of rules which Hume calls 'the laws of nations'. 'Under his head we may comprise the sacredness of the person of ambassadors, the declaration of war, the abstaining from poisoned arms, with other duties of that kind, which are evidently calculated for the commerce that is peculiar to different societies.'[28]

These 'laws of nations' have the same foundation as the

'laws of nature', namely, utility or advantage, and they do not abolish the latter. Princes are, indeed, bound by moral rules. 'The same *natural* obligation of interest takes place among independent kingdoms, and gives rise to the same *morality*; so that no one of ever so corrupt morals will approve of a prince who voluntarily and of his own accord breaks his word or violates any treaty.'[29] At the same time, although the moral obligation of princes has the same extent as that of private persons, it does not possess the same *force*. For intercourse between different States is not so necessary or advantageous as that between individuals. Without society of some kind human life cannot subsist; but there is not the same degree of necessity for intercourse between States. Accordingly, the natural obligation to justice is not so strong with regard to the behaviour of one political society towards another as it is with regard to the mutual relations of two private members of the same society. And from this there follows a similar difference of strength in moral obligation. Hence, 'we must necessarily give a greater indulgence to a prince or minister who deceives another than to a private gentleman who breaks his word of honour'.[30] But if one is asked to state the exact proportion which obtains between the morality of princes and the morality of private persons, one can give no precise answer. 'One may safely affirm that this proportion finds itself, without any art or study of men; as we may observe on many other occasions.'[31] Hume is thus ready to find some truth in the principles of Machiavellian politics; but he is not prepared to state that there is one morality for princes and another for private persons.

6. One salient feature of Hume's political theory is his attention to empirical data and his refusal to accept philosophical hypotheses which are not confirmed by the known facts. This is particularly true of his attitude towards the contract theory or theories. He does, indeed, accept this theory to some extent as far as the first origins of government are concerned. But there he is thinking of a tribe voluntarily gathering round a leader in an inter-tribal war rather than of any formal contract or promise. And, apart from this concession, he has no use for contract theories. In place of such rationalistic theories he substitutes the idea of 'felt' interest or advantage.

There is a strong element of what we may call 'positivism' in Hume's political philosophy. He appeals to what actually happens or to what everyone thinks as a criterion rather than to any *a priori* reasonings. For example, political authority is frequently the result of usurpation, rebellion or conquest, and if the authority is stable and not obviously tyrannical and oppressive, it is in practice accepted as legitimate by the vast majority of the governed. This is sufficient for Hume. Subtle discussions about the legitimacy of such authority, and attempts to prove its legitimacy by means of 'philosophical fictions', are a waste of time. It is more profitable to inquire what are the titles to authority which are actually accepted as titles. Again, Hume is not disposed to spend time discussing ideal forms of commonwealth. In his essay on the *Idea of a Perfect Commonwealth* he does, indeed, remark that it is advantageous to know what is most perfect of its kind, that we may amend existing forms of constitution and government 'by such gentle alterations and innovations as may not give too great disturbance to society'. And he himself makes some suggestions under this heading. But he also observes that 'all plans of government which suppose great reformation in the manners of mankind are plainly imaginary. Of this nature are the *Republic* of Plato and the *Utopia* of Sir Thomas More.' But apart from the essay in question he shows himself more concerned with understanding what has been and is rather than with suggesting what ought to be. And even when he does make suggestions towards improving the constitution, it is practical advantage and utility that he has in mind rather than conclusions deduced from eternal, abstract principles.

In his essay *Of the Original Contract* Hume mentions the position of those who maintain that since God is the origin of all authority the sovereign's authority is sacred and inviolable in all circumstances. He then comments as follows: 'That the Deity is the ultimate author of all government will never be denied by any who admit a general providence and allow that all events in the universe are conducted by an uniform plan and directed to wise purposes. . . . But since he (God) gave rise to it, not by any particular or miraculous interposition, but by his concealed and universal efficacy, a sovereign cannot, properly speaking, be called his vicegerent in any other sense than every power or force, being derived from him, may be said to act by his commission.' In other words, even if we grant the validity of the premiss, the conclusion drawn by those who maintain the divine right of kings does not follow. And, in general, it is clear that Hume did not think that there is much practical help to be gained by a process of deduction from metaphysical principles. God has made man so that government is highly advantageous, even necessary, to him; and in this sense God may be called the author of political authority. But in deciding what form of government to adopt or who possesses legitimate authority we must have recourse to other criteria than divine creation, preservation and providence.

But though Hume shows an admirable hard-headed common sense, his political theory seems to me to suffer from a weakness which is shared by his moral theory. It is all very well to appeal to utility and advantage and public benefit; but it is by no means self-evident what these terms mean in the concrete. And it is difficult to give them a meaning which will serve as a criterion without going further into a philosophical anthropology, and so into metaphysics, than Hume was prepared to go.

FOR AND AGAINST HUME

Introductory remarks — Adam Smith — Price — Reid — Campbell — Beattie — Stewart — Brown — Concluding remarks.

1. The title of this chapter is perhaps rather misleading. For it suggests that at any rate immediately after Hume's death, if not during his lifetime, controversy raged about the validity of his philosophical theories. But this would scarcely be an accurate picture of the situation. In France he was acclaimed as the leading British man of letters and during his visits to that country he was lionized in the *salons* of Paris. But though his essays and historical writings were appreciated, his philosophy was not a success in his own country during his lifetime. And, apart from the scandal caused by his reputation for theological unorthodoxy, no very great interest was taken in it. If Hume is now generally regarded as the chief British philosopher, and certainly as the leading British thinker of his period, this is largely because his theories have come into their own, so to speak, in modern empiricism. He has undoubtedly exercised a profound influence on philosophical thought; but, if we except the influence which Hume's empiricism exercised on the mind of Kant, its more important manifestations were reserved for a later period.

In Hume's lifetime there were, however, a few thinkers in his own country who gave a more or less favourable reception to his philosophical ideas. And among these the most remarkable and the most appreciative was his personal friend, Adam Smith. Again, among Hume's critics some were, indeed, moderate and polite; and these included the moral philosopher, Richard Price. Further, a more extensive answer to Hume was proposed by Thomas Reid, the founder of

the Scottish philosophy of common sense. It may be appropriate, therefore, to conclude the present part of the fourth
volume of this *History* with a brief chapter on Smith, Price,
Reid and Reid's followers.

2. Adam Smith (1723–90) went in 1737 to the University of Glasgow, where he attended Hutcheson's lectures.
Three years later he went to Balliol College, Oxford. He
seems to have become acquainted with Hume at Edinburgh
about 1749, and in due course he became the philosopher's
close friend, the friendship lasting until Hume's death. In
1751 Smith was elected to the chair of logic at Glasgow, but
in the following year he changed to the chair of moral philosophy, which had become vacant through the death of
Hutcheson's successor. In 1759 he published his *Theory of
Moral Sentiments*.

In 1764 Smith went to France as tutor-companion to the
duke of Buccleuch, after having resigned from his university
chair. While in Paris he consorted with Quesnay and other
'physiocrats' as well as with philosophers such as d'Alembert
and Helvetius. The physiocrats were an eighteenth-century
school of French economists who insisted that governmental
interference with individual liberty should be reduced to the
indispensable minimum. The reason for this insistence was
that they believed in natural economic laws which produce
prosperity and wealth if left to operate freely. Hence the
word 'physiocracy' or rule of nature. Smith was influenced
by them to some extent; but this influence should not be
exaggerated. He did not borrow from them his leading ideas.

On returning to England in 1766 Smith retired to Scotland, and in 1776 there appeared his great work, *An Inquiry
into the Nature and Causes of the Wealth of Nations*. He
received a warm letter of congratulation from Hume. In this
classic of economics Smith begins by insisting on the annual
labour of a nation as the source of its supply of the necessities and conveniences of life. And he goes on to discuss the
causes of improvement in the productiveness of labour and
the distribution of its produce. The second book treats of the
nature, accumulation and employment of stock; the third of
the different progress of wealth in different nations; the
fourth of systems of political economy; and the fifth of the
revenue of the sovereign or commonwealth. And there are a
large number of supplementary notes and dissertations.

In 1778 Smith was appointed one of the commissioners of

customs in Scotland. In 1787 he was elected Lord Rector of Glasgow University. He died on July 17th, 1790.

We are not concerned here with Smith's economic theories, but with his moral philosophy. It is worth mentioning, however, that when he was lecturing at Glasgow his course was divided into four parts: natural theology, ethics, the part of morality relating to justice, and those political institutions, including those relating to finance and commerce, which are founded on 'expediency' rather than on the principle of justice and which tend to increase the riches and power of a State. For Smith, therefore, economics was a member of a total body of knowledge, of which ethics was another member.

One salient feature of Adam Smith's moral theory is the central place accorded to sympathy. To attribute ethical importance to sympathy was not, indeed, a novel position in British moral philosophy. Hutcheson had attributed importance to it, and Hume, as we have seen, made great use of the concept of sympathy. But Smith's use of it is more obvious in that he begins his *Theory of Moral Sentiments*[1] with this idea and thus gives his ethics from the very start a social character. 'That we often derive sorrow from the sorrow of others is a matter of fact too obvious to require any instances to prove it.'[2] The sentiment of sympathy is not confined to the virtuous and humane; it is found in all men to some degree.

Smith explains sympathy in terms of the imagination. 'As we have no immediate experience of what other men feel, we can form no idea of the manner in which they are affected, but by conceiving what we ourselves should feel in the like situation.'[3] When we sympathize with someone's great pain, 'by the imagination we place ourselves in his situation. . . .'[4] Thus sympathy, which means or can be used to mean 'our fellow-feeling with any passion whatever',[5] arises not so much from a view of the passion 'as from that of the situation which excites it'.[6] For example, when we feel sympathy with a madman, that is to say when we feel compassion and pity for his state, it is primarily his situation, that of being deprived of the normal use of reason, which excites our sympathy. For the madman himself may not feel any sorrow at all. He may even laugh and sing and appear quite oblivious of his pitiful condition. Again, 'we sympathize even with the dead'.[7]

However, if we assume the causes of sympathy, whatever they may be, we can say that it is an original sentiment of human nature. It is often excited so directly and immediately that it cannot reasonably be derived from self-interested affection, that is, from self-love. And there is no need to postulate a distinct 'moral sense' which expresses itself in moral approval or disapproval. For 'to approve of the passions of another, as suitable to their objects, is the same thing as to observe that we entirely sympathize with them; and not to approve of them as such is the same thing as to observe that we do not entirely sympathize with them'.[8] Moral approbation and disapprobation, therefore, can ultimately be referred to the operation of sympathy. There are, indeed, cases in which we seem to approve without any sympathy or correspondence of sentiments. But even in these cases it will be found upon examination that our approbation is ultimately founded upon sympathy. Smith takes an example of what he calls a very frivolous nature. I may approve a jest and the consequent laughter, even though, for some reason or other, I do not myself laugh. But I have learned by experience what sort of pleasantry is most capable of amusing me and making me laugh, and I observe that the jest in question is one of this kind. And even though I am not now in the mood for laughing, I approve of the jest and of the company's merriment, this approval being the expression of 'conditional sympathy'. I know that, were it not for my present mood or perhaps illness, I should certainly join in the laughter. Again, if I see a passing stranger who shows signs of distress and sorrow and I am told that he has just lost his father or mother or wife, I approve of his sentiments, even though I may not actually share his distress. For I know by experience that a bereavement of this kind naturally excites such sentiments, and that if I were to take time to consider and enter into his situation, I should doubtless feel sincere sympathy.

Smith makes the sense of propriety the essential element in our moral judgments. And he speaks frequently of the suitableness or unsuitableness, propriety or impropriety of sentiments, passions and affections. Thus, he says that 'in the suitableness or unsuitableness, in the proportion or disproportion which the affection seems to bear to the cause or object which excites it, consists the propriety or impropriety, the decency or ungracefulness of the consequent action'.[9] Further, 'in the beneficial or hurtful nature of the effects which the affection aims at, or tends to produce, consists the merit or demerit of the action, the qualities by which it is entitled to reward, or is deserving of punishment'.[10] But when I disapprove of a man's resentment as being disproportionate to its exciting cause, I disapprove of his sentiments because they do not tally with my own or with what I think my own would be in a like situation. My sympathy does not reach to the man's degree of resentment, and I therefore disapprove of it as excessive. Again, when I approve of a man's act as meritorious, as entitled to reward, I sympathize with the gratitude which the action naturally tends to excite in the beneficiary of the action. Or, more accurately, my sense of the merit of the action is compounded of my sympathy with the agent's motive together with my sympathy with the gratitude of the beneficiary.

It may appear, says Smith, that it is the utility of qualities which first commends them to us. And consideration of utility, when we do come to consider it, doubtless enhances the value of qualities in our eyes. 'Originally, however, we approve of another man's judgment, not as something useful, but as right, as accurate, as agreeable to truth and reality, and it is evident we attribute those qualities to it for no other reason but because we find that it agrees with our own. Taste, in the same manner, is originally approved of, not as useful, but as just, as delicate, and as precisely suited to its object. The idea of the utility of all qualities of this kind is plainly an afterthought, and not what first recommends them to our approbation.'[11] If Smith rejected the idea of an original and distinct moral sense, so also did he reject utilitarianism. The concept of sympathy reigns supreme. Smith does, indeed, agree with an 'ingenious and agreeable author' (Hume) that 'no qualities of the mind are approved of as virtuous, but such as are useful or agreeable either to the person himself or to others; and no qualities are disapproved of as vicious but such as have a contrary tendency'.[12] Indeed, 'nature seems to have so happily adjusted our sentiments of approbation and disapprobation to the conveniency both of the individual and of the society that after the strictest examination it will be found, I believe, that this is universally the case'.[13] But it is not this utility which is the first or principal source of moral approbation or disapprobation. 'It seems impossible that the approbation of virtue should be a sentiment of the same kind with that by which we approve of a convenient and well-contrived building; or that we should have no other reason for praising a man than that for which we commend a chest of drawers.'[14] 'The sentiment of approbation always involves in it a sense of propriety quite distinct from the perception of utility.'[15]

To enter upon Smith's analyses of virtues and passions would be to devote to his ethics an excessive amount of space. But it is necessary to ask how he interprets the moral judgment which we pass about ourselves if moral approbation is an expression of sympathy. And the answer is that in his opinion we cannot approve or disapprove of our own sentiments, motives or conduct except by placing ourselves in the position of another man and viewing our conduct from without, as it were. If a man were brought up on a desert island and had never at any time enjoyed human society, he could no more think 'of the propriety or demerit of his own sentiments and conduct than of the beauty or deformity of his own face'.[16] Our first moral judgments are made about the characters and conduct of other people. But we soon learn that they make judgments about us. Hence we become anxious to know how far we deserve their praise or blame; and we begin to examine our own conduct by imagining ourselves in the position of others, supposing ourselves to be the spectators of our own conduct. Hence, 'I divide myself, as it were, into two persons. . . . The first is the spectator. . . . The second is the agent, the person whom I properly call myself, and of whose conduct, under the character of a spectator, I was endeavouring to form some opinion.'[17] I can thus have sympathy with or antipathy towards my own qualities, motives, sentiments and actions.

One of the obvious objections against Smith's ethical theory of sympathy is that it seems to leave no room for any objective standard of right or wrong, good or evil. In answer to an objection of this kind Smith stresses the idea of the 'impartial spectator'. For example, he says that 'the natural misrepresentation of self-love can be corrected only by the eye of this impartial spectator'.[18] At the same time 'the violence and injustice of our own selfish passions are sometimes sufficient to induce the man within the breast to make a report very different from what the real circumstances of the case are capable of authorizing'.[19] Nature, however, has not left us to the delusions of self-love. We gradually and insensibly form for ourselves general rules concerning what is right and what is wrong, these rules being founded on experience of particular acts of moral approbation and disapprobation. And these general rules of conduct, 'when they have been fixed in our mind by habitual reflection, are of great use in correcting the misrepresentations of self-love concerning what is fit and proper to be done in our particular situation'.[20] Indeed, these rules are 'the only principle by which the bulk of mankind are capable of directing their actions'.[21] Further, nature impresses upon us an opinion, 'afterwards confirmed by reasoning and philosophy, that these important rules of morality are the commands and laws of the Deity, who will finally reward the obedient and punish the transgressors of their duty'.[22] And 'that our regard to the will of the Deity ought to be the supreme rule of our conduct can be doubted of by nobody who believes his existence'.[23] Conscience is thus the 'vicegerent' of God. Smith does not, however, claim infallibility for the moral judgment. He speaks at some length of the influence of custom on the moral sentiments.[24] Moreover, he tells us that the 'general rules of almost all the virtues . . . are in many respects loose and inaccurate, admit of many exceptions and require so many modifications, that it is scarce possible to regulate our conduct entirely by a regard to them'.[25] There is, indeed, one exception. 'The rules of justice are accurate in the highest degree.'[26]

As historians have pointed out, it is not always easy to reconcile Adam Smith's various statements. On the one hand, the impartial spectator, the man within the breast, will not deceive us if we listen to him attentively and respectfully. On the other hand, there are variations in moral approval from place to place and age to age, and bad customs can pervert or obscure the moral judgment. On the one hand, the majority of people are only capable of directing their conduct by general rules. On the other hand, as these rules, with the exception of the rules of justice, are loose and inaccurate and indeterminate, our conduct should be directed rather by a sense of propriety, by a certain taste for a particular way of acting, than by regard for a rule as such. It may, indeed, be possible to reconcile these diverse statements with one another. For example, it might be said that though the impartial spectator, if listened to attentively, never deceives, passion and bad custom (arising perhaps from external circumstances which seem to make the custom expedient) may very well prevent the requisite attention being given. In any case, however, it seems true to say with his critics that in his ethical treatise Smith displays his abilities to greater advantage as a psychological analyst than as a moral philosopher.

3. It has been already remarked that the philosophers of the moral sense theory tended to assimilate ethics to aesthetics, this tendency being connected, I think, with their concentration on qualities of character rather than with acts. And to the extent that they assimilated ethics to aesthetics they tended to overlook the specifically ethical features of the moral judgment. I use the word 'tended' deliberately; for I do not intend to assert that they identified ethics and aesthetics or that they made no effort to distinguish them by isolating the specific feature or features of the moral judgment.

Adam Smith cannot, of course, be properly called a philosopher of the moral-sense theory. For despite his admiration for Hutcheson and his appreciation of the latter's achievements as a moralist he explicitly rejected 'every account of the principle of approbation, which makes it depend upon a peculiar sentiment, distinct from every other'.[27] At the same time Smith is akin to the philosophers of the moral sense theory in his tendency to dissolve ethics in psychology. (Again I use the word 'tendency' deliberately.) This tendency can be observed also in Hume, though in his moral philosophy, as we have seen, there was present a conspicuous element of utilitarianism.

The early utilitarians (and the same can be said of utilitarianism in general) tended to reduce the moral judgment to a statement about consequences. That is to say, they tended to interpret the specifically moral judgment as an empirical statement or hypothesis.

On the one hand, therefore, we have the moral sense school, with its psychologizing tendencies and its tendency to assimilate ethics to aesthetics, while on the other hand we have utilitarianism, which in its own way tended to strip the moral judgment of its specific character. It was only natural, then, that some thinkers at least should react to these tendencies by insisting on the part played by reason in morality and on the intrinsic nature of the rightness and wrongness of certain actions, quite apart from the thought of reward and punishment and other utilitarian considerations. Such a thinker was Richard Price, who in certain respects anticipated the position of Kant.

Richard Price (1723–91) was the son of a Nonconformist minister and himself entered the ministry. Besides publishing some sermons, he also wrote on financial and political matters. In addition, he carried on a controversy with Priest-

ley, in which he upheld free-will and the immateriality of
the soul. We are here concerned, however, with his ethical
ideas as expressed in his *Review of the Principal Questions
in Morals* (1757). It shows clearly his debt to Cudworth and
Clarke on the one hand and to Butler on the other, for whom
he had a profound admiration.

Price disliked the moral sense theory, especially as developed by Hume. It favours subjectivism and abandons the
direction of human conduct to instinct and feeling. Reason,
not emotion, is authoritative in morals. And reason has every
title to this position in that it discerns objective moral distinctions. There are actions which are intrinsically right and
actions which are intrinsically wrong. Price does not mean
that in ethics we should consider actions without any regard
to the intention of the agent and the natural end of the action. But if we consider human acts in their totality, we can
discern by reason their rightness or wrongness, which belong
to the actions in question independently of consequences
such as reward or punishment. There are at least some actions
which are right in themselves and which need no further
justification in terms of extraneous factors, just as there are
some ultimate ends. 'There are, undoubtedly, some actions
that are ultimately approved, and for justifying which no
reason can be assigned; as there are some ends, which are
ultimately desired, and for choosing which no reason can be
given.'[28] If this were not the case, says Price, there would
be an infinite regress.

In expounding the idea of an intellectual intuition of objective moral distinctions Price was reviving the views held
by earlier writers such as Cudworth and Clarke. And the
historical source of the neglect of this intellectual operation
by the moral sense theorists and of the consequent subjectivism and empiricism of Hume was traced by Price to
Locke's theory of ideas and to his concept of the understanding. Locke derived all simple ideas from sensation and reflection. But there are simple and self-evident ideas which
are immediately perceived or intuited by the understanding.
Among them are the ideas of right and wrong. If we confuse
the understanding with the imagination, we shall necessarily
tend to confine unduly the scope of the former. 'The powers
of the imagination are very narrow; and were the understanding confined to the same limits, nothing could be known, and
the very faculty itself would be annihilated. Nothing is plainer
than that one of these often perceives where the other is

blind . . . and in numberless instances knows things to exist of which the other can frame no idea.'[29] Reasoning, considered as a distinct intellectual operation, studies the relations between ideas which we already possess; but the understanding intuits self-evident ideas which cannot be resolved into elements derived from sense-experience.

In defence of the assertion that the understanding has original and self-evident ideas, Price appeals to 'common sense'. If a man denies that there are such ideas, 'he is not further to be argued with, for the subject will not admit of argument, there being nothing clearer than the point itself disputed to be brought to confirm it'.[30] In appealing to common sense and self-evident principles Price anticipates to some extent the position of the Scottish philosophy of common sense. But his insistence that the ideas of right and wrong are simple or 'single' ideas which are not further analysable recalls to mind later ethical intuitionism.

By rejecting the moral sense theory Price does not commit himself to rejecting the emotional element in morals. Right and wrong are objective attributes of human actions, and these attributes are perceived by the mind; but we certainly have feelings with regard to actions and human qualities, and these feelings find expression in the subjective ideas of moral beauty and deformity. What Price does, therefore, is to oust feeling from a central position and to keep it as an accompaniment of rational intuition. Another accompaniment of the intellectual perception of right and wrong in actions is the perception of merit and demerit in agents. To perceive merit in the agent is simply to perceive that his action is right and that he ought to be rewarded. On this matter Price follows Butler. He also insists that merit depends on the intention of the agent. Unless the action possesses 'formal rightness', unless, that is to say, it is performed with a good intention, it is not meritorious.

Right and obligatory seem to be synonymous for Price. The obligatory character of an intrinsically right action is founded simply on its rightness, without regard to reward or punishment. Benevolence is certainly a virtue, though not the only one; and there is such a thing as rational self-love. But a man, as a rational being, ought, in principle at least, to act simply out of respect for the dictates of reason, and not from instinct, passion or emotion. 'The intellectual nature is its own law. It has, within itself, a spring and guide of action which it cannot suppress or reject. Rectitude is itself an end, an ultimate end, an end superior to all other ends, governing, directing, and limiting them, and whose existence and influence depend on nothing arbitrary. . . . To act from affection to it, is to act with light, and conviction, and knowledge. But acting from instinct is so far acting in the dark, and following a blind guide. Instinct *drives* and *precipitates*; but reason *commands*.'[31] Hence an agent cannot properly be called virtuous 'except he acts from a consciousness of rectitude, and with a regard to it as his *rule* and *end*'.[32] In any case an agent's virtue is always less in proportion as he acts from natural propensity and inclination or from instinct instead of according to purely rational principles.[33] Price does, indeed, bring in consideration of reward and punishment to the extent that he expresses surprise that anyone should forget that by acting virtuously he may gain an infinite reward while by acting otherwise he may suffer infinite loss. And he insists that virtue itself is 'the object of the chief complacency of every virtuous man; the exercise of it is his chief delight; and the consciousness of it gives him his highest joy'.[34] But his insistence on acting in accordance with purely rational principles and out of consideration of the rightness of right acts, which oblige the agent, and his view that the virtue of a man is less in proportion to the degree in which he acts from instinct or natural inclination clearly approximate to a Kantian position. And Kant himself did not exclude all thought of reward from ethics. For though he considered that we should not do right and obligatory actions simply with a view to reward, he certainly thought that virtue should ultimately produce or be united with happiness. So for Price we must conceive happiness as the end envisaged by divine Providence. And virtue will produce happiness. But this happiness depends on 'rectitude', and we cannot be truly virtuous unless we do right actions because they are right.

4. Thomas Reid (1710–96), son of a Scottish minister, studied at Aberdeen. After some years as minister in the parish of New Machar he was elected to a post at King's College, Aberdeen, and in 1764 he published *An Inquiry into the Human Mind on the Principles of Common Sense*. Thus although Reid was a year older than Hume, his first work (apart from an essay on quantity) appeared much later than Hume's *Treatise* and *Enquiries*. Shortly after the publication of this work Reid was elected professor of moral philosophy at Glasgow in succession to Adam Smith. In 1785

he published a volume of *Essays on the Intellectual Powers of Man*, which was followed in 1788 by *Essays on the Active Powers of Man*. These two sets of essays have been reprinted together several times as *Essays on the Powers of the Human Mind*.

After reading part of the manuscript of Reid's *Inquiry*, transmitted to him by a Dr. Blair, Hume wrote a letter to the author which contained some innocuous comments. In the course of his reply Reid remarks: 'Your system appears to me not only coherent in all its parts, but likewise justly deduced from principles commonly received among philosophers: principles which I never thought of calling in question, until the conclusions you draw from them in the *Treatise of Human Nature* made me suspect them.' It was Reid's contention that Hume's philosophy was 'a system of scepticism, which leaves no ground to believe any one thing rather than its contrary'.[35] In fact, it constituted, in Reid's opinion, the *reductio ad absurdum* of scepticism. At the same time it was the result of a consistent development of the implications of certain principles, or of a certain principle, which had been shared by writers such as Locke and Berkeley, and even by Descartes, who were not so consistent or rigorous as Hume in drawing the appropriate conclusions from their premisses. Hence it was necessary to examine the starting-point of the process of reasoning which had led in the end to a contradiction of the beliefs upon which all men of common sense must act in common life.

The root of the whole trouble Reid finds in what he calls 'the theory of ideas'. In his first essay,[36] as indeed elsewhere, Reid distinguishes several senses of the word 'idea'. In popular language the word signifies conception or apprehension. Reid means the act of conceiving or apprehending. 'To have an idea of anything is to conceive it. To have a distinct idea is to conceive it distinctly. To have no idea of it is not to conceive it at all. . . . When the word idea is taken in this popular sense, no man can possibly doubt whether he has ideas.'[37] But the word is also given a 'philosophical' meaning; and then 'it does not signify that act of the mind which we call thought or conception, but some object of thought'.[38] Thus according to Locke ideas are nothing but the immediate objects of the mind in thinking. Now, 'Bishop Berkeley, proceeding upon this foundation, demonstrated very easily that there is no material world. . . . But the Bishop, as became his order, was unwilling to give up the world of

spirits. . . . Mr. Hume shows no partiality in favour of the
world of spirits. He adopts the theory of ideas in its full extent; and, in consequence, shows that there is neither matter
nor mind in the universe; nothing but impressions and
ideas.'[39] In fact, 'Mr. Hume's system does not even leave him
a *self* to claim the property of his impressions and ideas'.[40]
Ideas, therefore, which 'were first introduced into philosophy
in the humble character of images or representatives of
things' have by degrees 'supplanted their constituents and un-
dermined the existence of everything but themselves', the
'triumph of ideas' being completed by Hume's *Treatise*,
which 'leaves ideas and impressions as the sole existence in
the universe'.[41]

In attacking the theory of ideas Reid characteristically
employs two ways of approaching the matter. One way is to
appeal to common sense, to the universal belief or persuasion
of ordinary people. Thus the ordinary man is convinced that
what he perceives is the sun itself, and not ideas or impressions. But Reid does not content himself with an appeal to
the beliefs of 'the vulgar'. He also argues, for example, that
there are no such things as ideas in the 'philosophical' sense
of the word; they are fictions of the philosophers, or of some
philosophers, and it is in no way necessary to postulate them.
Why, then, did philosophers invent this fiction? In Reid's
opinion one fundamental error was Locke's assumption that
'simple ideas' are the elementary data of knowledge. The
'ideal system' 'teaches us that the first operation of the mind
about its ideas is simple apprehension; that is, the bare
conception of a thing without any belief about it; and that
after we have got simple apprehensions, by comparing them
together, we perceive agreements or disagreements between
them; and that this perception of the agreement or disagreement of ideas is all that we call belief, judgment or knowledge. Now this appears to me to be all fiction, without any
foundation in nature. . . . Instead of saying that the belief
or knowledge is got by putting together and comparing the
simple apprehensions, we ought rather to say that the simple
apprehension is performed by resolving and analysing a natural and original judgment.'[42] Locke and Hume started with
the supposed elements of knowledge, simple ideas in the
case of the former and impressions in the case of the latter,
and then depicted knowledge as being essentially the result
of combining these elementary data and perceiving their
agreement or disagreement. But the so-called elementary

data are the result of analysis: we first have original, fundamental judgments. 'Every operation of the senses, in its very
nature, implies judgment or belief, as well as simple apprehension. . . . When I perceive a tree before me, my faculty
of seeing gives me not only a notion or simple apprehension
of the tree, but a belief of its existence, and of its figure,
distance, and magnitude; and this judgment or belief is not
got by comparing ideas, it is included in the very nature of
the perception.'[43]

These 'original and natural judgments are therefore a part
of that furniture which nature hath given to the human understanding. They are the inspiration of the Almighty, no
less than our notions or simple apprehensions. . . . They
are a part of our constitution, and all the discoveries of our
reason are grounded upon them. They make up what is
called *the common sense of mankind*; and what is manifestly
contrary to any of those first principles is what we call *absurd*.'[44] If philosophers maintain that ideas are the immediate objects of thought, they will be forced to conclude in the
end that ideas are the only objects of our minds. Locke did
not draw this conclusion. He used the word 'idea' in several
senses, and there are different, and indeed incompatible,
elements in his writings. But Hume eventually drew the logical conclusions from Locke's premisses (which can be referred
back to Descartes). And in so doing he has to deny the principles of common sense, the original and natural judgments
of mankind. His conclusions, therefore, were absurd. The
remedy is to recognize the principles of common sense, the
original judgments of mankind, and to acknowledge that the
'theory of ideas' is a useless and harmful fiction.

By judgments of nature and principles of common sense
Reid means self-evident principles. 'We ascribe to reason two
offices, or two degrees. The first is to judge of things self-
evident; the second to draw conclusions that are not self-
evident from those that are. The first of these is the province,
and the sole province of common sense.'[45] The name 'common sense' is appropriate because 'in the greatest part of
mankind no other degree of reason is to be found'.[46] The
power to deduce conclusions from self-evident principles in
an orderly and systematic way is not found in everyone,
though many people can learn to do so. But the power to see
self-evident truths is found in all beings who qualify for being
called rational. And it is 'purely the gift of Heaven':[47] it cannot be acquired if one does not possess it.

What relation does common sense in this special meaning of the term bear to common sense in the 'popular' meaning of the term? Reid's answer is that 'the same degree of understanding which makes a man capable of acting with common prudence in the conduct of life makes him capable of discovering what is true and what is false in matters that are self-evident and that he distinctly apprehends'.[48]

According to Reid, therefore, there are 'common principles which are the foundation of all reasoning and of all science. Such common principles seldom admit of direct proof, nor do they need it. Men need not to be taught them; for they are such as all men of common understanding know; or such, at least, as they give a ready assent to, as soon as they are proposed and understood.'[49] But what are these principles? Reid distinguishes between necessary truths, the opposite of which is impossible, and contingent truths, the opposite of which is possible. Each class includes 'first principles'. Among first principles belonging to the first class there are logical axioms (for example, every proposition is either true or false), mathematical axioms, and the first principles of morals and metaphysics. One of the examples of moral first principles given by Reid is that 'no man ought to be blamed for what it was not in his power to hinder'.[50] These moral axioms 'appear to me to have no less evidence than those of mathematics'.[51] Under the heading of metaphysical first principles Reid considers three, 'because they have been called in question by Mr. Hume'.[52] The first is that 'the qualities which we perceive by our senses must have a subject, which we call body, and that the thoughts we are conscious of must have a subject, which we call mind'.[53] This principle is recognized as true by all ordinary men, and this recognition is expressed in ordinary language. The second metaphysical principle is that 'whatever begins to exist must have a cause which produced it'.[54] And the third is that 'design and intelligence in the cause may be inferred from marks or signs of it in the effect'.[55]

Among the first principles of contingent truths we find 'that those things did really happen which I distinctly remember';[56] 'that those things do really exist which we distinctly perceive by our senses, and are what we perceive them to be';[57] 'that the natural faculties by which we distinguish truth from error are not fallacious';[58] and 'that in the phenomena of nature what is to be will probably be like to what has been in similar circumstances'.[59] That we have some degree of power over our actions and over the determinations of our will, and that there is life and intelligence in our fellow-men with whom we converse, are also among the first principles mentioned by Reid.

Now, it is evident, I think, that these first principles are of different types. Among logical axioms Reid mentions the proposition that whatever can be truly affirmed of a genus can be truly affirmed of the species. Here we have an analytic proposition. We have only to learn the meanings of the terms 'genus' and 'species' in order to see that the proposition is true. But can the same be said of the validity of memory or of the existence of the external world? Reid can hardly have thought that it could; for he classifies the relevant propositions as first principles of contingent truths. In what sense, then, are they self-evident? Reid obviously means at the very least that there is a natural propensity to believe them. Speaking of the statement that the things really exist which we perceive by the senses and that they are what we perceive them to be, he remarks: 'It is too evident to need proof, that all men are by nature led to give implicit faith to the distinct testimony of their senses, long before they are capable of any bias from prejudices of education or of philosophy.'[60] Again, when speaking of the principle relating to the uniformity, or probable uniformity, of nature, he observes that it cannot be simply the result of experience, though it is confirmed by experience. For 'the principle is necessary for us before we are able to discover it by reasoning, and therefore is made a part of our constitution, and produces its effects before the use of reason'.[61] In other words, we have a natural propensity to expect that the course of nature will probably prove to be uniform.

Propositions which are obviously tautological cause no difficulty. Given the meanings of the terms, they cannot be denied without absurdity. And though the existence of informative necessary propositions is a matter of controversy, Reid is perfectly entitled to his opinion that there are such propositions. I mean, the issue between Reid and Hume on this matter can be clearly expressed. But the issue is not at all so clear when it comes to natural belief in what Reid calls the first principles of contingent truths; nor has Reid made it clear. Hume never denied that there are natural beliefs; and he was perfectly well aware that these natural beliefs form a basis or framework for practical life. He does, indeed, sometimes make ontological assertions, as when he says that people are nothing but bundles or collections of different perceptions; but, generally speaking, he is concerned, not with denying a given proposition, but with examining our grounds for asserting the proposition. For instance, Hume does not say that there is no external world or that the course of nature will be so entirely unexpected that we can rely on no uniformity at all: he is concerned with examining the rationally assignable grounds for beliefs which he shares in common with other people. Hence in so far as Reid appeals to natural belief, to natural propensities and to the common consent of mankind, his observations have not much relevance as against Hume. Reid does, indeed, recognize that Hume speaks of natural beliefs; but he tends to represent the latter as denying what he does not in fact deny. If Reid had maintained that what he calls first principles were susceptible of proof, the issue with Hume would be sufficiently clear-cut. For example, can the validity of memory be proved or can it not? But Reid did not think that his first principles were susceptible of proof. Speaking of the validity (in principle) of memory, he says that the principle possesses one of the surest marks of a first principle, namely, that no one has pretended to prove it, though no sensible man questions it. But Hume was well aware that people are naturally prone to believe that memory is in principle reliable. Reid refers to the acceptance of testimony in the courts of law and remarks that 'what is absurd at the bar (that no heed at all should be paid to testimony) is so in the philosopher's chair'.[62] But Hume never dreamed, of course, of suggesting that testimony about remembered facts should never be accepted, and that no one should ever trust his or her memory. Reid does, indeed, proceed to admit that 'Mr. Hume has not, as far as I remember, directly called in question the testimony of memory',[63] though he adds immediately that Hume has laid down the premisses by which the authority of memory is overthrown, leaving it to his reader to draw the logical conclusion. But it is a mistake to assume that Hume intended, even by implication, to destroy that degree of reliance on memory which is given it by prudent common sense. He no more intended this than he intended to deny that there are any causal relations and to suggest that no reliance should in practice be put on causal laws. In general, then, we can say that Reid's criticism of Hume is sometimes deprived of force by his misunderstanding of what Hume was about.

It is not, of course, a fair presentation of Reid's position if he is depicted as appealing simply to the persuasion or opinion of nonphilosophers as a proof of the truth of his first principles. What he does is to regard universal consent, when coupled with an inability to doubt, save perhaps in the sceptical philosopher's chair, as an indication that a given proposition is a first principle. First principles cannot be proved; otherwise they would not be first principles. They are known intuitively. But Reid does not give, as it seems to me, any very clear and consistent account of the way or ways in which we come to know the different types of first principles. In some cases he does, indeed, explain his view. For example, 'the evidence of mathematical axioms is not discerned till men come to a certain degree of maturity of understanding. A boy must have formed the general conception of *quality*, and of *more* and *less* and *equal*, of *sum* and *difference*; and he must have been accustomed to judge of these relations in matters of common life, before he can perceive the evidence of the mathematical axiom, that equal quantities, added to equal quantities, make equal sums. In like manner our moral judgment, or conscience, grows to maturity from an imperceptible seed, planted by our Creator.'[64] Here we have a reasonably straightforward account. In the course of experience a man obtains certain notions or learns the meaning of certain terms, and he can then see the self-evident truth of certain propositions containing or presupposing those terms. If the principles are said to belong to the constitution of human nature, this means that we have a natural power of discerning the evident truth of these principles, but not that the latter are known antecedently to experience. But when talking about the proposition that perceived sensible qualities and thoughts of which we are conscious must have subjects, namely, body and mind, Reid speaks of 'principles of belief in human nature, of which we can give no other account but that they necessarily result from the constitution of our faculties'.[65] And this principle, like mathematical axioms, is classed as a first principle of necessary truths. And when we turn to first principles of contingent truths we find him saying with regard to the principle of the uniformity of nature, that it is 'a part of our constitution and produces its effects before the use of reason'.[66] The principle is antecedent to experience, 'for all experience is grounded upon a belief that the future will be like the past'.[67] We are determined by our nature to expect that the future will be like the past. There is a kind of irresistible natural expectation.

Perhaps these ways of speaking can be made consistent. Speaking of the principle that the natural faculties by which we distinguish truth from error are not fallacious, Reid remarks that 'we are under a necessity of trusting to our reasoning and judging powers', and that doubt on this point cannot be maintained 'because it is doing violence to our constitution'.[68] He also asserts that 'no man ever thinks of this principle, unless when he considers the grounds of scepticism; yet it invariably governs his opinions'.[69] He seems to be saying, therefore, first that there is a natural and irresistible propensity to trust our rational powers, and secondly that this proposition is not explicitly recognized as true from the beginning. And he might make analogous statements, not only about the principle of the uniformity of nature, but also about the principle of causality, which he regards as a metaphysical and necessary principle. But he tends, I think, to leave his readers with the impression that principles such as the validity of memory and the existence of the external world are self-evident in the sense that we have a natural and irresistible impulse to believe them, whereas mathematical axioms, for instance, are self-evident in the sense that once we have the meanings of certain terms we see necessary relations between them. What I suggest, therefore, is that Reid asserts the existence of a considerable number of first principles of different types without providing an unambiguous explanation of the precise sense or senses in which they are said to be self-evident, first principles, and a part of the constitution of our nature. It may be possible to reconcile his various ways of speaking and provide an account which will cover all his first principles; but I do not think that Reid provided it. And if he wished to give different accounts of the different sets of first principles, he might have made the point clearer than he in fact did.

Reid sometimes tends to play to the gallery by practically making fun of certain philosophers (Berkeley, for example) and by announcing that he takes his stand with 'the vulgar'. But his philosophy of common sense is by no means a mere acceptance of the opinions of the multitude and a rejection of academic philosophy. It was his view that philosophy must be grounded in common experience and that if it reaches paradoxical conclusions which contradict common experience and conflict with the beliefs on which everyone, even sceptical philosophers, necessarily base their lives in practice, there must be something wrong with it. And this is a perfectly reputable view of philosophy. It is not invalidated by Reid's historical inaccuracies and misrepresentations of other points of view.

It must be added that Reid did not adhere invariably to common sense, if by common sense we mean the spontaneous belief of the man in the street. For example, when speaking of colour he first says that 'by colour all men, who have not been tutored by modern philosophy, understand, not a sensation of the mind, which can have no existence when it is not perceived, but a quality or modification of bodies, which continues to be the same, whether it is seen or not'.[70] He then goes on to distinguish between 'the appearance of colour' and colour itself, as a quality of a body. The latter is cause of the former, and it is unknown in itself. But the appearance of scarlet, for example, is so closely united in imagination with its cause that 'they are apt to be mistaken for one and the same thing, although they are in reality so different and unlike that one is an idea in the mind, the other is a quality of body. I conclude, then, that colour . . . is a certain power or virtue in bodies that in fair daylight exhibits to the eye an appearance. . . .'[71] Indeed, Reid does not hesitate to say that 'none of our sensations are resemblances of any of the qualities of bodies'.[72] It is perhaps rather surprising to hear such utterances from the lips of a champion of 'the vulgar'. But the truth is, of course, that though Reid maintained that in the 'unequal contest betwixt common sense and philosophy the latter will always come off both with dishonour and loss',[73] he by no means confined himself to repeating the views of people innocent of all philosophy and science.

5. Among Reid's friends was George Campbell (1719–96), who became Principal of Marischal College, Aberdeen, in 1759 and professor of divinity at that college in 1771. In his *Philosophy of Rhetoric* he includes under the general heading of propositions the truth of which is known intuitively mathematical axioms, truths of consciousness and first principles of common sense. Some mathematical axioms, he points out, merely exhibit the meanings of terms, though this is not true, in his opinion, of all mathematical principles. Truths of consciousness include, for instance, assurance of one's existence. As for principles of common sense, these include the principle of causality, the principle of the uniformity of

nature, the existence of body, and the validity of memory when it is 'clear'. He thus gave to common sense a more restricted meaning than that given it by Reid.

6. Better known than Campbell are James Oswald (d. 1793), author of *An Appeal to Common Sense in behalf of Religion*, and James Beattie (1735–1803). In 1760 the latter was elected professor of moral philosophy and logic at Marischal College, Aberdeen; and in 1770 he published his *Essay on Truth*. In it he not only criticized Hume's opinions but also indulged in declamation and diatribe in passages which were doubtless the expression of sincere indignation but which seem rather out of place in a philosophical work. Hume was angry; and some of his comments have been reported. Of the *Essay on Truth* he remarked: 'Truth! there is no truth in it; it is a horrible large lie in octavo.' And of its author he spoke as 'that silly bigoted fellow, Beattie'. But the work enjoyed a great success. King George III was pleased, and he rewarded the author with an annual pension. Oxford University conferred on Beattie the doctorate of civil law.

In the first part of the *Essay on Truth* Beattie considers the standard of truth. He distinguishes between common sense, which perceives self-evident truth, and reason (reasoning). The first principles of truth, of which there are a considerable number, 'rest upon their own evidence, perceived intuitively by the understanding'.[74] But how are we to distinguish between first principles of common sense and mere prejudices? This question is treated in the second part. Reflection on mathematics shows us that the criterion of truth is that principle which forces our belief by its own intrinsic evidence.[75] In natural philosophy this principle is 'well-informed sense'. When is sense well-informed? First, I must be disposed, of my own accord, to confide in it without hesitation. Secondly, the sensations received must be 'uniformly similar in similar circumstances'.[76] Thirdly, I must ask myself 'whether, in acting upon the supposition that the faculty in question is well-informed, I have ever been misled to my hurt or inconvenience'.[77] Fourthly, the sensations communicated must be compatible with one another and with the perceptions of my other faculties. Fifthly, my sensations must be compatible with those of other men. The third part of the *Essay* is professedly devoted to answering objections against Beattie's theories. But the latter takes the opportunity of giving us his opinions about a large number of philosophers, and in most cases this opinion is very low.

For Aristotle he shows an obvious respect; and Reid is naturally immune from attack. But the Schoolmen are depicted as mere verbal wranglers, and the greater number of modern philosophical systems are represented as contributing to or as examples of sceptical systems, 'those unnatural productions, the vile effusions of a hard heart'.[78] Beattie tends to give the impression that he has very little use for philosophy except as a means of attacking philosophies and philosophers.

7. Of more account than Beattie was Dugald Stewart (1753–1828). After studying at Edinburgh University he taught mathematics there, and in 1778 he took the class in moral philosophy during the absence of the professor, Adam Ferguson.[79] When the latter resigned his chair in 1785, Stewart was appointed to succeed him. In 1792 he published the first volume of *Elements of the Philosophy of the Human Mind*, of which the second and third volumes did not appear until 1814 and 1827 respectively. *Outlines of Moral Philosophy* was published in 1793, and *Philosophical Essays* in 1810. In 1815 and 1821 appeared the two parts of his *Dissertation exhibiting the Progress of Metaphysical, Ethical and Political Philosophy since the Revival of Letters in Europe* which was written for the supplement of the *Encyclopaedia Britannica*. Finally, his *Philosophy of the Active and Moral Powers* was published in 1828, a few weeks before his death. Stewart was an eloquent and influential lecturer, attracting students even from abroad. And after his death a monument to his memory was erected in Edinburgh. He was not a particularly original thinker; but he was a man of wide culture, and he was gifted with a power of exposition.

In the introduction to his *Outlines of Moral Philosophy* Stewart remarks that 'our knowledge of the laws of nature is entirely the result of observation and experiment; for there is no instance in which we perceive such a necessary connection between two successive events, as might enable us to infer the one from the other by reasoning *a priori*. We find, from experience, that certain events are invariably conjoined, so that when we see the one, we expect the other, but our knowledge in such cases extends no farther than the fact.'[80] We have to use observation and controlled experiment to arrive inductively at general laws, from which we can reason deductively ('synthetically') to effects.

This point of view may seem to be very out of keeping with the outlook of Reid. But though Reid maintained that the truth of the proposition that everything which begins to be has a cause is known intuitively, he did not maintain that experience can inform us about particular necessary connections in Nature. 'General maxims, grounded on experience, have only a degree of probability proportioned to the extent of our experience, and ought always to be understood so as to leave room for exceptions if future experience shall discover any such.'[81] According to Reid, we can infer the existence of God, as cause of contingent and mutable things, with absolute certainty. But apart from this truth, from self-evident first principles and from what can be strictly deduced from them, we are left to experience and probability. He instances the law of gravitation as a probable law, in the sense that exceptions are in principle possible. Hence Stewart's view of natural philosophy is not so alien to Reid's outlook as might appear at first sight.

Stewart notes that the 'reformation' in physics which has taken place during the last two centuries has not been extended in the same degree to other branches of knowledge, in particular to the knowledge of the mind. 'As all our knowledge of the material world rests ultimately on facts ascertained by observation, so all our knowledge of the human mind rests ultimately on facts for which we have the evidence of our own consciousness. An attentive examination of such facts will lead in time to the general principles of the human constitution, and will gradually form a science of mind not inferior in certainty to the science of body. Of this species of investigation, the works of Dr. Reid furnish many valuable examples.'[82]

The general aim proposed by Stewart for inquiries into psychology is, therefore, that of giving to this branch of study the character of a science. And this involves applying to psychology the methods which have proved so successful in physics. The data studied are, of course, different from the data studied by physicists. But an analogous scientific method should be used. And if psychology is to acquire the character of a science, it is most important that it should not be confused with metaphysics. Natural philosophers or physicists 'have, in modern times, wisely abandoned to metaphysicians all speculations concerning the nature of that substance of which it (the material world) is composed; concerning the possibility or impossibility of its being created; . . . and even concerning the reality of its existence, independent of that of percipient beings: and have confined themselves to the humbler province of observing the phenomena it exhibits, and of

ascertaining their general laws. . . . This experimental philosophy no one now is in danger of confounding with the
metaphysical speculations already mentioned. . . . A similar
distinction takes place among the questions which may be
stated relative to the human mind. . . . When we have once
ascertained a general fact, such as the various laws which regulate the association of ideas, or the dependence of memory
on that effort of the mind which we call Attention; it is all we
ought to aim at in this branch of science. If we proceed no
farther than facts for which we have the evidence of our own
consciousness, our conclusions will be no less certain than
those in physics. . . .'[83]

Stewart restricts unduly the scope of psychology and regards as 'metaphysical' some inquiries which would not ordinarily be classified in this way.[84] But the interesting point
about his discussion of the science of mind is his inductive approach and his insistence on not confounding science with
speculation. And even though he tends sometimes to restrict
unduly the scope and range of psychological inquiry, this does
not mean that he is blind to the need for constructive hypotheses. On the contrary, he reproves those Baconians who reject
hypotheses and appeal to Newton's famous *Hypotheses non
fingo*, understood in a literal sense. We must distinguish between 'gratuitous' hypotheses and those which are supported
by presumptions suggested by analogy. The utility of an hypothesis is shown when conclusions derived from it are verified or confirmed. But even an hypothesis which is subsequently shown to be false may prove to have been of great
use. Stewart quotes[85] Hartley's remark in his *Observations
on Man*[86] that 'any hypothesis which possesses a sufficient
degree of plausibility to account for a number of facts, helps
us to digest these facts in proper order, to bring new ones to
light, and to make *experimenta crucis* for the sake of future
inquirers'.

In his approach to psychology, therefore, Stewart adopted
what we may call a frankly empiricist approach. But this does
not mean that he rejects Reid's theories of first principles or
principles of common sense. True, he regards the term 'common sense' as too vague and as calculated to give rise to misunderstanding and misrepresentation. But he accepts the idea
of principles, the truth of which is perceived intuitively.
These he classifies under three headings. First, there are axioms of mathematics and physics. Secondly, there are first
principles relating to consciousness, perception and memory.

Thirdly, there are 'those fundamental laws of human belief, which form an essential part of our constitution; and of which our entire conviction is implied, not only in all speculation, but in all our conduct as acting beings'.[87] Among 'laws' of this first class are the truths of the existence of the material world and of the uniformity of nature. 'Such truths no man ever thinks of stating to himself in the form of propositions; but all our conduct and all our reasonings proceed on the supposition that they are admitted. The belief of them is necessary for the preservation of our animal existence; and it is accordingly coeval with the first operations of the intellect.'[88] Stewart distinguishes, therefore, between judgments which 'are formed as soon as the terms of the proposition are understood' and judgments which 'result so necessarily from the earliest constitution of the mind, that we act upon them from our earliest infancy, without ever making them an object of reflection'.[89] In addition, there are judgments which are arrived at by reasoning.

The judgments which result from the earliest constitution of the mind are called by Stewart 'fundamental laws of human belief'. The word 'principle' is, in his opinion, misleading. For we cannot draw any inferences from them for the enlargement of human knowledge. 'Abstracted from other data, they are perfectly barren in themselves.'[90] They should not be confused with 'principles of reasoning'. They are involved in the exercise of our rational powers; but it is with the rise of philosophical reflection that they are thought about, becoming objects of the mind's attention. As for the criterion by which we can distinguish fundamental laws of belief, universality of belief is not the only one. Stewart mentions with approval two criteria proposed by Buffier.[91] First, the truths in question should be such that it is impossible either to attack or to defend them except by means of propositions which are neither more evident nor more certain than they are. Secondly, the practical influence of the truths must extend even to those who theoretically dispute their authority.

It is clear that Stewart is more careful than Reid in trying to state his position exactly. And this care can be frequently seen in his treatment of particular points. For example, he explains with care that though the immediate evidence of consciousness assures us of the present existence of sensations or of affections, desires, and so on, we are not immediately conscious of the mind itself in the sense of enjoying a direct intuition of the mind. True, 'the very first exercise' of consciousness necessarily implies a belief, not only of the present existence of what is felt, but of the present existence of *that* which feels and thinks. . . . Of these facts, however, it is the former alone of which we can properly be said to be conscious, agreeably to the rigorous interpretation of the expression.'[92] Consciousness of the self as subject of sensation or feeling is posterior in the order of nature, if not in the order of time, to consciousness of the sensation or feeling. In other words, awareness of our existence is 'a concomitant or accessory of the exercise of consciousness'.[93] Again, when writing about our belief in the uniformity of nature, Stewart is careful to discuss the meaning of the word 'law' when we talk about laws of nature. When used in experimental philosophy, 'it is more correctly logical to consider it as merely a statement of some general fact with respect to the order of nature—a fact which has been found to hold uniformly in our past experience, and on the continuance of which, in future, the constitution of our mind determines us confidently to rely'.[94] We should beware of conceiving so-called laws of nature as acting in the capacity of efficient causes.

The moral faculty is 'an original principle of our constitution which is not resolvable into any other principle or principles more general than itself; in particular, it is not resolvable into self-love or a prudential regard to our own interest'.[95] 'There are, in all languages, words equivalent to *duty* and to *interest*, which men have constantly distinguished in their signification.'[96] By this faculty we perceive the rightness or wrongness of actions. And we must distinguish between this perception and the accompanying emotion of pleasure or pain which varies according to the degree of a person's moral sensibility. We must also distinguish the perception of the merit or demerit of the agent. Hutcheson went wrong by making no distinction between the rightness of an action as approved by our reason and its aptitude to excite a man's moral emotions. Again, Shaftesbury and Hutcheson tended to neglect the fact that the objects of moral approbation are actions, not affections. In other words, Stewart disliked the tendency of the moral sense theorists to turn ethics into aesthetics, though he also thought that some writers, such as Clarke, had paid too little attention to our moral feelings. As for the term 'moral sense', considered in itself, Stewart has no objection to its retention. As he remarks, we habitually speak of a 'sense of duty' and it would be pedantic to object to 'moral sense'. At the same time he insists that when a man asserts that an act is right he intends to say something which is true. Moral discrimination is a rational operation, just as much as is perception of the fact that the three angles of a triangle together equal one right angle. 'The exercise of our reason in the two cases is very different; but in both cases we have a perception of *truth*, and are impressed with an irresistible conviction that the truth is immutable and independent of the will of any being whatever.'[97]

Stewart considers the obvious objection to the theory that rightness and wrongness are qualities of actions, which are perceived by the mind; namely, the objection that people's ideas of what is right and wrong have varied from country to country and from age to age. And he thinks that this variety can be explained in a manner which leaves his theory of objective moral qualities intact. Physical conditions, for instance, may influence the moral judgment. Where nature produces in abundance the necessities of life, it is only to be expected that men should have looser ideas about the rights of property than those which prevail elsewhere. Again, different speculative opinions or convictions can influence people's perceptions of right and wrong.

On the subject of moral obligation Stewart expresses his agreement with Butler's insistence on the supreme authority of conscience. And he commends the statement of a Dr. Adams that '*right* implies duty in its ideas'. Stewart's point is that 'it is absurd to ask *why* we are bound to practise virtue. The very notion of virtue implies the notion of obligation.'[98] Obligation cannot be interpreted simply in terms of the notions of reward and punishment. For these presuppose the existence of obligation. And if we interpret obligation in terms of the divine will and command, we shall find ourselves involved, in Stewart's opinion, in a vicious circle.

In conclusion, we can consider very briefly Stewart's line of argument for the existence of God. The process of reasoning, he tells us, 'consists only of a single step, and the premises belong to that class of first principles which form an essential part of the human constitution. These premises are *two* in number. The one is, that everything which begins to exist must have a cause. The other, that a combination of means conspiring to a particular end implies intelligence.'[99]

Stewart accepts Hume's contention that every attempt to demonstrate the truth of the first premiss involves assuming what has to be proved. He also accepts Hume's analysis of causality, so far as natural philosophy is concerned. 'In natural philosophy, when we speak of one thing being the cause of another, all that we mean is, that the two things are *constantly conjoined*, so that when we see the one we may expect the other. These conjunctions we learn from experience alone. . . .'[100] Causes in this sense can be called 'physical causes'. But there is also a metaphysical sense of causality, in which the word implies necessary connection. And causes in this sense can be called 'metaphysical or efficient causes'. As for the question how this idea of causation, power or efficacy is acquired, Stewart says that 'the most probable account of the matter seems to be that the idea of Causation or Power necessarily accompanies the perception of change in a way somewhat analogous to that in which sensation implies a being who feels, and thought a being who thinks'.[101] In any case the truth of the proposition that everything which begins to exist must have a cause is intuitively perceived. And in applying this principle Stewart is prepared to admit that all the events which constantly take place in the material universe are the immediate effects of divine causation and power, God being the constantly operative efficient cause in the material world. Stewart is thus in agreement with Clarke's view that the course of nature is, strictly speaking, nothing but the will of God producing certain effects in a continuous, regular and uniform manner. In other words, we can consider nature from the point of view either of the physicist or of the metaphysician. In the first case the empiricist analysis of causality is all that is required. In the second case (that is to say, if we grant the reality of active power in the material world), we must see natural events as effects of a divine agency. But for this argument to have any cogency, it is obviously necessary to suppose that we cannot discern active power and efficient causes (in Stewart's sense of the term) in nature. Further, as Stewart notes, this line of reasoning does not of itself show the unicity of God.

Stewart then turns to consider our apprehension of intelligence or design as manifested in the 'conspiration' of different means to a particular end. He argues first that we have intuitive knowledge of the connection between observed evidence of design and a designer or designers. That the combination of a variety of means to produce a particular effect implies design is not a generalization from experience; nor can it be demonstrated. We perceive its truth intuitively. Secondly, Stewart argues that there are evidences of design in the universe. He cites, for example, the way in which Nature repairs, in many cases, injuries to the human body. Thirdly, he argues that there is one uniform plan, which proves the unicity of God. He subsequently goes on to consider the moral attributes of the Deity.

In his writings Stewart manifests his wide reading and his power of using material taken from a great variety of philosophers in developing his system. But the essential features of his system are evidently derived mainly from Reid. What he does is to systematize and develop Reid's ideas, even though he criticizes him from time to time. Of Kant, Stewart knew comparatively little, as he himself observes. He shows, indeed, some appreciation of the German philosopher, and he concedes that Kant had a glimpse of the truth. But he was evidently both revolted and mystified by Kant's style, and in his *Philosophical Essays*[102] he speaks of Kant's 'scholastic barbarism' and of the 'scholastic fog through which he delights to view every object to which he turns his attention'. Reid, if he had been able to, might have learned something from Kant; but it is obvious that the former was, in Stewart's opinion, a superior philosophical thinker.

8. We have seen that Stewart, and indeed Reid before him, accepted Hume's analysis of causality as far as natural philosophy is concerned. Thomas Brown (1778–1820), a pupil of Stewart and his successor in the chair of moral philosophy at Edinburgh, proceeded further in the empiricist direction. Indeed, he may be regarded as a link between the Scottish philosophy of common sense and the nineteenth-century empiricism of J. S. Mill and Alexander Bain.

In his *Inquiry into the Relation of Cause and Effect* (1804, later revised and enlarged), Brown defines a cause as 'that which immediately precedes any change, and which, existing at any time in similar circumstances, has been always, and will be always, immediately followed by a similar change'.[103] The elements, and the only elements combined in the idea of cause are priority in the observed sequence and invariable antecedence. Power is only another word for expressing 'the antecedent itself, and the invariableness of the relation'.[104] When, therefore, we say 'that A is the cause of B, it may be allowed that we mean only that A is followed by B, has always been followed by B, and, we believe, will be always followed by B'.[105] Similarly, 'when I say that I have mentally the power of moving my hand, I mean nothing more than that, when my body is in a sound state, and no foreign force is imposed on me, the motion of my hand will always follow my desire to move it'.[106] Thus in mental phenomena, as in physical phenomena, causality is to be analysed in the same way.

Brown rejects Stewart's distinction between physical and efficient causality. 'The *physical* cause which has been, is, and always will be, followed by a certain change is the *efficient* cause of that change; or if it be not the efficient cause of it, it is necessary that a definition of efficiency should be given us, which involves more than the certainty of a particular change, as consequent in instant sequence. Causation is efficiency; and a cause which is not efficient, is truly no cause whatever.'[107] The defenders of the distinction between efficient and physical causes have merely asserted that there is a distinction without explaining its nature. It is true that God is the ultimate cause of all things; but this is no reason for saying that there are no other efficient causes.

Given this analysis of causality, it may well be asked with what justification Brown is classified with the philosophers of 'common sense' rather than as a follower of Hume. The answer is that though Brown accepts Hume's analysis of causal relation in terms of invariable or uniform sequence, he rejects the latter's account of the origin of our belief in necessary connection and in causation in general. According to Brown, there is an original belief in causation, which is antecedent to any effects of custom and association. 'The belief of regularity of sequence is so much the result of an original principle of the mind, that it arises constantly, on the observation of change, whatever the observed antecedents and consequents may have been, and requires the whole counteracting influence of our past knowledge to save us from the mistakes into which we should thus, at every moment, be in danger of falling.'[108] Further, 'the uniformity of the course of Nature, in the similar returns of future events, is not a conclusion of reason . . . but is a single intuitive judgment that, in certain circumstances, rises in the mind inevitably and with irresistible conviction. Whether true or false, the belief is in these cases felt, and it is felt without even the possibility of a perceived customary conjunction of the particular antecedent and the particular consequent.'[109] Belief in the uniformity of nature is not the result of custom and association; it is antecedent to observed sequences. What experience of customary succession does is to enable us to determine particular antecedents and their particular consequents. The trouble with Hume is his determination to derive all ideas from impressions, which forces him to explain belief in necessary connection and in the uniformity of nature in terms of observation of single sequences. But this belief is prior to such observation, and it is intuitive in character. 'In ascribing the belief of efficiency to such a principle, we place it, then, on a foundation as strong as that on which we suppose our belief of an external world, and even of our own identity, to rest.'[110] Brown goes further than Reid or Stewart in accepting Hume's analysis of causality, which he is prepared to extend to the mental sphere, and even to divine power. But he endeavours to combine this acceptance with an acceptance of the doctrine of intuitive beliefs, which was characteristic of the Scottish philosophy of common sense. In so doing he gives a new colouring to Reid's first principles. He tells us, for instance, that 'the proposition, *Everything which begins to exist must have had a cause of its existence*, is not itself an independent axiom, but is reducible to this more general law of thought, *Every change has had a cause of its existence in some circumstance, or combination of circumstances, immediately prior*'.[111]

In his *Lectures on the Philosophy of the Human Mind*, which were published after his death, Brown assimilates the study of mental phenomena to that of physical phenomena. 'The same great objects are to be had in view, and no other—the analysis of what is complex, and the observation and arrangement of the sequences of phenomena, as respectively antecedent and consequent.'[112] In both cases our knowledge is confined to phenomena. 'The philosophy of mind and the philosophy of matter agree in this respect, that our knowledge is, in both, confined to the mere phenomena.'[113] Brown does not question the existence of matter or the existence of mind; but we use these words, he insists, to connote the unknown causes of the respective sets of phenomena. Our knowledge of mind and matter is relative. We know matter as it affects us and mind in the varying mental phenomena of which we are conscious. A science of mind, therefore, so far as it is open to us, will consist in the analysis of mental phenomena and in the observation and systematic arrangement of causal sequences, that is, of regular sequences, in these phenomena.

The announcement of this programme does not mean, however, that Brown has abandoned belief in primary truths or intuited principles. He does, indeed, remark that the assertion of such principles can be carried to 'an extravagant and ridiculous length—as, indeed, seems to me to have been the case in the works of Dr. Reid and some other Scotch philosophers, his contemporaries and friends'.[114] If this habit is indulged, it only encourages mental laziness. At the same time 'it is not less certain that of our mental nature such principles are truly a part'.[115] Brown does not attempt to give a list of those principles, but among first principles of belief he mentions 'that on which I conceive the conviction of our identity to be founded'.[116] Our belief in our identities as permanent beings is universal, irresistible and immediate; and it is prior to, or presupposed by, reasoning. It is, therefore, an intuitive belief. Brown finds that it is 'another form of the faith which we put in memory':[117] it is 'founded on an essential principle of our constitution, in consequence of which it is impossible for us to consider our successive feelings[118] without regarding them as truly our successive feelings, states, or affections of our thinking substance'.[119]

In the same *Lectures* Brown vigorously criticizes Reid's refutation of the 'theory of ideas'. In his opinion Reid attributed to the majority of philosophers a view which they did not in fact maintain, namely, that ideas are entities which occupy a position intermediate between perceptions and the things perceived. In reality, Brown maintains, these philosophers understood by ideas the perceptions themselves. Further, he finds himself in agreement with the view of these philosophers that it is sensations and perceptions of which we are immediately aware, and not of an independent material world. Sensations, when referred to an external cause, are called perceptions. The question arises, therefore, what is this reference, in consequence of which a new name is given to sensations? For Brown, 'it is the suggestion of some extended resisting object, the presence of which had before been found to be attended with that particular sensation, which is now again referred to it'.[120] In other words, our primary knowledge of the material is due to touch. More accurately, it is due to muscular sensations. The child encounters resistance and, guided by the principle of causation, it finds the cause of this resistance in something other than itself. Brown distinguished between muscular sensations and other feelings commonly ascribed to the sense of touch. 'The feeling of resistance is, I conceive, to be ascribed, not to our organ of touch, but to our muscular frame, to which I have already more than once directed your attention as forming a distinct organ of sense.'[121] Our notion of extension is originally due

to muscular sensations as known in time. If a child gradually
stretches its arm or closes its hand, it has a succession of feelings, and this gives it the notion of length. The notions of
breadth and depth can be analogously explained. But in order to arrive at belief in an independent material reality the
muscular feeling of resistance must be added to the notion
of extension. 'Extension, resistance—to combine these simple
notions into something which is not ourselves, and to
have the notion of matter, are precisely the same thing.'[122]
The feelings of extension and resistance are referred to an
external, material world; but this independent world, considered in itself, is unknown to us.

From what has been said hitherto it is clear that Brown
was very far from simply carrying on the positions adopted
by Reid and Stewart. Indeed, he frequently adopted a critical
attitude towards their opinions. We would expect him, then,
to show a similar vigorous independence in his ethical reflections. In Brown's opinion moral philosophy has suffered from
the making of distinctions which seemed to those who made
them to be the result of accurate analysis, but which were
only verbal. For example, some have thought that questions
such as, what makes an action virtuous, what constitutes the
moral obligation to perform certain actions, and what constitutes the merit of the agent of such actions, are distinct
questions. But 'to say that any action which we are considering is right or wrong, and to say that the person who performed it has moral merit or demerit, are to say precisely the
same thing'.[123] 'To have merit, to be virtuous, to have done
our duty, to have acted in conformity with obligation—all
have reference to one feeling of the mind, that feeling of
approbation which attends the consideration of virtuous actions. They are merely, as I have said, different modes of
stating one simple truth; that the contemplation of anyone,
acting as we have done in a particular case, excites a feeling of
moral approval.'[124] We can ask, of course, why it seems to
us virtuous to act in this or that way. Why do we have a feeling of obligation? And so on. But 'the only answer which we
can give to these questions is the same to all, that it is impossible for us to consider the action without feeling that, by
acting in this way, we should look upon ourselves, and others
would look on us, with approving regard; and that if we were
to act in a different way we should look upon ourselves, and
others would look upon us, with abhorrence, or at least with
disapprobation'.[125] If we say that we regard an action as vir-

tuous because it tends to the public good or because it represents the divine will, similar questions will recur, and a like answer will have to be given. Certainly, we can and do consider actions in themselves, apart from any particular agent, and we can and do consider virtuous qualities or dispositions in themselves; but here we have abstractions, useful abstractions no doubt, but still abstractions.

Brown insists, however, that when he says that it is vain to ask why we feel the obligation to perform certain actions, he is speaking of inquiry into the nature of the mind. If we look beyond the mind itself, we can find the answer. The case of our belief in the uniformity of nature presents us with an analogous situation. If we consider the mind alone, we cannot say why we expect future events to resemble past events: we can only say that the mind is so constituted. But there are obvious reasons why the mind has been so constituted. For example, if we had been constituted with the opposite expectation, we could not live; we could not provide for the future, nor could we take steps to avoid dangers by learning from past experience. Similarly, if we had no feelings of moral approbation and disapprobation, if there were no virtue or vice, no love of God or man, human life would be wretched in the extreme. 'We know, then, in this sense, why our mind has been so constituted as to have these emotions; and our inquiry leads us, as all other inquiries ultimately lead us, to the provident goodness of him by whom we were made.'[126]

Given this view of moral approbation, Hume's utilitarian interpretation of morality is naturally rejected by Brown. 'That virtuous actions do all tend in some greater or less degree to the advantage of the world, is indeed a fact, with respect to which there can be no doubt.'[127] But 'the approbation which we give to actions as virtuous, whether we be ourselves the agents, or merely consider the actions of others, is not given to them simply as useful. Utility, in either case, is not the measure of moral approbation. . . .'[128] For the matter of that, conduciveness to the public good is itself an object of moral approbation. The reason why thinkers such as Hume find it easy to slip into a utilitarian interpretation of morality is that there is an 'independent pre-established relation of virtue and utility',[129] established, that is to say, by God.

Does this mean that Brown accepts the theory of a moral sense? If by the word 'sense' were meant merely susceptibility, then, inasmuch as we undoubtedly possess a susceptibility for moral feelings, we could speak of a moral sense. In this case, however, we should have to speak of as many 'senses' as there are distinguishable kinds of feeling. But the moral sense theorists understood something more by 'sense' than mere susceptibility. They were thinking of a peculiar moral sense analogous to the various senses such as sight and touch. And Brown can 'discover no peculiar analogy to perceptions or sensations, in the philosophical meaning of those terms, and the phrase "moral sense", therefore, I consider as having had a very unfortunate influence on the controversy as to the original moral differences of actions, from the false analogies which it cannot fail to suggest'.[130] Hutcheson's great mistake was to believe that there are certain moral qualities in actions, which excite in us ideas of those qualities in the same way that external things give us ideas of colour, form and hardness. But right and wrong are not qualities of things. 'They are words expressive only of relation, and relations are not existing parts of objects or things. . . . There is no right nor wrong, virtue nor vice, merit or demerit, existing independently of the agents who are virtuous or vicious; and, in like manner, if there had been no moral emotions to arise on the contemplation of certain actions, there would have been no virtue, vice, merit or demerit, which express only relations to these emotions.'[131]

There is another error to which some philosophers have been prone. In considering the aesthetic emotions they suppose that there is a universal beauty which is diffused, as it were, in all beautiful things. Similarly, they have imagined that there must be one universal virtue, diffused in all virtuous actions. Hence some have made of benevolence a universal virtue. 'There is no virtue, however, as I have already repeatedly said; there are only virtuous actions; or, to speak still more correctly, only virtuous agents: and it is not one virtuous agent only, or any number of virtuous agents, acting in one uniform manner, that excite our moral emotion of regard; but agents acting in many different ways—in ways that are not less different in themselves, on account of the real or supposed simplicity of the generalizations and classifications which we may have made.'[132] Brown does not deny, of course, that we can generalize and classify. But he rejects any attempt to reduce all virtuous actions to one class.

Brown's 'empiricist' tendency shows itself in what he has to say on evidence for God's existence. He remarks several times that he rejects all *a priori* reasonings on this matter, and, indeed, all metaphysical arguments except in so far as they can be reduced to what he calls the physical argument. 'The arguments commonly termed metaphysical I have always regarded as absolutely void of force, unless in as far as they proceed on a tacit assumption of the physical argument.'[133] By the physical argument Brown means the argument from design. 'The universe exhibits indisputable marks of design, and is, therefore, not self-existing, but the work of a designing mind. There exists, then, a great designing mind.'[134] Brown argues that the universe exhibits a harmony of relations, and that to perceive this harmony is to perceive design. 'That is to say, it is impossible for us to perceive them without feeling immediately, that the harmony of parts with parts, and of their results with each other, must have had its origin in some designing mind.'[135] But Brown seems to take it for granted that this argument also shows the existence of God as maker or author of the universe. He does not appear to realize that the argument from design, considered by itself, shows only that there is a designer, not that there is, in the strict sense, a creator.

When speaking of the divine unity, Brown again rejects all metaphysical arguments as, at best, 'a laborious trifling with words, which either signify nothing or prove nothing'.[136] Hence the only divine unity which we can prove is 'wholly relative to that one design which we are capable of tracing in the frame of the universe'.[137] And this anti-metaphysical attitude comes out again in his treatment of the divine goodness. That God is not malevolent 'the far greater proportion of the marks of benevolent intention sufficiently indicates'.[138] In other words, Brown argues that if we weigh the proportion of good to evil in the universe, we shall find that the former exceeds the latter. As for the moral goodness of God, His character is manifested in His gift to man of moral feelings. And we on our part are led by our very nature to regard what we look on with moral approbation or disapprobation as 'objects of approbation or disapprobation, not to all mankind only, but to every being whom we imagine to contemplate the actions, and especially to him who, as quickest to perceive and to know, must, as we think, by this very superiority of discernment, be quickest also to approve and condemn'.[139]

Obviously, if anyone accepts the kind of metaphysical arguments which Brown rejects, he will look on the latter's natural theology as constituting one of the weakest, or more probably the weakest, parts of his philosophy. If, however, he thinks that propositions about God are at best empirical hypotheses, he will presumably sympathize with Brown's general attitude, even if he does not regard the latter's arguments as cogent.

9. Kant's opinion of the Scottish philosophers of common sense was not a high one. His remarks about them in the introduction to the *Prolegomena to any Future Metaphysic* have been often quoted. Hume's opponents, says Kant, such as Reid, Oswald and Beattie, missed the point altogether. For they assumed what he doubted and undertook to prove what he never thought of disputing. Further, they appealed to common sense as to an oracle, using it as a criterion of truth when they had no rational justification to offer for their opinions. In any case 'I should think Hume might fairly have laid as much claim to sound sense as Beattie, and besides to a critical understanding such as the latter did not possess. . . .'

This judgment was doubtless prompted primarily by Beattie's performance; and he was far from being the best representative of the Scottish School. However, there is obviously some justification for Kant's remarks. After all, Brown, himself a Scottish philosopher, drew attention to the undesirability of laying down a multitude of inviolable first principles of common sense. We cannot set bounds in this dogmatic way to critical analysis. Further, both Stewart and Brown noted that Hume had often been misunderstood by the earlier philosophers of the common-sense tradition. And they were justified in doing so.

Further, it may appear that the development of the Scottish common-sense philosophy provides empirical evidence for the soundness of Kant's criticism. For, as we have seen, this movement which began, in large part at least, as a vigorous reaction against Hume's theories, gradually came nearer, on several important points, to the latter's philosophy. Moreover, from some of Brown's positions to the position of J. S. Mill there was no great step to be taken. For example, though Brown affirmed the existence of an independent material world, matter in itself was, in his opinion, unknown by us. We know sensations, and belief in the independent material world arises through a combination of the acquired notion of extension and the notion of external reference acquired by muscular experience of resistance. The distance does not seem to be so very great from this position to Mill's view of the world as a permanent possibility of sensations.

It is thus arguable that in proportion as the employment of critical analysis advanced within the common-sense School, this philosophy approximated more and more to empiricism, and that this is an indication of its untenable character in the earlier forms which were attacked by Kant.

Yet the common-sense philosophy obviously had something to say for itself. Reid's attack on the 'theory of ideas' was not entirely without point. It is true, as Brown remarks, that Reid inclined to treat the philosophers who spoke of perceiving ideas as though they all held pretty much the same theory, namely, that the ideas which we perceive are intermediate entities between minds and things. And this interpretation does not fit Berkeley, for instance, who called sensible things 'ideas'. But it is applicable to Locke, if we concentrate on one of his ways of speaking. In any case it is arguable that the language of ideas was unfortunate, that the philosophers who used this language became victims of their own way of speaking and that what Reid was doing was to recall philosophers to the position of common sense and to underline the need for delimiting carefully the meanings of terms such as 'idea' and 'perception'. Again, when Reid objected to the epistemological atomism of Locke and Hume and drew attention to the fundamental role of judgment, maintaining that the supposed elements of cognition were obtained by analytic abstraction from a larger whole, he was putting forward a point of view which certainly merited attention.

As for the general recall to common sense, some distinctions must, I think, be made. In so far as the Scottish philosophers were suggesting that we should regard with some suspicion those theories which are incompatible with common experience or which are plainly at variance with the beliefs and presuppositions which are necessary for life, their point of view was sound. At the same time people like Beattie do not seem to have understood that David Hume was not concerned to reject natural beliefs or to deny the standpoint of common sense. He was concerned to examine the theoretical reasons which can be adduced to support these beliefs. And even when he thought that no valid theoretical reasons or proofs could be adduced, he did not suggest that we should abandon these beliefs. Indeed, his point of view was that in practice belief must prevail over the dissolvent effects of the critical reason. Hence the Scottish philosophers' criticism of Hume frequently missed the mark altogether. It was not sufficient to offer a large number of principles of common sense, especially when the tendency was to depict these principles as representing inevitable propensities of the human mind. What they should have done, if they wished to refute Hume, was to show either that the validity of Hume's natural beliefs, which he accounted for with the aid of association, could be theoretically proved or that the so-called principles of common sense really were intuitively perceived self-evident rational principles. Or, more accurately, they should have concentrated on the second alternative, since in their view the first principles of common sense could not be demonstrated. It was not enough merely to assert the principles. For it would have been open to Hume to retort that in some cases at least what were called principles of common sense simply expressed natural beliefs which could be accounted for psychologically but which could not be philosophically proved, however necessary they might be for practical life. It is really no great matter for surprise that the Scottish philosophy of common sense was overshadowed in the nineteenth century by empiricism on the one hand and idealism on the other. And when something resembling a philosophy of common sense came again to the fore in contemporary British thought it took a new form, namely, the form of linguistic analysis.

On the continent of Europe the Scottish movement was not without success. Through Victor Cousin (1792–1867) in particular it exercised a very considerable influence on what was for a time the official philosophy of France. The French philosophers who were influenced by the Scottish movement saw further than the features which excited Kant's critical comments. They saw, for example, and approved the direction of the mind towards ethical and practical questions, the use of the experimental method, and the tendency to concentrate on available factual data rather than on abstract speculations. And it is true in a sense that for the Scottish thinkers philosophy was less of a game than it was for their great compatriot, Hume. It would, indeed, be misleading to suggest that for Hume philosophy was no more than a game. He thought, for example, that an analytic and critical philosophy can be a powerful instrument for diminishing fanaticism and intolerance. And, on the positive side, he envisaged the rise of a science of man which might be analogous to the physical science of Galileo and Newton. At the same time he did sometimes speak of his philosophy, especially in what appeared to Reid as its more destructive aspects, as a matter for the study, as having little connection with practical life. Reid and Stewart, however, evidently regarded philosophy as of importance for man's ethical and political life; and they were concerned not merely to investigate why people think and speak as they do, but to reinforce the convictions which they regarded as valuable. And their French admirers, accustomed to see in philosophy a guide to life, found this element in their thought congenial.

Reid's great thesis, so far as his attack on Hume was concerned, was that the latter simply drew in a clear and consistent manner the conclusions which followed from the premisses laid down by his predecessors. And he was thus partly responsible for a common and influential interpretation of the development of classical British empiricism. To a certain extent this thesis was shared by Kant, to the extent at least of considering that a fresh hypothesis should be prepared and that a fresh explanation was needed of man's cognitive life and of his moral and aesthetic judgments. But though Hume provided, in part, a point of departure not only for Reid but also for Kant, the latter is of vastly more importance in the history of philosophy than the philosopher of common sense. And his system will be considered at some length in the next volume.

APPENDIX

A Short Bibliography

For general remarks and for General Works see the Bibliography at the end of A HISTORY OF PHILOSOPHY, Volume 4, *Modern Philosophy: Descartes to Leibniz.*

Chapters Eleven–Thirteen: Berkeley

Texts

The Works of George Berkeley, Bishop of Cloyne. Edited by A. A. Luce and T. E. Jessop. 9 vols. London, 1948 (critical edition).

The Works of George Berkeley. Edited by A. C. Fraser. 4 vols. Oxford, 1901 (2nd edition).

Philosophical Commentaries, generally called the Commonplace Book. An editio diplomatica edited with introduction and notes by A. A. Luce. London, 1944.
(The *Philosophical Commentaries* are also contained in the critical edition of the Works, vol. 1.)

A New Theory of Vision and other Select Philosophical Writings (*Principles of Human Knowledge* and *Three Dialogues*), with an introduction by A. D. Lindsay. London (E.L.).

Berkeley: Selections. Edited by M. W. Calkins. New York, 1929.

Berkeley: Philosophical Writings. Selected and edited by T. E. Jessop. London, 1952.

Berkeley: Alciphron ou le Pense-menu. Translated with introduction and notes by J. Pucelle. Paris, 1952.

Studies

Baladi, N. *La pensée religieuse de Berkeley et l'unité de sa philosophie.* Cairo, 1945.

Bender, F. *George Berkeley's Philosophy re-examined*. Amsterdam, 1946.

Broad, C. D. *Berkeley's Argument about Material Substance*. London, 1942.

Cassirer, E. *Berkeley's System*. Giessen, 1914.

Del Bocca, S. *L'unità del pensiero di Giorgio Berkeley*. Florence, 1937.

Fraser, A. C. *Berkeley*. Edinburgh and London, 1881.

Hedenius, I. *Sensationalism and Theology in Berkeley's Philosophy*. Oxford, 1936.

Hicks, G. Dawes. *Berkeley*. London, 1932.

Jessop, T. E. *Great Thinkers: XI, Berkeley* (in *Philosophy* for 1937).

Johnston, G. A. *The Development of Berkeley's Philosophy*. London, 1923.

Joussain, A. *Exposé critique de la philosophie de Berkeley*. Paris, 1920.

Laky, J. J. *A Study of George Berkeley's Philosophy in the Light of the Philosophy of St. Thomas Aquinas*. Washington, 1950.

Luce, A. A. *Berkeley and Malebranche: A Study in the Origins of Berkeley's thought*. New York, 1934.

  Berkeley's Immaterialism: A Commentary on His Treatise concerning the Principles of Human Knowledge. London, 1945.

  The Life of George Berkeley, Bishop of Cloyne. London, 1949.

Metz, R. G. *Berkeleys Leben und Lehre*. Stuttgart, 1925.

Oertel, H. J. *Berkeley und die englische Literatur*. Halle, 1934.

Olgiati, F. *L'idealismo di Giorgio Berkeley ed il suo significato storico*. Milan, 1926.

Penjon, A. *Étude sur la vie et sur les œuvres philosophiques de George Berkeley, évêque de Cloyne*. Paris, 1878.

Ritchie, A. D. *George Berkeley's 'Siris'* (British Academy Lecture). London, 1955.

Sillem, E. A. *George Berkeley and the Proofs for the Existence of God*. London, 1957.

Stäbler, E. *George Berkeleys Auffassung und Wirkung in der deutschen Philosophie bis Hegel*. Dresden, 1935.

Stammler, G. *Berkeleys Philosophie der Mathematik*. Berlin, 1922.

Testa, A. *La filosofia di Giorgio Berkeley*. Urbino, 1943.

Warnock, G. J. *Berkeley*. Penguin Books, 1953.

Wild, J. *George Berkeley: A Study of His Life and Philosophy*. London, 1936.

Wisdom, J. O. *The Unconscious Origins of Berkeley's Philosophy*. London, 1953.

See also *Hommage to George Berkeley*. A commemorative issue of *Hermathena*. Dublin, 1953. And the commemorative issue of the *British Journal for the Philosophy of Science*. Edinburgh, 1953.

Chapters Fourteen–Seventeen: Hume

Texts

The Philosophical Works of David Hume. Edited by T. H. Green and T. H. Grose. 4 vols. London, 1874–5.

A Treatise of Human Nature. Edited by L. A. Selby-Bigge. Oxford, 1951 (reprint of 1888 edition).

A Treatise of Human Nature. With an introduction by A. D. Lindsay. 2 vols. London (E.L.).

An Abstract of a Treatise of Human Nature, 1740. Edited by J. M. Keynes and P. Sraffa. Cambridge, 1938.

Enquiries concerning the Human Understanding and concerning the Principles of Morals. Edited by L. A. Selby-Bigge. Oxford, 1951 (reprint of second edition, 1902).

Dialogues concerning Natural Religion. Edited with an introduction by N. K. Smith. London, 1947 (2nd edition).

The Natural History of Religion. Edited by H. Chadwick and with an introduction by H. E. Root. London, 1956.

Political Essays. Edited by C. W. Hendel. New York, 1953.

Hume: Theory of Knowledge. (Selections.) Edited by D. C. Yalden-Thomson. Edinburgh and London, 1951.

Hume: Theory of Politics. (Selections.) Edited by E. Watkins. Edinburgh and London, 1951.

Hume: Selections. Edited by C. W. Hendel. New York, 1927.

The Letters of David Hume. Edited by J. V. T. Grieg. 2 vols. Oxford, 1932.

New Letters of David Hume. Edited by R. Klibansky and E. C. Mossner. Oxford, 1954.

Studies

Bagolini, L. *Esperienza giuridica e politica nel pensiero di David Hume*. Siena, 1947.

Brunius, T. *David Hume on Criticism*. Stockholm, 1952.

Church, R. W. *Hume's Theory of the Understanding*. London, 1935.

Corsi, M. *Natura e società in David Hume*. Florence, 1954.

Dal Pra, M. *Hume*. Milan, 1949.

Della Volpe, G. *La filosofia dell' esperienza di David Hume*. Florence, 1939.

Didier, J. *Hume*. Paris, 1912.

Elkin, W. B. *Hume, the Relation of the Treatise Book I to the Inquiry*. New York, 1904.

Glatke, A. B. *Hume's Theory of the Passions and of Morals*. Berkeley, U.S.A., 1950.

Greig, J. V. T. *David Hume*. (Biography.) Oxford, 1931.

Hedenius, L. *Studies in Hume's Aesthetics*. Uppsala, 1937.

Hendel, C. W. *Studies in the Philosophy of David Hume*. Princeton, U.S.A., 1925.

Huxley, T. *David Hume*. London, 1879.

Jessop, T. E. *A Bibliography of David Hume and of Scottish Philosophy from Francis Hutcheson to Lord Balfour*. London, 1938.

Kruse, V. *Hume's Philosophy in His Principal Work, A Treatise of Human Nature*. Translated by P. E. Federspiel. London, 1939.

Kuypers, M. S. *Studies in the Eighteenth-Century Background of Hume's Empiricism*. Minneapolis, U.S.A., 1930.

Kydd, R. M. *Reason and Conduct in Hume's* Treatise. Oxford, 1946.

Laing, B. M. *David Hume*. London, 1932.
    Great Thinkers: XII, Hume (in *Philosophy* for 1937).

Laird, J. *Hume's Philosophy of Human Nature*. London, 1932.

Leroy, A-L. *La critique et la religion chez David Hume*. Paris, 1930.

MacNabb, D. G. *David Hume: His Theory of Knowledge and Morality*. London, 1951.

Magnino, B. *Il pensiero filosofico di David Hume*. Naples, 1935.

Maund, C. *Hume's Theory of Knowledge: A Critical Examination*. London, 1937.

Metz, R. *David Hume, Leben und Philosophie*. Stuttgart, 1929.

Mossner, E. C. *The Forgotten Hume: Le bon David*. New York, 1943.
    The Life of David Hume. London, 1954. (The fullest biography to date.)

Passmore, J. A. *Hume's Intentions.* Cambridge, 1952.
Price, H. H. *Hume's Theory of the External World.* Oxford, 1940.
Smith, N. K. *The Philosophy of David Hume.* London, 1941.

Chapter Eighteen: For and Against Hume

1. Adam Smith

Texts

Collected Works. 5 vols. Edinburgh, 1811–12.
The Theory of Moral Sentiments. London, 1759, and subsequent editions.
The Wealth of Nations. 2 vols. London, 1776, and subsequent editions.
The Wealth of Nations. With an introduction by E. R. A. Seligman. 2 vols. London (*E.L.*).

Studies

Bagolini, L. *La simpatia nella morale e nel diritto: Aspetti del pensiero di Adam Smith.* Bologna, 1952.
Chevalier, M. *Étude sur Adam Smith et sur la fondation de la science économique.* Paris, 1874.
Hasbach, W. *Untersuchungen über Adam Smith.* Leipzig, 1891.
Leiserson, A. *Adam Smith y su teoría sobre il salario.* Buenos Aires, 1939.
Limentani, L. *La morale della simpatia di Adam Smith nella storia del pensiero inglese.* Genoa, 1914.
Paszhowsky, W. *Adam Smith als Moralphilosoph.* Halle, 1890.
Rae, J. *Life of Adam Smith.* London, 1895.
Schubert, J. *Adam Smiths Moralphilosophie.* Leipzig, 1890.
Scott, W. R. *Adam Smith as Student and Professor.* Glasgow, 1937.
Small, A. W. *Adam Smith and Modern Sociology.* London, 1909.

2. Price

Text

A Review of the Principal Questions in Morals. Edited by D. Daiches Raphael. Oxford, 1948.

Study

Raphael, D. Daiches. *The Moral Sense.* Oxford, 1947. (This

work deals with Hutcheson, Hume, Price and Reid.)

3. Reid

Texts

Works. Edited by D. Stewart. Edinburgh, 1804.

Works. Edited by W. Hamilton. 2 vols. Edinburgh, 1846.
  (6th edition, with additions by H. L. Mansel, 1863.)

Œuvres complètes de Thomas Reid. Translated by T. S.
  Jouffroy. 6 vols. Paris, 1828–36.

Essays on the Intellectual Powers of Man. (Abridged.) Edited by A. D. Woozley. London, 1941.

Philosophical Orations of Thomas Reid. (Delivered at Grad-
  uation Ceremonies.) Edited by W. R. Humphries. Aberdeen, 1937.

Studies

Bahne-Jensen, A. Gestaltanalytische Untersuchung zur Erk-
  enntnislehre Reids. Glückstadt, 1941.

Dauriac, L. Le réalisme de Reid. Paris, 1889.

Fraser, A. C. Thomas Reid. Edinburgh and London, 1898.

Latimer, J. F. Immediate Perception as held by Reid and
  Hamilton considered as a Refutation of the Scepticism of
  Hume. Leipzig, 1880.

Peters, R. Reid als Kritiker von Hume. Leipzig, 1909.

Sciacca, M. F. La filosofia di Tommaso Reid con un'appen-
  dice sui rapporti con Gallupi e Rosmini. Naples, 1936.

4. Beattie

Texts

Essay on the Nature and Immutability of Truth. Edinburgh,
  1770, and subsequent editions.

Dissertations Moral and Critical. London, 1783.

Elements of Moral Science. 2 vols. Edinburgh, 1790–3.

Study

Forbes, W. An Account of the Life and Writings of James
  Beattie. 2 vols. Edinburgh, 1806 (2nd edition, 3 vols.,
  1807).

5. Stewart

Texts

Collected Works. Edited by W. Hamilton. 11 vols. Edinburgh, 1854–8.

Elements of the Philosophy of the Human Mind. 3 vols. Edinburgh, 1792–1827, and subsequent editions.
Outlines of Moral Philosophy. Edinburgh, 1793 (with notes by J. McCosh, London, 1863).
Philosophical Essays. Edinburgh, 1810.
Philosophy of the Active and Moral Powers of Man. Edinburgh, 1828.

Study

A Memoir by J. Veitch is included in the 1858 edition of Stewart's *Works.* The latter's eldest son, M. Stewart, published a Memoir in *Annual Biography and Obituary,* 1829.

6. *Brown*

Texts
An Inquiry into the Relation of Cause and Effect. London, 1818.
Lectures on the Philosophy of the Human Mind. Edited by D. Welsh. 4 vols. Edinburgh, 1820, and subsequent editions.
Lectures on Ethics. London, 1856.

Study
Welsh, D. *Account of the Life and Writings of Thomas Brown.* Edinburgh, 1825.

7. *General Works*

Text
Selections from the Scottish Philosophy of Common Sense. Chicago, 1915.

Studies
Jessop, T. E. *A Bibliography of David Hume and of Scottish Philosophy from Francis Hutcheson to Lord Balfour.* London, 1938.
Laurie, H. *Scottish Philosophy in its National Development.* Glasgow, 1902.
McCosh, J. *Scottish Philosophy from Hutcheson to Hamilton.* London, 1875.
Pringle-Pattison, A. S. *Scottish Philosophy: A Comparison of the Scottish and German Answers to Hume.* Edinburgh and London, 1885 and subsequent editions.

NOTES

CHAPTER ELEVEN

1 *Philosophical Commentaries*, 751; I, p. 91. References to Berkeley's writings by volume and page are to the critical edition of his Works by Professors A. A. Luce and T. E. Jessop. The *Philosophical Commentaries* will be referred to as *P.C.*; the *Essay towards a New Theory of Vision* as *E.*; the *Principles of Human Knowledge* as *P.*; the *Three Dialogues* as *D.*; the *De motu* as *D.M.*; *Alciphron* as *A.*

2 *P.C.*, 491; I, pp. 61–2.

3 Berkeley was not, indeed, indifferent to ecclesiastical preferment. And he had a family to maintain. But his plans for the evangelization of America, however abortive they may have proved, reveal him as an idealist, certainly not as a place-hunter.

4 *P.*, 1, 156; II, p. 113.

5 *D.*, sub-title; II, p. 147.

6 *E.*, 1; II, p. 171.

7 *E.*, 11; II, p. 173.

8 *E.*, 21; II, p. 175.

9 *E.*, 55; II, p. 191.

10 *E.*, 61; II, p. 194.

11 *E.*, 65; II, p. 195.

12 *E.*, 129; II, p. 223.

13 *Ibid.*

14 *E.*, 144; II, p. 229.

15 *E.*, 147; II, p. 231.

16 *E.*, 55; II, p. 191.

CHAPTER TWELVE

1 *P.C.*, 162; I, p. 22.

2 *P.C.*, 178; I, p. 24.

3 *Ibid.*

4 *P.C.*, 591; I, p. 73.

5 *P.C.*, 553; I, p. 69.

6 *P.C.*, 642; I, p. 78.

7 *P.C.*, 492; I, p. 62.

8 *P.C.*, 581; I, p. 72.

9 *P.C.*, 517; I, p. 64.

10 *P.C.*, 593; I, p. 74.

11 *P.*, Introduction, 6; II, p. 27.

12 *Ibid.*, 20; II, p. 37.

13 *Ibid.*, 24; II, p. 40.

14 *Ibid.*, 12; II, p. 31.

15 *Ibid.*, 10; II, p. 29.

16 *Ibid.*, 13; II, p. 33.

17 *Essay concerning Human Understanding*, 4, 7, 9.

18 *Ibid.*, 3, 3, 6.

19 *P.*, Introduction, 11; II, p. 31.

20 *Ibid.*, 12; II, p. 32.

21 *Ibid.*, 15; II, pp. 33–4.

22 *Ibid.*, 16; II, p. 35.

23 *P.*, 1, 3; II, p. 42.

24 *Ibid.*

25 *P.C.*, 429; I, p. 53.

26 P.C., 593; I, p. 74.
27 Cf., for example, Chapters III and IV of my *Contemporary Philosophy* (London, Burns and Oates, 1956).
28 P.C., 378; I, p. 45.
29 *Ibid.*
30 *Ibid.*
31 P.C., 24; I, p. 10.
32 P., 1, 3; II, p. 42.
33 P., 1, 1; II, p. 41.
34 P., 1, 4; II, p. 42.
35 *Ibid.*
36 P., 1, 5; II, p. 42.
37 P., 1, 9; II, pp. 44–5.
38 P., 1, 10; II, p. 45.
39 P., 1, 11; II, p. 46.
40 P., 1, 17; II, pp. 47–8.
41 The word 'supporting' must be understood, of course, in an active sense. Material substance, that is to say, is said to support accidents.
42 P., 1, 16; II, p. 47.
43 D., 1; II, p. 197.
44 *Ibid.*, p. 199.

45 Hylas might perhaps have replied that the reason why he could not satisfy Philonous's request for a clear and definite meaning was that the latter was asking him to describe the relation between substance and accidents in terms of some relation other than itself. But Philonous (Berkeley) held, of course, that phenomena are ideas. And in this case they cannot inhere in unthinking, senseless substance.
46 P., 1, 24; II, p. 51.
47 P.C., 807; I, p. 97.
48 P.C., 105; I, p. 38.
49 P., 1, 34; II, p. 55.
50 *Ibid.*
51 P., 1, 38; II, p. 57.
52 P., 1, 39; II, p. 57.
53 P., 1, 35; I, p. 55.
54 P., 1, 33; II, p. 54.
55 P.C., 606; I, p. 75.
56 P.C., 660; I, p. 80.

CHAPTER THIRTEEN

1 It may seem that Berkeley is contradicting himself. But when he said, as mentioned in the last chapter, that the term 'supporting accidents' is meaningless, he was referring to the alleged relation between material substance and ideas. Here he is speaking of the relation between spiritual substance or mind and ideas.
2 P., 1, 89; II, pp. 79–80.
3 P., 1, 139; II, p. 105.
4 P., 1, 135; II, p. 103.
5 *Ibid.*
6 P., 1, 27; II, p. 52.
7 P., 1, 140; II, p. 105.
8 *Ibid.*
9 P., 1, 138; II, p. 104.

10 P.C., 581; I, p. 72.
11 P., 1, 89; II, p. 80.
12 P., 1, 145; II, p. 107.
13 A., 4, 5; III, p. 147.
14 P., 1, 148; II, p. 109.
15 *Ibid.*
16 A., 4, 5; III, p. 147.
17 P., 1, 147; II, p. 108.
18 P.C., 580; I, p. 72.
19 P., 1, 138; II, p. 104.
20 If the existence of bodies is defined as *percipi*, then it is natural to define the existence of spirits or minds as *percipere*. For the two are correlative. But inasmuch as bodies are said to be ideas which are imprinted on minds and perceived by them, it is natural

to maintain that minds are substances which 'support' ideas and subjects which perceive ideas. Berkeley does not tidy up the confusion caused by his different ways of speaking.

21 P., 1, 141; II, p. 105.
22 Ibid., p. 106.
23 Ibid., p. 105.
24 Ibid., p. 106.
25 Ibid., p. 105.
26 P., 1, 34; II, p. 55.
27 P., 1, 62; II, p. 67.
28 D., 2; II, p. 211.
29 P., 1, 107; II, p. 88.
30 P., 1, 103; II, p. 86.
31 D.M., 1; IV, p. 11.
32 D.M., 53; IV, p. 24.
33 D.M., 66; IV, p. 28.
34 D.M., 17; IV, p. 15.
35 D.M., 39; IV, p. 20.
36 D.M., 35; IV, p. 19.
37 D.M., 69; IV, p. 29.
38 D.M., 36; IV, p. 20.
39 D.M., 72; IV, p. 30.
40 D.M., 71; IV, p. 30.
41 D.M., 4 and 6; IV, p. 32.
42 D.M., 7; IV, p. 12.
43 P.C., 782; I, p. 94.
44 A., 4, 2; III, p. 142.
45 P., 1, 146; II, pp. 107-8.
46 D., 2; II, p. 212.
47 P., 1, 148; II, p. 109.
48 P., 1, 152; II, p. 111.
49 A., 4, 23; III, p. 172.
50 Ibid.
51 A., 4, 16; III, p. 163.
52 A., 4, 17; III, p. 164.
53 Ibid.
54 Ibid.
55 A., 4, 20; III, pp. 168-9.
56 Ibid.
57 A., 4, 22; III, p. 171.
58 D., 3; II, pp. 231-2.
59 P., 1, 57; II, p. 65.
60 P., 1, 90; II, p. 80: cf. P.,

1, 1; II, p. 41.
61 D., 2; II, p. 215.
62 A., 4, 14; III, p. 159.
63 Ibid., pp. 159-60.
64 D., 3; II, pp. 245-7.
65 D., 2; II, p. 212.
66 Ibid.
67 D., 3; II, pp. 230-1.
68 Ibid., p. 252.
69 Ibid., p. 254.
70 Ibid., p. 252.
71 Siris, 253; V, p. 120.
72 Siris, 266; V, p. 125.
73 Siris, 289; V, pp. 134-5.
74 D., 3; II, p. 241.
75 P., 1, 65; II, p. 69.
76 A., 4, 14; III, p. 160.
77 D., 3; II, p. 237.
78 Ibid.
79 P.C., 800; I, p. 96.
80 P.C., 548; I, p. 69.
81 D., 2; II, p. 214.
82 P.C., 686; I, p. 83.
83 D., 3; II, p. 230.
84 D., 2; II, p. 213.
85 P.C., 824; I, p. 98.
86 P.C., 825; I, p. 98.
87 P.C., 822; I, p. 98.
88 I, pp. 251 f.
89 P.C., 688; I, p. 84.
90 E., 125; I, p. 221.
91 P.C., 717; I, p. 87.
92 P.C., 697; I, p. 85.
93 P.C., 755; I, p. 92.
94 P.C., 690; I, p. 84.
95 P.C., 853; I, p. 101.
96 P.C., 769; I, p. 93.
97 P.C., 773; I, p. 93.
98 P.C., 776; I, p. 93.
99 P., 1, 100; II, pp. 84-5.
100 A., 5, 4; III, p. 178.
101 Passive Obedience, 7; VI, p. 21.
102 A., 3, 10; III, p. 129.
103 A., 1, 12; III, p. 52.
104 Passive Obedience, 5; VI, p. 19.

105 *Ibid.*
106 *Ibid.*, 6; VI, p. 20.
107 *Ibid.*, 7; VI, p. 20.
108 *Ibid.*, 11; VI, p. 22.
109 *Ibid.*, 12; VI, p. 23.

110 *Ibid.*, 53; VI, p. 45.
111 P., 1, 92; II, p. 81.
112 *Dissertations and Discussions*, 4, 155.

CHAPTER FOURTEEN

1 Page-references to Hume's *Treatise* and *Enquiries* will be given according to the editions by L. A. Selby-Bigge (Oxford, 1951 reprint of 1888 edition of the *Treatise* and 1951 impression of 1902 edition of the *Enquiries*). The *Treatise* will be referred to as *T.*; the *Enquiry concerning Human Understanding* as *E.*, and the *Enquiry concerning the Principles of Morals* as *E.M.* Page-references to the *Dialogues concerning Natural Religion* will be given according to the edition by Norman Kemp Smith (Edinburgh, second edition, 1947), and the work will be referred to as *D.*
2 *T.*, Introduction, p. xx.
3 *Ibid.*
4 *Ibid.*, p. xxiii.
5 *E.*, 1, 2, p. 6.
6 *E.*, 1, 7, p. 12.
7 *E.*, 1, 9, p. 14.
8 *T.*, 1, 1, 1, p. 3.
9 *Ibid.*, p. 1.
10 *Ibid.*, p. 2.
11 *E.*, 2, 11, p. 17.
12 *T.*, 1, 1, 1, p. 3.
13 *Ibid.*
14 *Ibid.*, p. 5.
15 *Ibid.*, p. 6.
16 *T.*, 1, 1, 2, p. 7.
17 *E.*, 2, 17, p. 21.
18 *Ibid.*, p. 22.
19 2, 12, p. 18.

20 *E.*, 2, 17, note, p. 22.
21 *Ibid.*
22 *Ibid.*
23 *T.*, 1, 1, 3, p. 10.
24 *T.*, 1, 1, 4, p. 10.
25 *Ibid.*, p. 13.
26 *Ibid.*, p. 11.
27 *Ibid.*
28 *T.*, 1, 1, 6, p. 16.
29 *T.*, 1, 1, 5, p. 13.
30 *Ibid.*, pp. 14–15; cf. *T.*, 1, 3, 1, p. 69.
31 *T.*, 1, 1, 7, p. 17.
32 *Ibid.*, p. 18.
33 *Ibid.*, p. 20.
34 *Ibid.*, p. 22.
35 *E.*, 4, 1, 20–1, p. 25.
36 *T.*, 1, 3, 1, p. 70.
37 *Ibid.*, p. 71.
38 *Ibid.*
39 *Ibid.*
40 *E.*, 4, 1, 20, p. 25.
41 *E.*, 4, 1, 21, pp. 25–6.
42 *T.*, 1, 3, 2, p. 73.
43 *Ibid.*, p. 74.
44 *E.*, 4, 1, 22, p. 26.
45 *T.*, 1, 3, 2, p. 75.
46 *Ibid.*
47 *Ibid.*
48 *T.*, 1, 4, 5, p. 236.
49 *T.*, 1, 3, 2, p. 76.
50 *Ibid.*
51 *Ibid.*, p. 77.
52 *Ibid.*, p. 78.
53 *T.*, 1, 3, 3, p. 80.
54 *T.*, 1, 1, 3, 6, pp. 86–7.
55 *Ibid.*, p. 87.
56 *Ibid.*
57 *E.*, 7, 2, 59, pp. 74–5.

58 E., 7, 2, 60, p. 76.
59 T., 1, 3, 6, p. 89.
60 T., 1, 3, 12, p. 134.
61 Abstract, 16.
62 T., 1, 3, 6, p. 88.
63 T., 1, 3, 14, pp. 632-3, Appendix.
64 Ibid., p. 163.
65 Ibid., p. 165.
66 Ibid., p. 170.
67 Ibid.
68 T., 1, 3, 6, p. 94.
69 T., 1, 3, 3, p. 82.
70 T., 1, 3, 14, p. 172.
71 E., 8, 1, 74, p. 95.

72 Ibid.
73 T., 1, 3, 12, p. 132.
74 T., 1, 3, 14, p. 171.
75 Ibid.
76 For Nicholas of Autrecourt vol. III of this History may be consulted (pp. 147 f.).
77 T., 1, 3, 7, p. 96.
78 Ibid., p. 97.
79 Ibid., p. 629, Appendix.
80 Ibid.
81 T., 1, 3, 9, pp. 116-17.
82 T., 1, 3, 8, p. 103.
83 T., 1, 4, 1, p. 183.
84 E., 11, 110, p. 142.

CHAPTER FIFTEEN

1 T., 1, 2, 6, pp. 67-8.
2 T., 1, 4, 2, p. 187.
3 Ibid., p. 191.
4 Ibid., p. 193.
5 Ibid.
6 Ibid., p. 194.
7 Ibid., p. 195.
8 Ibid., p. 198.
9 Ibid., p. 199.
10 T., 1, 4, 1, p. 205.
11 Ibid.
12 Ibid.
13 Ibid., pp. 207-8.
14 Ibid., p. 209.
15 Ibid., p. 218.
16 T., 1, 4, 4, p. 228.
17 Ibid., p. 231.
18 Ibid.
19 E., 12, 1, 122, p. 155, note.
20 T., 1, 4, 5, p. 232.
21 Ibid., p. 234.
22 Ibid., p. 239.
23 Ibid., p. 235.
24 Ibid., p. 250.
25 T., 1, 4, 6, pp. 251-2.
26 Ibid., p. 252.
27 Ibid., p. 253.
28 Ibid., p. 261.
29 Ibid., p. 262.
30 T., pp. 635-6.

31 He seems to imply, verbally at least, that we attribute identity to our perceptions. But we obviously do not do this, even if we regard them as acts of a persistent subject.
32 E., 11, 104, p. 135.
33 E., 11, 105, pp. 135-6.
34 E., 11, 110, p. 142.
35 E., 11, 114, p. 148.
36 E., 11, 110, p. 142.
37 D., Preface, p. 128.
38 D., XII, p. 228.
39 D., II, p. 143.
40 D., IX, p. 190.
41 E., 11, 115, p. 148.
42 D., XII, p. 227.
43 E., 12, 1, 116, p. 149.
44 E., 12, 1, 117, p. 150.
45 Ibid.
46 T., 1, 4, 1-2, pp. 180-218.
47 E., 12, 1, 117, p. 151.
48 E., 12, 1, 118, p. 151.
49 Ibid., p. 152.
50 E., 12, 1, 119, p. 153.
51 E., 12, 1, 121, p. 153.
52 E., 12, 2, 124, p. 156.
53 E., 12, 2, 125, p. 157.
54 E., 12, 2, 126, pp. 158-9.
55 Ibid., p. 159.

56 *E.*, 12, 2, 125, pp. 157–8.
57 Cf. *E.*, 12, 2, 125, note, p. 158, and *T.*, 1, 2, 1–2.
58 *T.*, 1, 4, 2, p. 218.
59 *E.*, 12, 2, 128, pp. 159–60.
60 *T.*, 1, 4, 7, p. 269.
61 *E.*, 12, 3, 129, p. 161.
62 *E.*, 12, 3, 131, p. 163.
63 *E.*, 12, 3, 132, p. 164.
64 *Ibid.*, p. 165.
65 *Ibid.*
66 *Ibid.*
67 *T.*, 1, 4, 7, p. 273.
68 *E.*, 12, 2, 128, p. 160.
69 *E.*, 1, 4, p. 9.

CHAPTER SIXTEEN

1 p. xx.
2 *T.*, 1, 4, 6, p. 263.
3 *T.*, 1, 4, 7, p. 263.
4 *T.*, 3, 1, 3, p. 455.
5 *E.*, 1, 1–2, pp. 5–6.
6 *T.*, 1, 1, 3, p. 282.
7 *Ibid.*
8 *T.*, 2, 3, 3, p. 415.
9 *T.*, 2, 1, 1, p. 275.
10 *Ibid.*, p. 276.
11 *Ibid.*
12 *T.*, 2, 3, 9, p. 439.
13 *Ibid.*
14 *T.*, 2, 1, 2, p. 277.
15 *T.*, 2, 2, 1, p. 329.
16 *T.*, 2, 1, 3, p. 280.
17 *Ibid.*, p. 281.
18 *T.*, 2, 1, 4, p. 283.
19 *Ibid.*, p. 284.
20 *T.*, 2, 1, 5, p. 289.
21 *T.*, 2, 1, 11, p. 317.
22 *Ibid.*
23 *Ibid.*, p. 318.
24 *Ibid.*
25 *Ibid.*, p. 320.
26 *T.*, 3, 3, 1, p. 576.
27 *T.*, 2, 3, 1, p. 399.
28 *Ibid.*, p. 404.
29 *Ibid.*, p. 407.
30 *T.*, 2, 3, 3, p. 413.
31 *Ibid.*
32 *Ibid.*
33 *Ibid.*, p. 414.
34 *Ibid.*
35 *Ibid.*, pp. 414–15.
36 *Ibid.*, p. 415.
37 Here Hume uses the word 'emotion' in a literal sense to mean a felt or apparent movement.
38 *T.*, 2, 3, 3, p. 417.
39 *Ibid.*
40 *Ibid.*, p. 418.
41 *E.M.*, 1, 133, p. 170.
42 *E.M.*, 1, 134, p. 170.
43 *E.M.*, 1, 137, pp. 172–3.
44 *E.M.*, Appendix 1, 237, p. 287.
45 *T.*, 3, 1, 1, p. 463.
46 *Ibid.*, pp. 468–9.
47 *Ibid.*, p. 463.
48 *Ibid.*, p. 468.
49 *E.M.*, Appendix 1, 239, pp. 288–9.
50 *T.*, 3, 1, 2, p. 470.
51 *Ibid.*, p. 471.
52 *Ibid.*, p. 472.
53 *Ibid.*
54 *E.M.*, Appendix 1, 239, p. 289.
55 *T.*, 3, 2, 9, p. 552.
56 *T.*, 3, 1, 2, p. 475.
57 *E.M.*, 1, 138, p. 174.
58 *E.M.*, Appendix 1, 244, p. 293.
59 *Ibid.*
60 *Ibid.*, 245, pp. 293–4.
61 *E.M.*, 2, 1, 139, p. 176.
62 *E.M.*, 2, 2, 141, p. 178.
63 *Ibid.*, p. 179.
64 *E.M.*, Appendix 2, 251, p. 299.

65 *Ibid.*, 252, p. 300.
66 *Ibid.*, 253, p. 301.
67 *E.M.*, 5, 1, 177, p. 218.
68 *E.M.*, 5, 2, 178, p. 219.
69 *E.M.*, 5, 2, 178 note, pp. 219–20.
70 *T.*, 3, 2, 1, p. 481.
71 *Ibid.*
72 *E.M.*, 3, 1, 145, p. 183.
73 *T.*, 3, 2, 2, p. 489.
74 *Ibid.*, p. 490.
75 *Ibid.*
76 *Ibid.*, p. 491.
77 *Ibid.*, p. 498.

78 *Ibid.*
79 *Ibid.*, pp. 499–500.
80 *E.M.*, Appendix 3, 256, p. 304.
81 *T.*, 3, 2, 6, p. 526.
82 *T.*, 3, 2, 1, p. 477.
83 *T.*, 3, 2, 2, p. 489.
84 *T.*, 3, 2, 1, p. 483.
85 *E.M.*, 3, 1, 149, p. 188.
86 *T.*, 3, 2, 1, p. 484.
87 *E.M.*, Appendix 3, 255–6, pp. 303–4.
88 *T.*, 3, 2, 2, p. 496.

CHAPTER SEVENTEEN

1 *T.*, Introduction, pp. xix–xx.
2 *E.*, 12, 3, 132, pp. 164–5.
3 *Ibid.*, p. 165.
4 *D.*, I, p. 135.
5 *T.*, 3, 2, 2, p. 485.
6 *Ibid.*, p. 490.
7 *Ibid.*, p. 486.
8 *Ibid.*
9 *Ibid.*, p. 493.
10 *E.M.*, 3, 1, 151, p. 190.
11 *E.M.*, 4, 164, p. 205.
12 *T.*, 3, 2, 7, p. 539.
13 *T.*, 3, 2, 8, p. 541.
14 *Ibid.*, pp. 539–40.
15 *Of the Original Contract.*
16 *Ibid.*

17 *T.*, 3, 2, 8, p. 546.
18 *Ibid.*, p. 547.
19 *T.*, 3, 2, 9, pp. 550–1.
20 *E.M.*, 4, 164, p. 205.
21 *T.*, 3, 2, 9, p. 551.
22 *T.*, 3, 2, 10, p. 554.
23 *Ibid.*, p. 556.
24 *Ibid.*
25 *Ibid.*
26 *Ibid.*, p. 557.
27 *Ibid.*, p. 566.
28 *T.*, 3, 2, 11, p. 567.
29 *Ibid.*, pp. 568–9.
30 *Ibid.*, p. 569.
31 *Ibid.*

CHAPTER EIGHTEEN

1 This work will be referred to as *T.M.S.*
2 *T.M.S.*, 1, 1, 1, p. 2; 1812 edition.
3 *Ibid.*
4 *Ibid.*
5 *Ibid.*, p. 5.
6 *Ibid.*, p. 7.
7 *Ibid.*, p. 8.
8 *T.M.S.*, 1, 1, 3, p. 16.
9 *Ibid.*, p. 20.

10 *Ibid.*
11 *T.M.S.*, 1, 1, 4, p. 24.
12 *T.M.S.*, 4, 2, p. 325.
13 *Ibid.*
14 *Ibid.*, p. 326.
15 *Ibid.*
16 *T.M.S.*, 3, 1, p. 190.
17 *Ibid.*, p. 193.
18 *T.M.S.*, 3, 8, p. 231.
19 *T.M.S.*, 3, 4, p. 266.
20 *Ibid.*, p. 273.

21 *T.M.S.*, 3, 5, p. 276.
22 *Ibid.*, p. 279.
23 *Ibid.*, p. 291.
24 *T.M.S.*, 5, 2.
25 *T.M.S.*, 3, 6, p. 299.
26 *Ibid.*, p. 301.
27 *T.M.S.*, 7, 3, p. 579.
28 *Review*, 1, 3.
29 *Review*, 1, 2.
30 *Ibid.*
31 *Review*, 8.
32 *Ibid.*
33 *Ibid.*
34 *Review*, 9.
35 Dedication to the *Inquiry*.
36 References to the *Essays on the Powers of the Human Mind* are given according to the three-volume edition of 1819, while references to the *Inquiry* are also given according to 1819 edition.
37 *Essays*, 1, 1, 10; I, p. 38.
38 *Ibid.*, p. 39.
39 *Essays*, 2, 12; I, pp. 266–7.
40 *Ibid.*, p. 267.
41 *Inquiry*, 2, 6, pp. 60–1.
42 *Inquiry*, 2, 4, pp. 52–3.
43 *Inquiry*, 7, 4, p. 394.
44 *Ibid.*, pp. 394–5.
45 *Essays*, 6, 2; II, pp. 233–4.
46 *Ibid.*, p. 234.
47 *Ibid.*, p. 234.
48 *Ibid.*, p. 223.
49 *Essays*, 1, 2; I, p. 57.
50 *Essays*, 8, 3, 5; II, p. 338.
51 *Ibid.*
52 *Essays*, 8, 3, 6; II, p. 339.
53 *Ibid.*
54 *Ibid.*, p. 342.
55 *Ibid.*, p. 352.
56 *Essays*, 6, 5, 3; II, p. 304.
57 *Essays*, 6, 5, 5; II, p. 308.
58 *Essays*, 6, 5, 7; II, p. 314.
59 *Essays*, 6, 5, 12; II, p. 328.
60 *Essays*, 6, 5, 5; II, p. 308.
61 *Essays*, 6, 5, 12; II, p. 329.
62 *Essays*, 6, 5, 3, p. 305.
63 *Ibid.*
64 *Essays*, 5, 1; III, p. 451.
65 *Essays*, 6, 6, 6; II, p. 341.
66 *Essays*, 6, 5, 12; II, p. 329.
67 *Ibid.*
68 *Essays*, 6, 5, 7; II, p. 316.
69 *Ibid.*, p. 317.
70 *Inquiry*, 6, 4, p. 153.
71 *Ibid.*, pp. 156–7.
72 *Inquiry*, 6, 6, p. 163.
73 *Inquiry*, 1, 4, p. 32.
74 *Essay*, 1, 2, 9, p. 93; 1820 edition.
75 *Essay*, 2, 1, 1; p. 117.
76 *Essay*, 2, 1, 2, p. 140.
77 *Ibid.*, p. 141.
78 *Essay*, 3, 3, p. 385.
79 Adam Ferguson (1723–1816) published an *Essay on the History of Civil Society* (1767), *Institutes of Moral Philosophy* (1769), a *History of the Progress and Termination of the Roman Republic* (1783) and *Principles of Moral and Political Science* (1792). Hume had a high opinion of him and left him a legacy in his will.
80 *Outlines*, Introduction, 1, 3; II, p. 6. All page references are to the edition of Stewart's *Collected Works* by Sir William Hamilton, 1854–8.
81 *Essays*, 6, 6, 6; II, p. 345.
82 *Outlines*, Introduction, 2, 11; II, p. 8.
83 *Elements*, Introduction, 1; II, pp. 48–52.
84 In another sense psychology has a very broad range for Stewart.
85 *Elements*, 2, 1, 4, p. 301.
86 1, 5.
87 *Outlines*, 1, 9, 71; II, p. 28.
88 *Ibid.*
89 *Outlines*, 1, 9, 70; p. 27.

90 *Elements*, 2, 1, 1, 2, 4; III, p. 45.
91 Claude Buffier (1661–1737), a French Jesuit, published a *Traité des vérités premières* (1717) in which he treated of the maxims of common sense.
92 *Elements*, 2, 1, 1, 2, 1; III, p. 41.
93 *Ibid.*
94 *Elements*, 2, 1, 2, 4, 2; III, pp. 159–60.
95 *Active and Moral Powers*, 2, 3; VI, p. 233.
96 *Ibid.*, 2, 2; VI, p. 220.
97 *Ibid.*, 2, 5, 1; VI, p. 299.
98 *Ibid.*, 2, 6; VI, p. 319.
99 *Ibid.*, 3, 1; VII, p. 11.
100 *Ibid.*, 3, 2, 1; VII, p. 24.
101 *Ibid.*, p. 18.
102 Cf., *Works*, V, pp. 117–18, note, and p. 422.
103 1, 1; 1835 edition, p. 13.
104 *Ibid.*, p. 14.
105 *Ibid.*, 1, 3, p. 32.
106 *Ibid.*, p. 38.
107 *Ibid.*, 1, 5, p. 89.
108 *Ibid.*, 4, 2, pp. 286–7.
109 *Ibid.*, p. 290.
110 *Ibid.*, 4, 7, pp. 377–8.
111 *Ibid.*, Note H, p. 435.
112 *Lectures on the Philosophy of the Human Mind*, Lecture 9; vol. I, p. 178, 1824 edition.
113 *Ibid.*, Lecture 10; I, p. 194.
114 *Ibid.*, Lecture 13; I, p. 265.
115 *Ibid.*, p. 268.
116 *Ibid.*
117 *Ibid.*, p. 273.
118 Brown gives to the word 'feeling' a very wide range of meaning.
119 *Ibid.*, p. 275.
120 *Ibid.*, Lecture 25; I, p. 546.
121 *Ibid.*, Lecture 22; I, p. 460.
122 *Ibid.*, Lecture 24; I, p. 508.
123 *Ibid.*, Lecture 73; III, p. 529.
124 *Ibid.*, p. 532.
125 *Ibid.*, p. 533.
126 *Ibid.*, p. 543.
127 *Ibid.*, Lecture 77; IV, p. 29.
128 *Ibid.*, p. 51.
129 *Ibid.*, p. 54.
130 *Ibid.*, Lecture 82; IV, pp. 149–50.
131 *Ibid.*, pp. 161–2.
132 *Ibid.*, p. 169.
133 *Ibid.*, Lecture 93; IV, p. 387.
134 *Ibid.*, Lecture 92; IV, p. 369.
135 *Ibid.*, Lecture 93; IV, pp. 387–8.
136 *Ibid.*, p. 391.
137 *Ibid.*
138 *Ibid.*, p. 407.
139 *Ibid.*, Lecture 95; IV, p. 444.

INDEX

(Asterisked numbers refer to bibliographical information. References to a continuous series of pages, e.g. 33–43, do not necessarily indicate continuous treatment. References to two persons together are usually under the person criticized or influenced. Note abbreviations given in italics, e.g. *A.*, are referred to the pages explaining them fully.)

---

[1] At the time dealt with in this book philosophy and science were not so clearly distinguished as they are today. Hence identical matters may be mentioned and indexed under different names. This should be borne in mind when looking up any of the following subjects: natural philosophy; philosophy, experimental; philosophy of Nature; physics; science, experimental.

---

[1] See footnote on page 227.

OTHER IMAGE BOOKS

THE IMITATION OF CHRIST – Thomas à Kempis. Edited with an Introduction by Harold C. Gardiner, S.J. (D17) – $1.25

SAINT THOMAS AQUINAS – G. K. Chesterton (D36) – $1.45

ST. FRANCIS OF ASSISI – G. K. Chesterton (D50) – $1.25

VIPER'S TANGLE – François Mauriac. A novel of evil and redemption (D51) – 95¢

THE CITY OF GOD – St. Augustine. Edited by Vernon J. Bourke. Introduction by Étienne Gilson. Specially abridged (D59) – $2.45

RELIGION AND THE RISE OF WESTERN CULTURE – Christopher Dawson (D64) – $1.95

THE LITTLE FLOWERS OF ST. FRANCIS – Translated by Raphael Brown (D69) – $1.75

DARK NIGHT OF THE SOUL – St. John of the Cross. Edited and translated by E. Allison Peers (D78) – $1.25

THE CONFESSIONS OF ST. AUGUSTINE – Translated with an Introduction by John K. Ryan (D101) – $1.75

A HISTORY OF PHILOSOPHY: VOLUME 1 – GREECE AND ROME (2 Parts) – Frederick Copleston, S.J. (D134a, D134b) – $1.75 ea.

A HISTORY OF PHILOSOPHY: VOLUME 2 – MEDIAEVAL PHILOSOPHY (2 Parts) – Frederick Copleston, S.J. Part I – Augustine to Bonaventure. Part II – Albert the Great to Duns Scotus (D135a, D135b) – $1.75 ea.

A HISTORY OF PHILOSOPHY: VOLUME 3 – LATE MEDIAEVAL AND RENAISSANCE PHILOSOPHY (2 Parts) – Frederick Copleston, S.J. Part I – Ockham to the Speculative Mystics. Part II – The Revival of Platonism to Suárez (D136a, D136b) – $1.45 ea.

A HISTORY OF PHILOSOPHY: VOLUME 4 – MODERN PHILOSOPHY: Descartes to Leibniz – Frederick Copleston, S.J. (D137) – $1.75

A HISTORY OF PHILOSOPHY: VOLUME 5 – MODERN PHILOSOPHY: The British Philosophers, Hobbes to Hume (2 Parts) – Frederick Copleston, S.J. Part I – Hobbes to Paley (D138a) – $1.45. Part II – Berkeley to Hume (D138b) – $1.75

A HISTORY OF PHILOSOPHY: VOLUME 6 – MODERN PHILOSOPHY (2 Parts) – Frederick Copleston, S.J. Part I – The French Enlightenment to Kant (D139a) – $1.45; (D139b) – $1.75

A HISTORY OF PHILOSOPHY: VOLUME 7 – MODERN PHILOSOPHY (2 Parts) – Frederick Copleston, S.J. Part I – Fichte to Hegel. Part II – Schopenhauer to Nietzsche (D140a, D140b) – $1.75 ea.

These prices subject to change without notice

OTHER IMAGE BOOKS

A HISTORY OF PHILOSOPHY: VOLUME 8 — MODERN PHILOSOPHY: Bentham to Russell (2 Parts) — Frederick Copleston, S.J. Part I — British Empiricism and the Idealist Movement in Great Britain. Part II — Idealism in America, the Pragmatist Movement, the Revolt against Idealism (D141a, D141b) — $1.45 ea.

THE SPIRITUAL EXERCISES OF ST. IGNATIUS — Translated by Anthony Mottola, Ph.D. Introduction by Robert W. Gleason, S.J. (D170) — 95¢

LIFE AND HOLINESS — Thomas Merton. Exposition of the principles of the spiritual life (D183) — 85¢

WITH GOD IN RUSSIA — Walter J. Ciszek, S.J., with Daniel L. Flaherty, S.J. (D200) — $1.45

THE TWO-EDGED SWORD — John L. McKenzie, S.J. Outstanding interpretation of the Old Testament (D215) — $1.45

NO MAN IS AN ISLAND — Thomas Merton (D231) — $1.45

CONJECTURES OF A GUILTY BYSTANDER — Thomas Merton. A collection of notes, opinions, reflections (D234) — $1.75

THE NOONDAY DEVIL: Spiritual Support in Middle Age — Bernard Basset, S.J. A funny-serious book of spiritual direction (D237) — $1.25

HEALTH OF MIND AND SOUL — Ignace Lepp (D239) — 95¢

RELIGION AND PERSONALITY — Adrian van Kaam, C.S.Sp. (D240) — $1.45

RELIGIONS OF THE WORLD (2 Volumes) — John A. Hardon, S.J. An account of the history, beliefs, and practices of the major religions of the world (D241a) — $1.75; (D241b) — $1.45

CHRISTIAN SACRAMENTS AND CHRISTIAN PERSONALITY — Bernard J. Cooke, S.J. (D246) — $1.25

THOUGHTS IN SOLITUDE — Thomas Merton (D247) — 95¢

NEW TESTAMENT ESSAYS — Raymond E. Brown, S.S. (D251) — $1.45

TEILHARD DE CHARDIN AND THE MYSTERY OF CHRIST — Christopher Mooney, S.J. (D252) — $1.45

THE NEW TESTAMENT OF THE JERUSALEM BIBLE: Reader's Edition — Alexander Jones, General Editor (D253) — $1.65

THE FOUR GOSPELS: AN INTRODUCTION (2 Volumes) — Bruce Vawter, C.M. (D255a, D255b) — $1.25 ea.

THE PROTESTANT CHURCHES OF AMERICA — Revised Edition — John A. Hardon (D259) — $1.95

These prices subject to change without notice

OTHER IMAGE BOOKS

EXISTENTIAL FOUNDATIONS OF PSYCHOLOGY – Adrian van Kaam (D260) – $1.75

THE CATHOLIC EXPERIENCE – An Interpretation of the History of American Catholicism – Andrew M. Greeley (D261) – $1.45

MORALITY FOR OUR TIME – Marc Oraison (D266) – $1.25

SUMMA THEOLOGIAE – Thomas Aquinas – Thomas Gilby, O.P., General Editor
   Volume 1: The Existence of God; Part One: Questions 1–13 (D270) – $1.45

THE GOSPELS AND THE JESUS OF HISTORY – Xavier Léon-Dufour, S.J. (D276) – $1.75

INTRODUCTION TO THE OLD TESTAMENT (2 Volumes) – André Robert and André Feuillet (D278a, D278b) – $1.95 ea.

THE SEVEN STOREY MOUNTAIN – Thomas Merton (D281) – $1.95

THE PSALMS OF THE JERUSALEM BIBLE – Alexander Jones, General Editor (D283) – $1.45

CONTEMPLATIVE PRAYER – Thomas Merton (D285) – 95¢

THE CHALLENGES OF LIFE – Ignace Lepp (D286) – $1.25

THE ROMAN CATHOLIC CHURCH – John L. McKenzie (D287) – $1.75

BEING TOGETHER: OUR RELATIONSHIPS WITH OTHER PEOPLE – Marc Oraison (D289) – $1.25

THE ABORTION DECISION – Revised Edition – David Granfield (D294) – $1.45

AUTHORITY IN THE CHURCH – John L. McKenzie (D296) – $1.25

CHRIST IS ALIVE! – Michel Quoist (D298) – $1.25

THE MAN IN THE SYCAMORE TREE: The Good Times and Hard Life of Thomas Merton – Edward Rice (D299) – $1.95

THE NEW TESTAMENT OF THE NEW AMERICAN BIBLE (D300) – $1.75

TOWARD A NEW CATHOLIC MORALITY – John Giles Milhaven (D302) – $1.45

THE POWER AND THE WISDOM – John L. McKenzie (D303) – $1.75

INFALLIBLE? AN INQUIRY – Hans Küng (D304) – $1.45

THE DECLINE AND FALL OF RADICAL CATHOLICISM – James Hitchcock (D305) – $1.25

IN THE SPIRIT, IN THE FLESH – Eugene C. Kennedy (D306) – $1.25

THE GOD OF SPACE AND TIME – Bernard J. Cooke (D308) – $1.45

AN AQUINAS READER (Image Original) – Edited with an Intro. by Mary T. Clark (D309) – $2.45

These prices subject to change without notice

OTHER IMAGE BOOKS